Table of contents

04 ABOUT USAFACTS

07 GOVERNMENT FINANCES

19 POPULATION

24 IMMIGRATION & BORDER SECURITY

36 ECONOMY

44 STANDARD OF LIVING

54 WEALTH & SAVINGS

61 HEALTH

70 INFRASTRUCTURE

77 OTHER KEY TOPICS

- **78** DEFENSE, VETERANS, & FOREIGN AID
- **80** CRIME
- **82** DISASTERS
- **84** ENERGY
- **86** ENVIRONMENT & NATURAL RESOURCES
- **88** EDUCATION

90 RECOMMENDATIONS

94 SOURCES & NOTES

USAFACTS

USAFacts is founded and funded by Steve Ballmer, Ballmer Group co-founder, Chairman of the LA Clippers, and former CEO of Microsoft.

USAFacts Institute
PO Box 1558, Bellevue, WA 98009-1558

ISBN-13: 979-8-9904493-0-5

About USAFacts

About USAFacts

Our mission: Empower Americans with facts.

USAFacts provides a data-driven portrait of the American population, governments' finances, and governments' impact on society. We are a nonpartisan, not-for-profit civic initiative without a political agenda.

Our principles

UNBIASED
We rely only on numbers from government agencies and present them without bias. You can use the data to judge the country's direction for yourself. We don't answer to a board or political group. We have no agenda other than improving debates — and, by extension, American democracy — with government facts that every American deserves to know.

UNDERSTANDABLE
We gather metrics from government sources and standardize them so they're easy to grasp. That means detailed reports and clear, vibrant visualizations illustrating the data.

COMPREHENSIVE
We offer a complete view of government finances and impact, from the federal level to the community where you live. We're always collecting and adding metrics from the nation's more than 90,000 governments.

CONTEXTUAL
We use government data from many different sources, allowing you to see the big picture in one place. Our reports include historical context and our visualizations are simple to navigate so that you can measure changes over time.

TRANSPARENT
We are open about our data sources and methods. We cite our sources and note if we have made any changes, such as adjusting for inflation or population.

About this report

In this, the second year of USAFacts' *America in Facts: A Data-Driven Report for Congress,* we interviewed more than 20 congressional staff (and more than 70 over the span of the 118th Congress) to understand the pressing issues facing policymakers. These discussions — which spanned, the House of Representatives and the Senate, committees, and both parties — helped shape the structure of the latest report.

In this report, we leverage nonpartisan government data to inform critical policy debates. While excellent nonpartisan, unbiased government data is available to illuminate some of these debates, in other instances, there is only limited or deficient data. The final section of this report documents some of the problems with government data we encountered and suggests potential areas of improvement.

We envision this report serving as a catalyst for informed policy discussions among members of Congress and their teams. Congress also has a unique role in shaping government data through legislation and oversight. **Where data is limited or deficient, we hope that Congress will take action to make improvements.** The resulting data will be valuable to policymakers and the American public alike.

We are excited to continue our work with Congress. For more information about USAFacts' data, reports, and recommendations, email us at congress@usafacts.org.

USAFacts' approach to the data

All Americans are stakeholders in this democracy. To find solutions to issues affecting the United States, everyone, from regular citizens to top policymakers, needs data to understand how the government serves the people. At USAFacts, we believe a vibrant democracy requires informed debate grounded in facts. We exclusively use publicly available government data to provide this grounding.

USAFacts organizes its view of government and its data into four missions, based on the framework set out in the Constitution's preamble.

Preamble to the US Constitution

We the people of the United States, in order to form a more perfect union,

Establish justice, insure domestic tranquility,

Crime and disasters: physical safety of Americans

Consumer and employee safeguards: protection from financial crime, wrongdoing, or malfeasance by businesses

Child safety and miscellaneous social services: protection of children from dangerous family situations

Provide for the common defense,

National defense and support for veterans: military forces and services to support our veterans

Foreign affairs and foreign aid: economic, military, and other support to countries around the world

Immigration and border security: immigration policy and protection of our nation's borders

Promote the general welfare,

Economy and infrastructure: economic stimulus, including policies and investments in infrastructure, and research and development

Standard of living and aid to the disadvantaged: income, taxes, transfers to citizens, and what people can purchase

Health: public health and the healthcare industry, which is affected by government regulation and payments

Government-run businesses: operation of the post office, hospitals, and airports, among others

Secure the blessings of liberty to ourselves and our posterity,

Education: investment in children, our workforce, and human capital

Wealth and savings: financial security, savings policy, mandating investment in Social Security and Medicare, and debt

Energy and environment: regulation, policies, and taxes on industry to help protect the planet and ensure energy and food supply

The American Dream: promoting equality and a chance to move up economically, and participation in democracy

Do ordain and establish this Constitution for the United States of America.

Government finances

Government finances facts

Government revenue

- Federal, state, and local governments combined collected $8.6 trillion in FY 2021, a nearly threefold increase since FY 1980, adjusted for inflation. The largest revenue source was individual income taxes.
- Federal revenue reached nearly $4.5 trillion in FY 2023, with 49% from individual income taxes and 37% from payroll taxes.
- Federal revenue decreased by 15% in FY 2023 but was still 8% higher than in FY 2019.
- More than one-quarter of state and local governments' revenue came from investment earnings in FY 2021, the most recent year for which there is data.

Government employment

- In 2022, the government employed over 20.9 million people, with 79% in state or local positions.
- Fifty-five percent of state and local employees worked in education, while half of federal employees were in national defense and international affairs.

Government spending

- In FY 2021, combined government spending in the US was $10.4 trillion, more than three times the amount in FY 1980, adjusted for inflation. The federal government spent 61% of this total directly on operations, people, and programs and it transferred another 14% to states and local governments.
- The federal government spent nearly $6.2 trillion in FY 2023, including money transferred to states and local governments.
- Federal spending decreased by 8% in FY 2023 but was 16% above FY 2019 levels.

Fiscal trends and deficit

- The federal government spent 38% more than it collected in FY 2023, resulting in a $1.7 trillion deficit. The deficit was higher than in FY 2022 but lower than the peaks of FY 2020 and FY 2021.
- Federal debt reached $33.2 trillion in FY 2023. More than $26 trillion of this debt was held by the public, equivalent to 95.4% of GDP, or $79,000 per person.

About the data

What are the primary sources of data on this topic?

- Office of Management and Budget
- Census Bureau
- Bureau of Economic Analysis
- Department of the Treasury

What adjustments did USAFacts make to this data?

- USAFacts categorizes government finances according to the four missions outlined in the US Constitution. This approach is modeled after what businesses do for management accountability and shareholder reporting.
- Finance data is adjusted for inflation so comparisons can be made over time.
- USAFacts recategorizes federal employee data from the Office of Management and Budget to capture the types of jobs these employees hold and to make it comparable with state and local employee data from the Census Bureau.
- To learn more about the financial analysis methodology, visit usafacts.org/methodology.

Other things to know about the data

- Due to collection time differences, state and local government data is not as current as federal data. The most recent state and local government data available ends in 2021.
- The data in this section is in fiscal years. The federal fiscal year is October through September, while state and local fiscal years are generally July through June. For example, the 2023 fiscal year covers the period of October 2022 through September 2023.

How much revenue do federal, state, and local governments collect in the United States?

Combined, US governments collected $8.6 trillion in FY 2021, three times what they collected in FY 1980 (adjusted for inflation). Individual income taxes were the largest source of revenue.

COMBINED GOVERNMENT REVENUE

FEDERAL, STATE, AND LOCAL

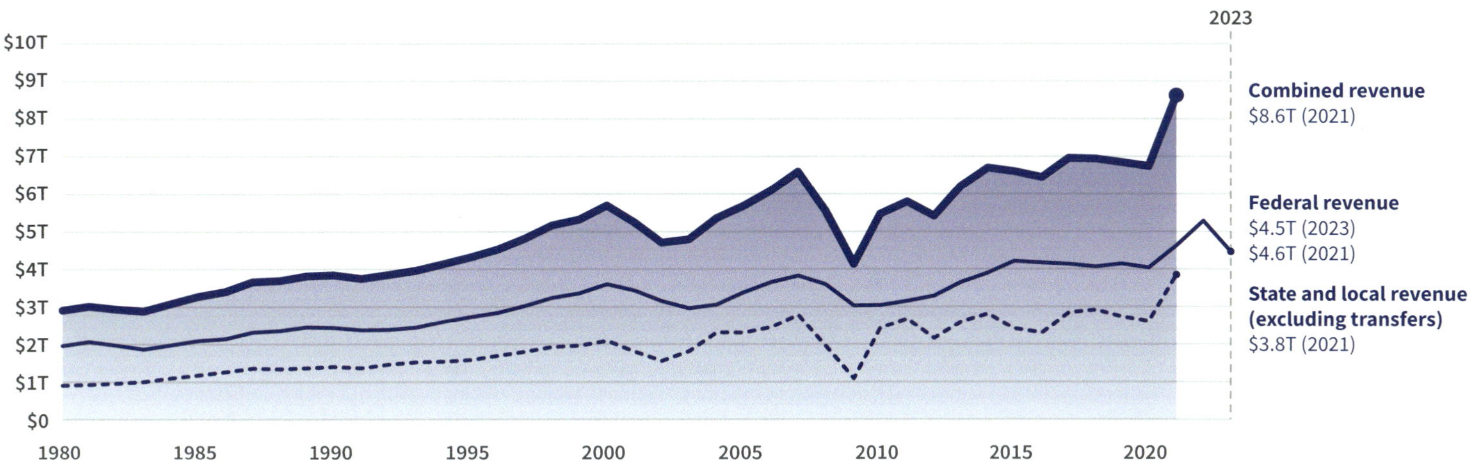

Source: USAFacts aggregation of data from Office of Management and Budget (OMB), Census Bureau, and Bureau of Economic Analysis (BEA)
Adjusted for inflation (FY 2023 dollars)
Note: Numbers may not add up due to the discrepancy between grants from the federal government to state and local governments as reported by the federal government versus as reported by state and local governments.

How much money do federal, state, and local governments spend?

Combined, US governments spent $10.4 trillion in FY 2021, 3.3 times more than in FY 1980 (adjusted for inflation). Spending peaked in FY 2020 due to COVID-19 relief efforts, and although it decreased slightly in FY 2021, it remained higher than in any fiscal year before 2020. Direct federal spending accounted for 61% of this spending. The federal government transferred another 14% for state and local governments to spend.

COMBINED GOVERNMENT SPENDING

FEDERAL, STATE, AND LOCAL

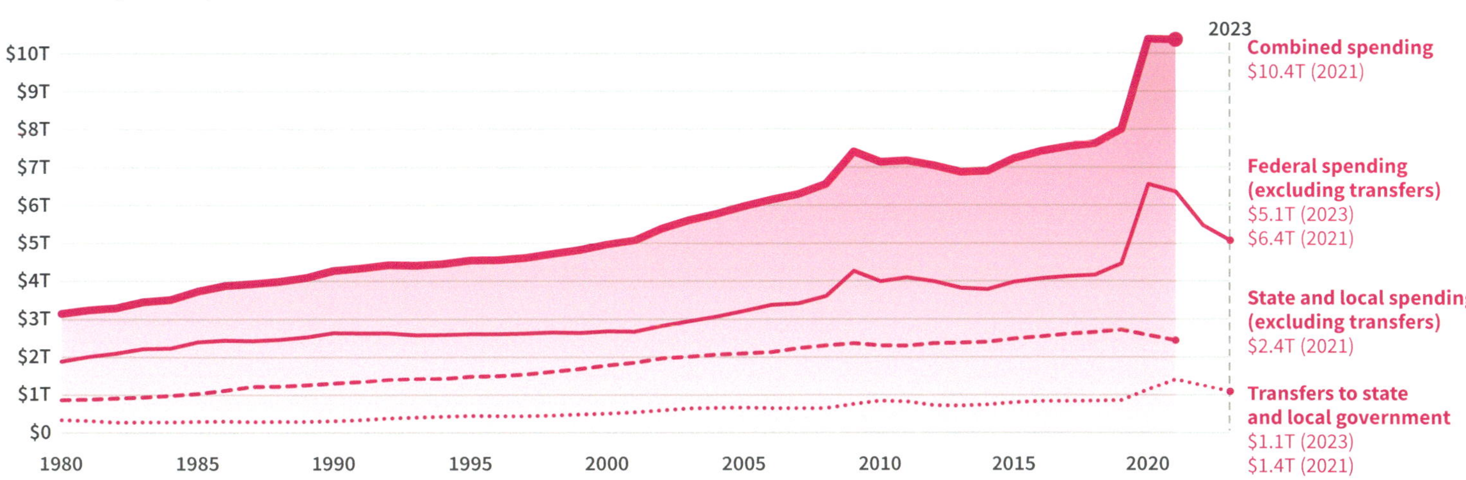

Source: USAFacts aggregation of data from Office of Management and Budget (OMB), Census Bureau, and Bureau of Economic Analysis (BEA)
Adjusted for inflation (FY 2023 dollars)
Note: Numbers may not add up due to the discrepancy between grants from the federal government to state and local governments as reported by the federal government versus as reported by state and local governments.

How did federal government revenue and spending compare in 2023?

In FY 2023, the federal government spent 38% more than it collected, resulting in a $1.7 trillion deficit.

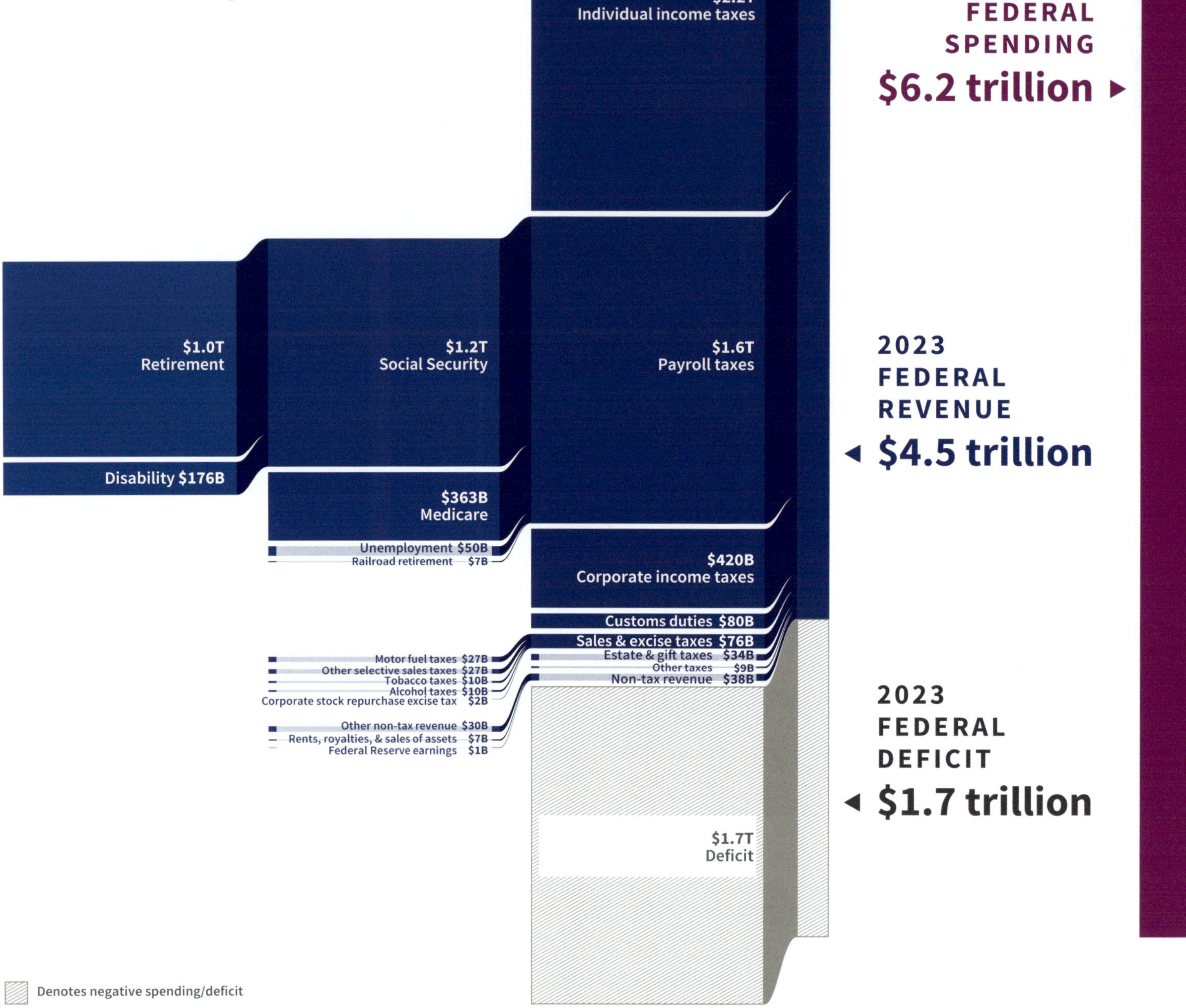

FEDERAL GOVERNMENT FINANCES (FY 2023)

Source: USAFacts aggregation of data from Office of Management and Budget (OMB), the Census Bureau, and the Bureau of Economic Analysis (BEA)
Adjusted for inflation (FY 2023 dollars)
Note: Charts are shown to scale for comparison. Numbers may not add due to rounding. The cost of President Biden's original student loan forgiveness executive order appeared as spending in the FY 2022 budget, but that anticipated spending was reversed in the FY 2023 budget after the Supreme Court's ruling that it was unconstitutional. As a result, total federal education spending in the FY 2023 budget was negative.

$103B Establish justice & ensure domestic tranquility
$93B Crime & disaster
$8B Consumer & employee safety
$2B Child & social services
$41B Disaster relief
$33B Law enforcement & corrections
$19B Justice system
$24B Law enforcement
$8B Corrections
$1.2T Provide for the common defense
$1.1T National defense & support for veterans
$820B National defense
$299B Support for veterans
$151B Veteran pensions & disability
$123B Veteran medical care
$25B Veteran readjustment benefits, housing, & other services
$70B Foreign affairs & foreign aid
$23B Immigration & border security
$804B Promote the general welfare
$496B Standard of living & aid to individuals
$257B Non-cash programs
$124B SNAP & other nutrition programs
$83B Other medical assistance to poor
$31B Pell Grants
$19B Housing assistance
$200M Child care assistance
$205B Cash programs
$62B Supplemental Security Income (SSI)
$59B Refugee assistance, TANF, & other
$55B Earned Income Tax Credit (EITC)
$29B Child tax credit
$30B Unemployment insurance
$3B Employment & training
$205B Economy & infrastructure
$92B Banking & finance
$39B Transportation
$24B Space
$17B Technology infrastructure
$17B General science & basic research
$7B Community & regional development
$6B Postal service
$3B General commerce
$24B Air transportation
$12B Water transportation
$2B General & other transportation (incl. highway, railroad, & unallocable)
$103B Health (excluding Medicaid/Medicare)
$102B Public health
$1B Other health, hospitals, & medical assistance (including unallocable)
$2.9T Secure the blessings of liberty to ourselves & our posterity
$3.0T Wealth & savings
$1.4T Social Security
$1.2T Retirement (FOASI)
$151B Disability (FDI)
$51B Other Social Security
$848B Medicare
$766B Obligations
$658B Net interest on debt
$107B Net employee retirement & disability benefits
$51B General retirement programs
-$22B Housing support
$35B Agriculture
$35B Environment & natural resources
-$1B Energy
$4B Education outside the classroom
-$136B Education inside the classroom
$48B Elementary & secondary education
$300M Vocational education
-$184B Higher education
$68B Sustainability & self-sufficiency
-$132B Education
$26B General government
$1.1T Transfers to state & local governments
$634B Medicaid & CHIP
$144B Other non-cash programs & aid to individuals
$90B All other transfers
$88B Transportation
$62B Elementary & secondary education
$37B Child & social services
$20B Cash programs
$11B Community & regional development

How has federal government revenue changed over time?

Federal government revenue increased 2.3 times between FY 1980 and FY 2023, while the population increased 1.5 times.

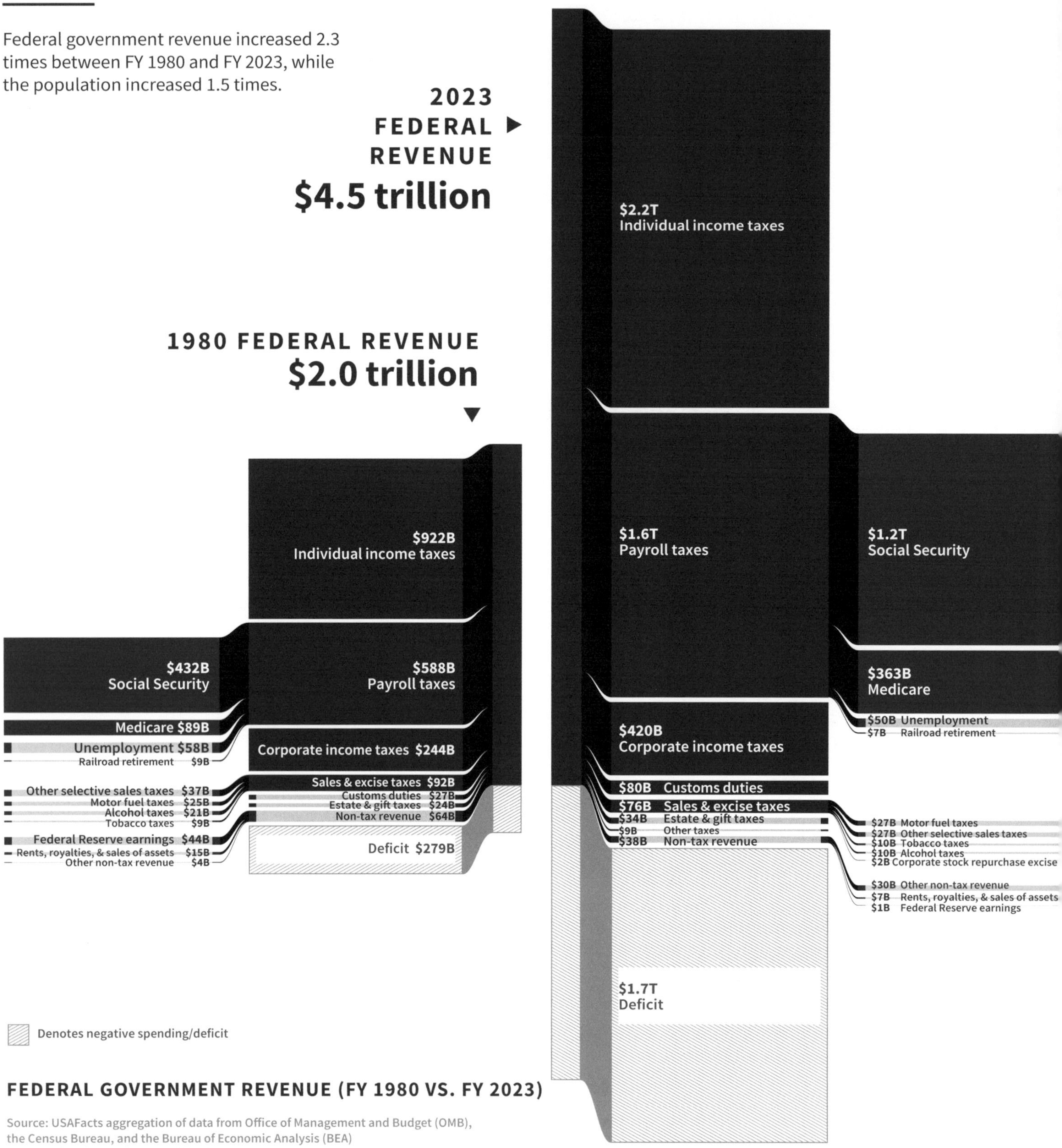

FEDERAL GOVERNMENT REVENUE (FY 1980 VS. FY 2023)

Source: USAFacts aggregation of data from Office of Management and Budget (OMB), the Census Bureau, and the Bureau of Economic Analysis (BEA)
Adjusted for inflation (FY 2023 dollars)
Note: Charts are shown to scale for comparison. Numbers may not add due to rounding.

What are the federal government's primary revenue sources?

The federal government collected nearly $4.5 trillion in revenue in FY 2023. Nearly half (49%) was collected through individual income taxes, while 37% was through payroll taxes. Other revenue sources included corporate income taxes, customs duties, and sales taxes. Federal revenue decreased 15% in FY 2023 but remained 8% higher than in FY 2019. The drop was due to lower revenue from individual income taxes (partly due to lower capital gains income) and non-tax sources. Non-tax sources include Federal Reserve earnings and proceeds from selling government resources.

FEDERAL GOVERNMENT REVENUE

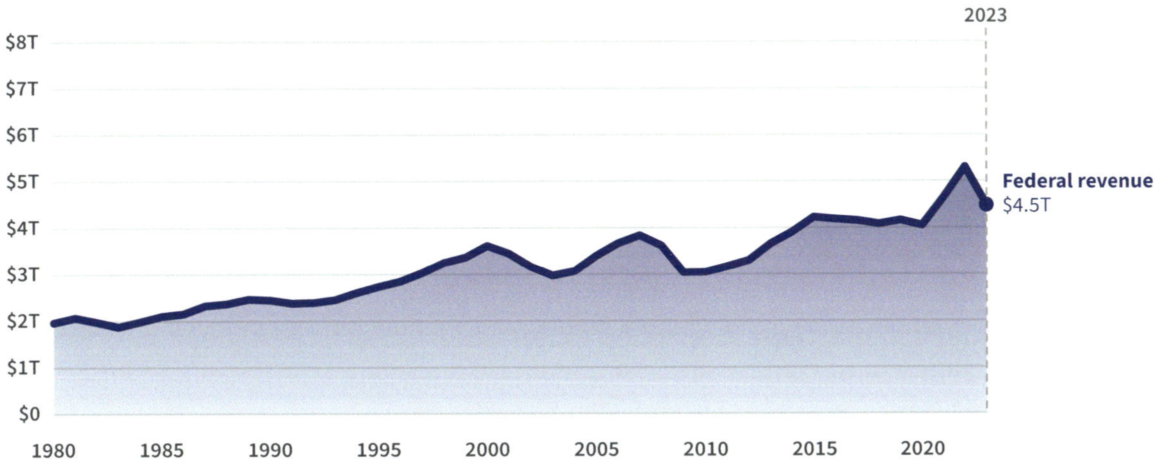

MOST FEDERAL GOVERNMENT REVENUE IN FY 2023 CAME FROM SIX AREAS

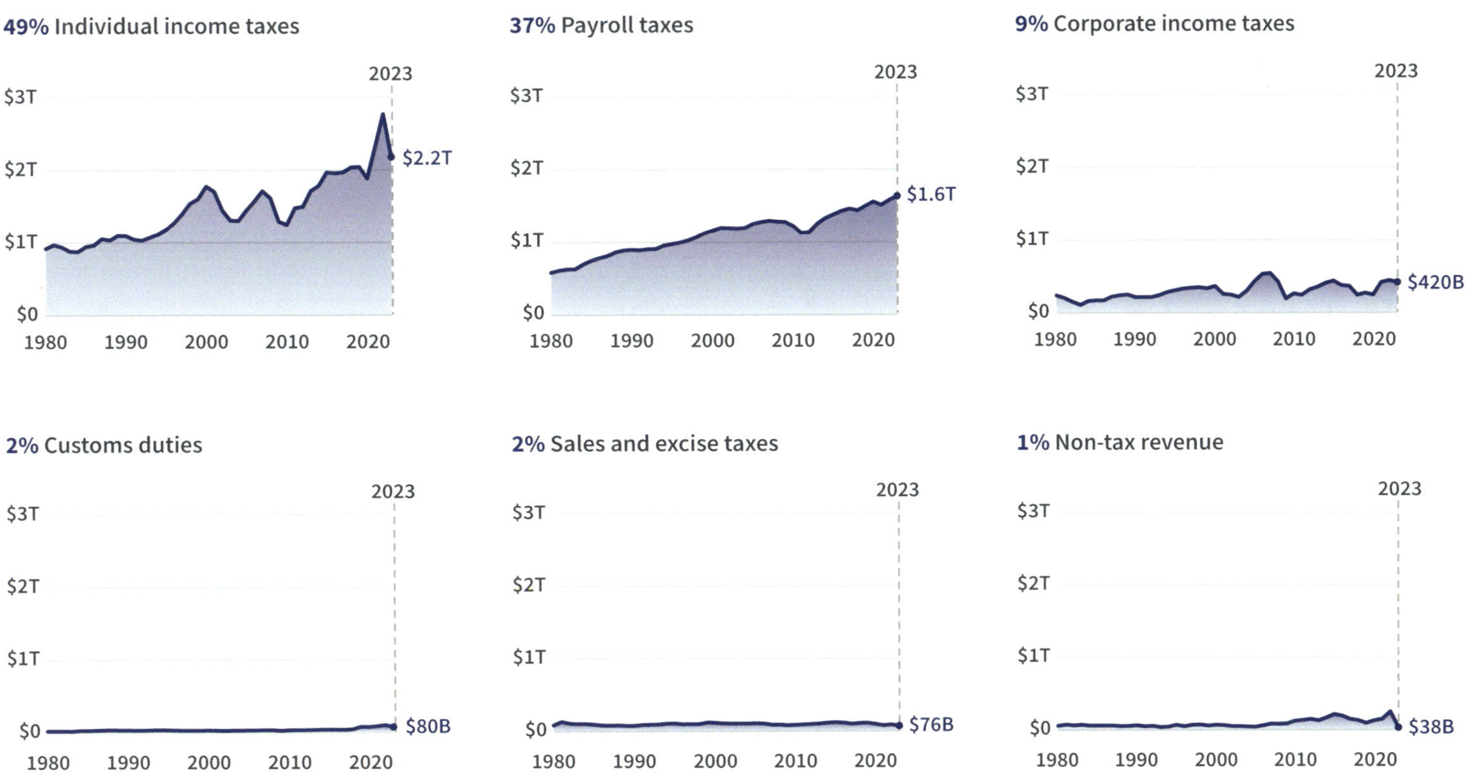

Source: USAFacts aggregation of data from Office of Management and Budget (OMB), Census Bureau, and Bureau of Economic Analysis (BEA)
Adjusted for inflation (FY 2023). Numbers have been rounded.

How has federal government spending changed over time?

Federal government spending increased 2.8 times between FY 1980 and FY 2023, when adjusted for inflation, while the population increased 1.5 times.

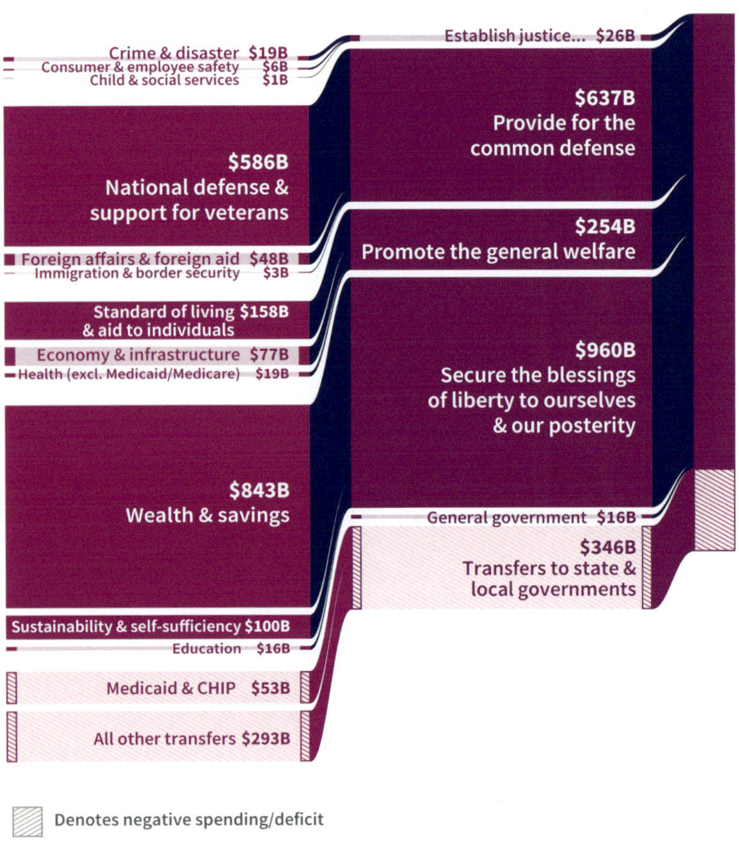

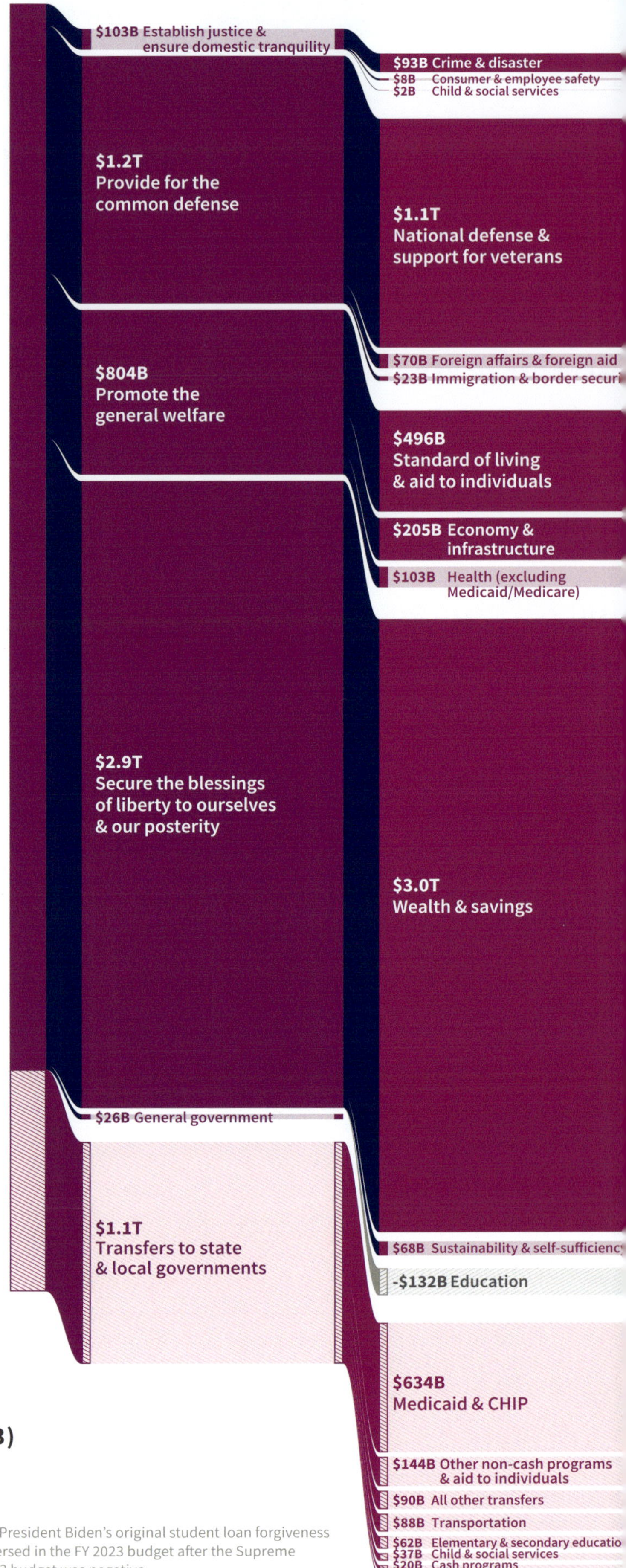

FEDERAL GOVERNMENT SPENDING (FY 1980 VS. FY 2023)

Source: USAFacts aggregation of data from Office of Management and Budget (OMB), the Census Bureau, and the Bureau of Economic Analysis (BEA)
Adjusted for inflation (FY 2023 dollars)
Note: Charts are shown to scale for comparison. Numbers may not add due to rounding. The cost of President Biden's original student loan forgiveness executive order appeared as spending in the FY 2022 budget, but that anticipated spending was reversed in the FY 2023 budget after the Supreme Court's ruling that it was unconstitutional. As a result, total federal education spending in the FY 2023 budget was negative.

On what does the federal government spend the most money?

The federal government spent almost $6.2 trillion in FY 2023, including transfers to states. Social Security (22%), transfers to states and local governments (18%), and defense and veterans (18%) accounted for more than half of spending. Federal spending decreased by 8% in FY 2023, the second year of decreased spending since a record high in FY 2021. Federal spending remained 16% above that of FY 2019.

FEDERAL GOVERNMENT SPENDING

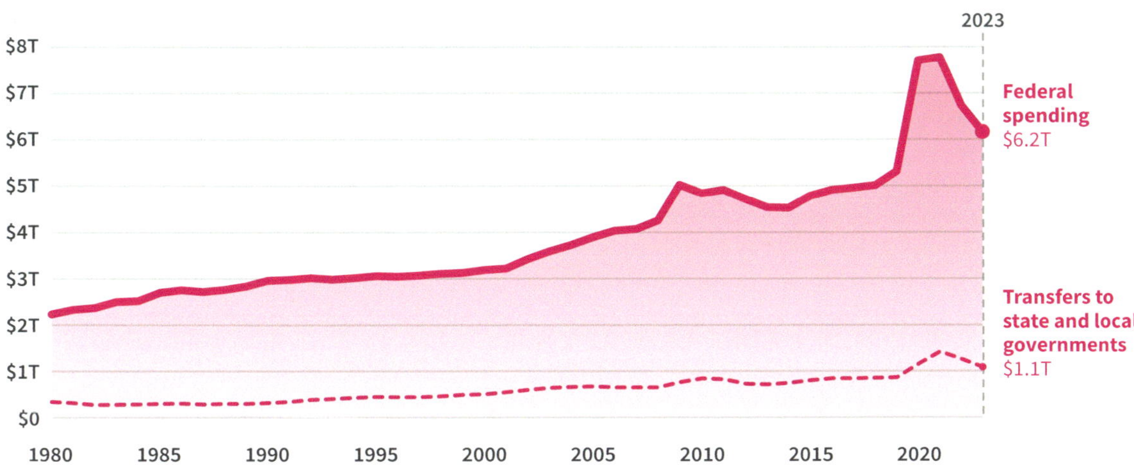

Most federal spending happens in two ways: direct spending on federal programs (such as for the military) and indirect spending through transfers to state and local governments in the form of grants (such as for infrastructure) that those governments then spend.

92% OF ALL FEDERAL GOVERNMENT SPENDING IN FY 2023 WENT TO SIX AREAS

22% Social Security

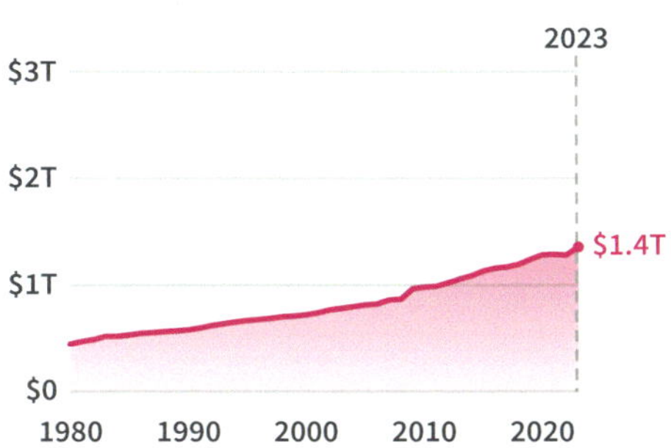

18% National defense & veterans

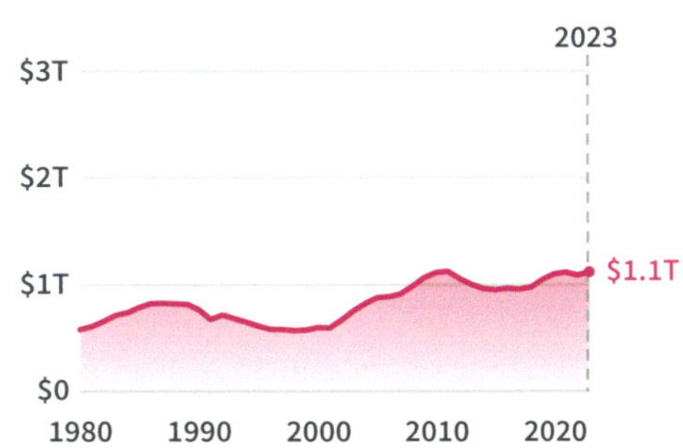

18% Transfers to state & local governments (including Medicaid)

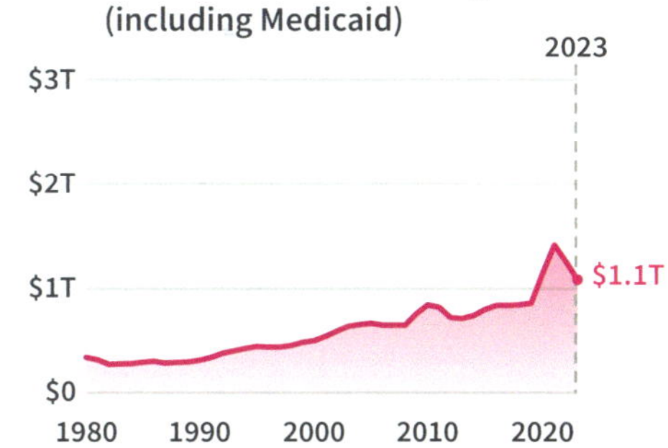

14% Medicare

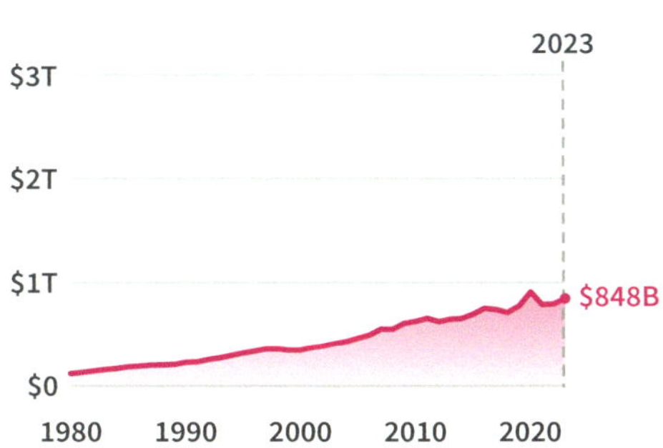

12% Obligations (including debt interest)

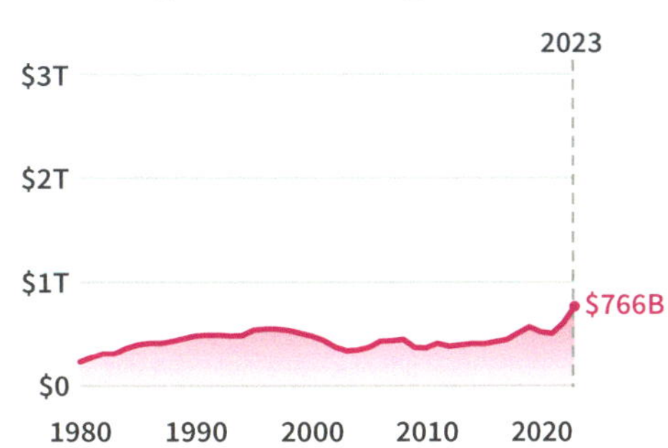

8% Standard of living & aid to individuals

Source: USAFacts aggregation of data from Office of Management and Budget (OMB), Census Bureau, and Bureau of Economic Analysis (BEA)
Adjusted for inflation (FY 2023). Numbers have been rounded.

How has federal government spending changed since the onset of the COVID-19 pandemic?

FY 2023 federal government spending was down from a peak of $7.8 trillion in FY 2021, but still $847.1 billion higher than pre-pandemic levels (adjusted for inflation). Economy and infrastructure spending was twice as high in FY 2023 as it was in FY 2019. Obligations were also 34% higher, mostly driven by increased net interest on the national debt. President Biden's original student loan forgiveness executive order affected FY 2022 and FY 2023 education spending. Loan forgiveness costs appeared as spending in the FY 2022 budget. The Supreme Court reversed this anticipated spending for the FY 2023 budget by ruling the program unconstitutional in Biden vs. Nebraska. As a result, total federal education spending in the FY 2023 budget was negative.

FEDERAL GOVERNMENT SPENDING (FY 2019 TO FY 2023)

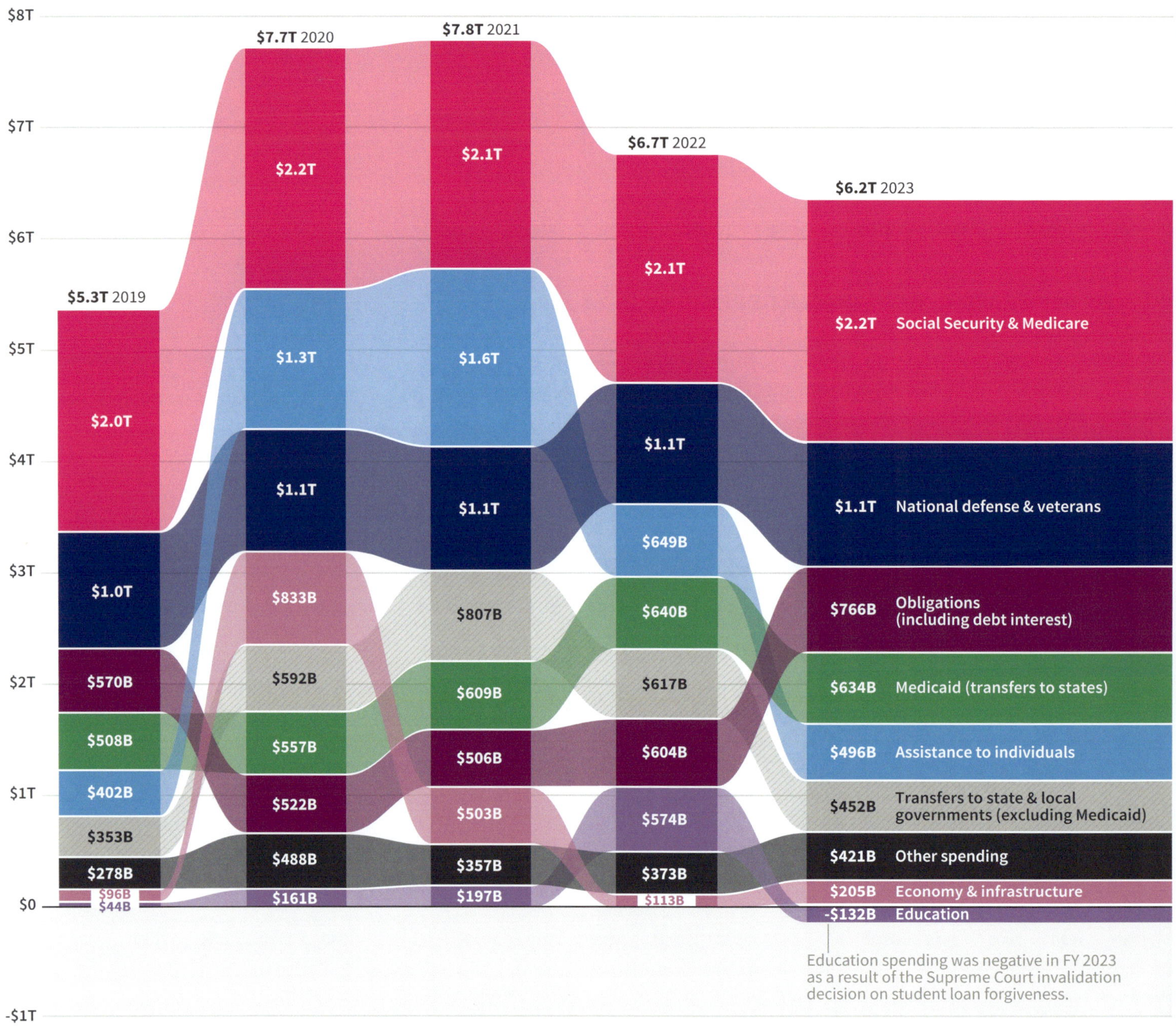

Source: USAFacts aggregation of data from Office of Management and Budget (OMB), Census Bureau, and Bureau of Economic Analysis (BEA)
Adjusted for inflation (FY 2023 dollars)
Note: Numbers may not add due to rounding.

How has federal government revenue and spending changed over time?

Although spending in FY 2023 dropped by $571.0 billion (adjusted for inflation) compared to FY 2022, revenue also decreased by $819.2 billion. As a result, the budget deficit increased to $1.7 trillion from $1.4 trillion in FY 2022. However, it did not reach FY 2020 and FY 2021 highs (both exceeding $3.0 trillion).

FEDERAL GOVERNMENT FINANCES

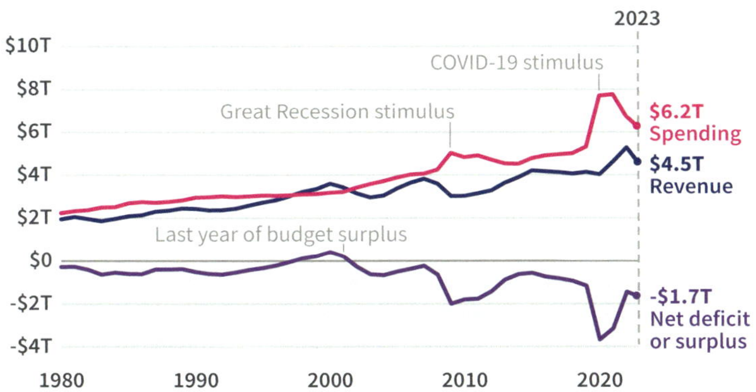

Source: USAFacts aggregation of data from Office of Management and Budget, the Census Bureau, and the Bureau of Economic Analysis
Adjusted for inflation (FY 2023 dollars)

FEDERAL GOVERNMENT DEBT

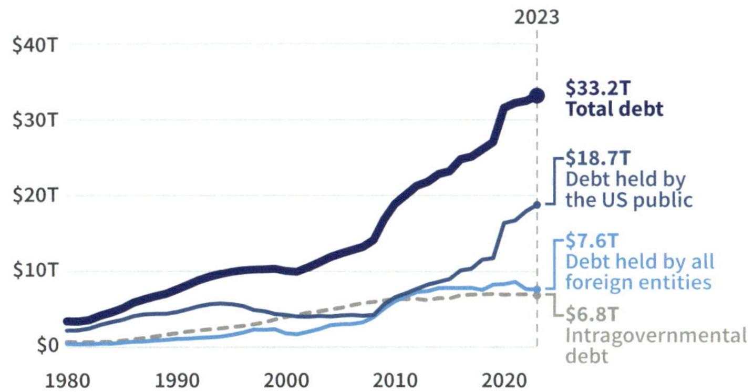

Source: Department of the Treasury
Adjusted for inflation (FY 2023 dollars)

How much debt does the federal government have?

The total debt owed by the federal government reached $33.2 trillion in FY 2023. The $26.3 trillion in federal debt held by the public, including foreign entities, totaled 95.4% of GDP, or $79,000 per person in the US. Debt as a percentage of GDP reached a peak in FY 2020, when debt held by the public was 97.2% of GDP. Debt held by the public per person was $57,000 higher in FY 2023 than in FY 2000, and nearly $18,000 more than in FY 2019.

FEDERAL GOVERNMENT DEBT HELD BY THE PUBLIC

AS A PERCENT OF GDP

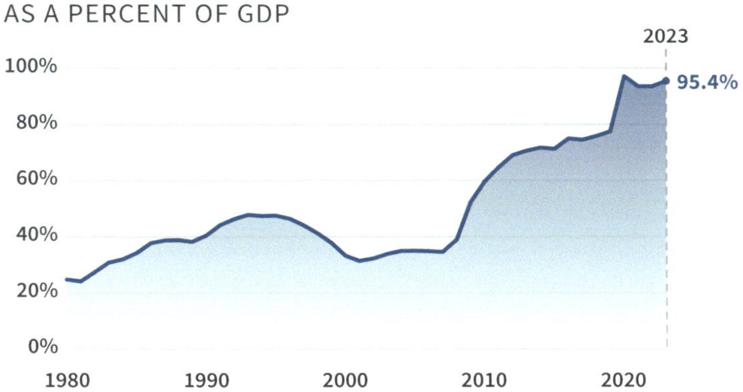

Source: Department of the Treasury
Adjusted for inflation (FY 2023 dollars)

FEDERAL GOVERNMENT DEBT HELD BY THE PUBLIC

PER CAPITA

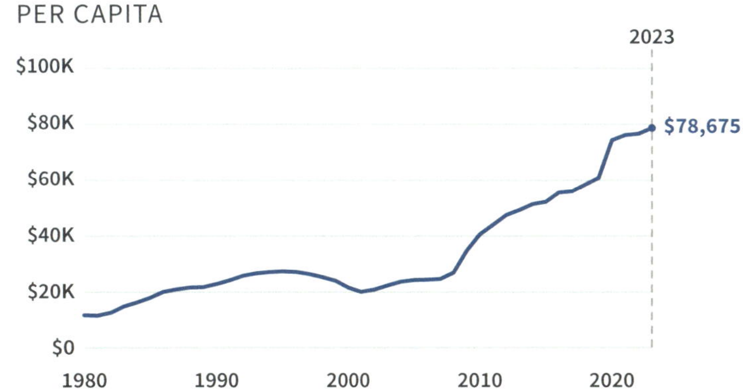

Source: Department of the Treasury
Adjusted for inflation (FY 2023 dollars)

How many people work for government?

In 2022, the government employed over 20.9 million people, 79% of whom were employed by state or local governments. Fifty-five percent of state and local employees worked in education. Half of federal employees worked in national defense and international affairs.

GOVERNMENT EMPLOYMENT (2022)[1]

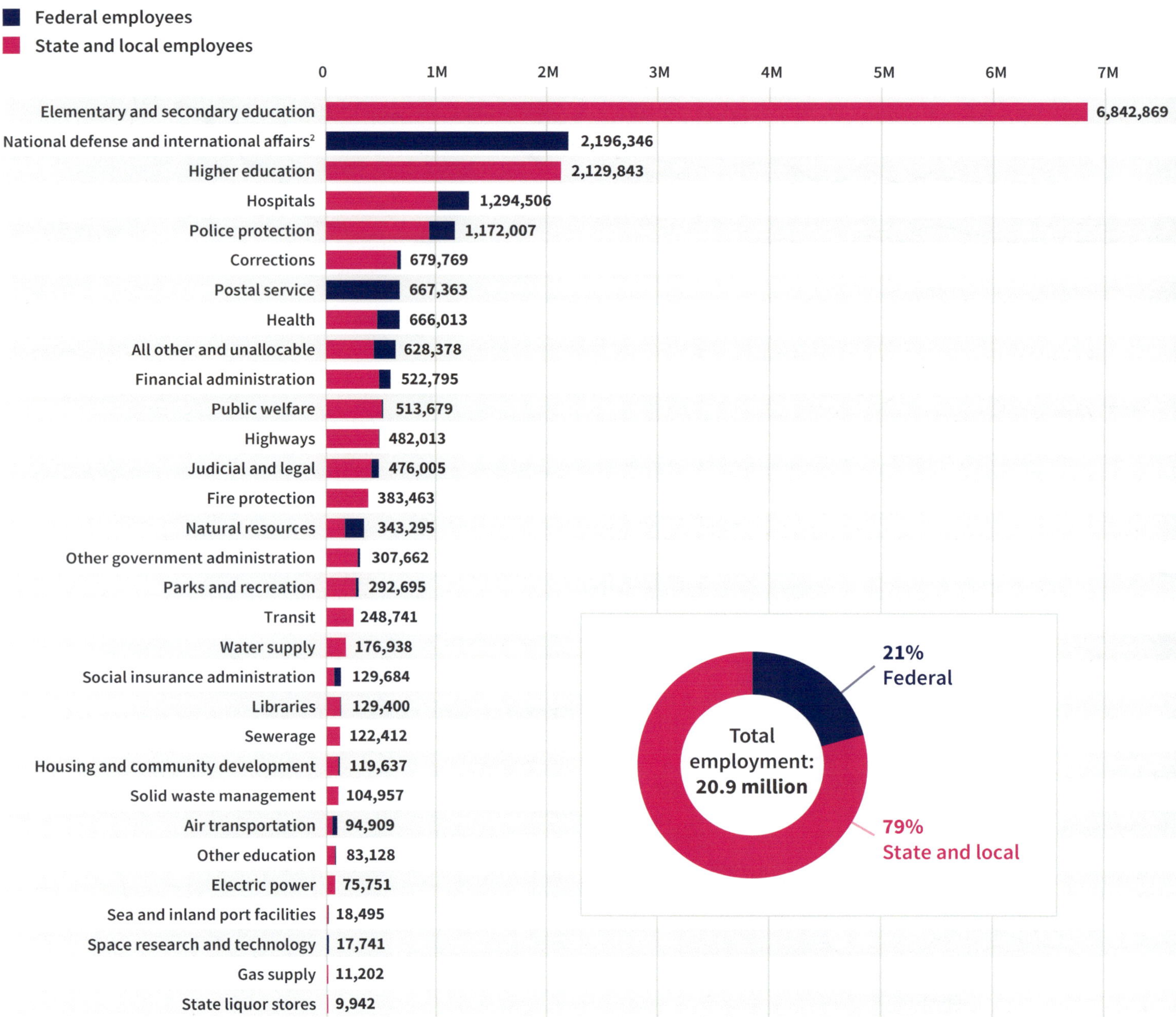

Source: USAFacts calculations using data from the Census Bureau and Office of Management and Budget

Notes:

1) Employment numbers here are full-time equivalent. Includes civilian and non-civilian employees.

2) Civilian military employees are included in "National defense and international affairs."

Population

Population facts

Population growth

- The US population was 334.9 million people in 2023.
- The population grew by 1.6 million in 2023, a growth rate of 0.5%.
- Over the last three years, net migration has accounted for 74% of US population growth.
- Net migration accounted for more than half of population growth in 2021, the first year this has been the case since the beginning of available data in 1991. Net migration continued to outpace natural population growth in 2022 and 2023.
- Between 2022 and 2023, Texas, Florida, North Carolina, and Georgia had the highest overall population growth, each gaining more than 100,000 people. New York lost the most residents, about 101,000.

Deaths and births

- In 2023, the death rate decreased for the second consecutive year, reaching 927 deaths per 100,000 people.
- The birth rate slightly decreased to 1,101 births per 100,000 people in 2022 and again to 1,078 in 2023, according to preliminary data.
- The 2023 birth rate was the lowest since records began, falling slightly below the previous record low of 1,097 births per 100,000 people in 2020.

Changing demographics

- The US population is aging. As of 2023, 18% of people are 65 and older, up from 11% in 1980.
- The share of households led by parents with children decreased in 2023, continuing a decades-long trend.
- In 2022, white non-Hispanic people made up 59% of the US population, down from 76% in 1990 and 69% in 2000. Between 2000 and 2022, the multi-racial population increased the fastest of any demographic, rising 132% from 3.5 million to 8.0 million people.

About the data

What are the primary sources of data on this topic?

- Census Bureau
- Centers for Disease Control and Prevention (CDC)

Other things to know about the data

- USAFacts relies upon Census population estimates as of July 1 of each year whenever possible. These estimates are known as intercensal or postcensal estimates and may differ from decennial census counts.
- The Census Bureau releases population estimates by different geographies and demographic characteristics at various times throughout each year. For example, it typically releases population by age and sex in April of each year, while it releases race and ethnicity data in June.
- At the time of this publishing, the CDC's deaths and births data for 2023 were provisional and subject to revision.

What is the US population?

Is the population growing?

The US population reached 334.9 million people in 2023. Population growth reached a low in 2021 when the population grew by 522,000 people. The population then grew by 1.2 million in 2022 and 1.6 million in 2023, both fewer than any year between at least 1980 and 2018. Population growth from net migration (the net effect of people moving into and out of the country) exceeded natural population growth (the effect of births and deaths) over the last three years. It has been responsible for 74% of population growth from 2021 through 2023.

POPULATION

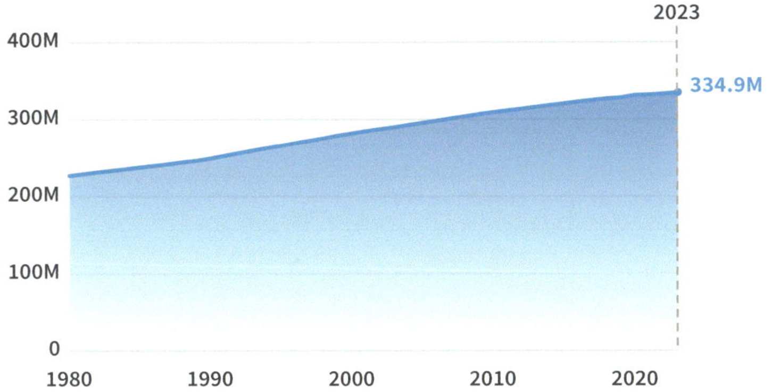

Source: Census Bureau

POPULATION GROWTH
BY COMPONENT

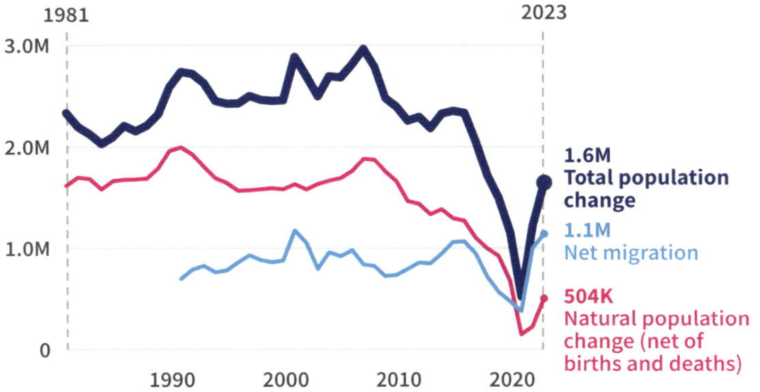

Source: Census Bureau

How have death and birth rates changed over time?

According to preliminary data, the death rate fell in 2023 for the second consecutive year to 927 deaths per 100,000 people, but is still above pre-pandemic levels. Meanwhile, the birth rate fell slightly to 1,101 births per 100,000 people in 2022 and again in 2023 to 1,078, according to preliminary data, lower than any previous year since at least 1980.

DEATH RATE
PER 100,000 PEOPLE

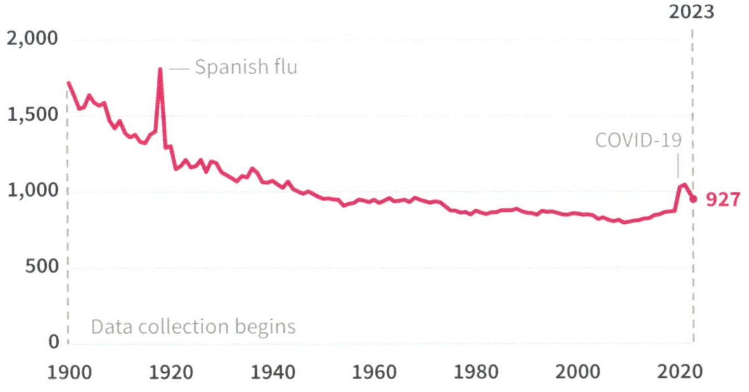

Source: Centers for Disease Control and Prevention
Note: Data for 2023 is provisional and may be revised.

BIRTH RATE
PER 100,000 PEOPLE

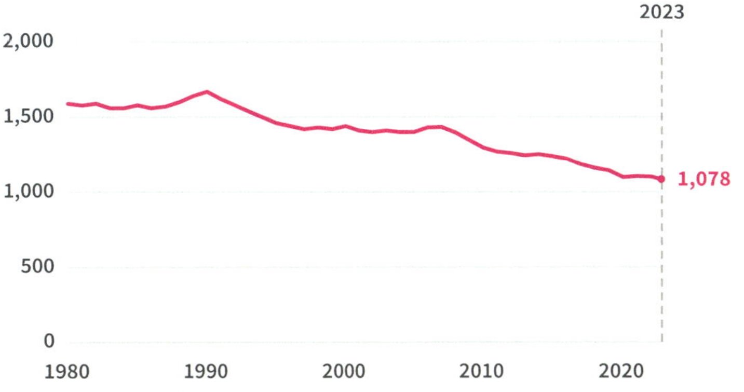

Source: Centers for Disease Control and Prevention
Note: Data for 2023 is provisional and may be revised.

How have state populations changed in the last year?

From 2022 to 2023, the populations of 10 states and Washington, DC, grew by more than 1%. Texas, Florida, North Carolina, and Georgia had the largest population increases, each gaining more than 100,000 people. Populations declined in eight states. New York lost the most residents, about 101,000.

COMPONENTS OF POPULATION CHANGE (2022 VS. 2023)

BY STATE

	PERCENT CHANGE IN POPULATION	NATURAL CHANGE (BIRTHS MINUS DEATHS)	NET DOMESTIC MIGRATION	NET INTERNATIONAL MIGRATION
Alabama	0.7%	-1,562	30,744	5,384
Alaska	0.0%	3,685	-5,543	2,004
Arizona	0.9%	7,702	36,179	21,635
Arkansas	0.7%	-907	18,106	4,096
California	-0.2%	111,416	-338,371	150,982
Colorado	0.6%	17,399	7,236	11,931
Connecticut	0.2%	2,115	-9,016	15,264
Delaware	1.2%	-172	10,320	2,277
District of Columbia	1.2%	2,607	-1,509	6,969
Florida	1.6%	-7,603	194,438	178,432
Georgia	1.1%	27,817	58,206	30,119
Hawaii	-0.3%	2,355	-11,193	4,627
Idaho	1.3%	5,639	15,389	4,664
Illinois	-0.3%	10,453	-83,839	40,492
Indiana	0.4%	7,508	4,599	17,869
Iowa	0.2%	3,779	-3,603	7,112
Kansas	0.1%	4,439	-4,574	3,932
Kentucky	0.3%	-2,005	8,965	7,627
Louisiana	-0.3%	6,115	-29,692	9,274
Maine	0.5%	-5,053	9,216	2,209
Maryland	0.3%	14,199	-30,905	32,977
Massachusetts	0.3%	6,983	-39,149	50,647
Michigan	0.0%	-4,030	-15,051	22,817
Minnesota	0.4%	13,843	-4,686	14,575
Mississippi	0.0%	-1,404	-2,614	4,800
Missouri	0.3%	-55	11,171	7,852
Montana	0.9%	-171	9,485	609
Nebraska	0.5%	5,699	-834	5,441
Nevada	0.5%	3,733	8,642	4,266
New Hampshire	0.2%	-2,109	4,298	859
New Jersey	0.3%	25,492	-44,666	49,298
New Mexico	0.0%	-1,616	-1,088	3,642
New York	-0.5%	41,536	-216,778	73,867
North Carolina	1.3%	12,657	97,264	29,448
North Dakota	0.6%	2,704	-9	2,298
Ohio	0.2%	-2,462	637	28,081
Oklahoma	0.9%	2,567	23,587	8,380
Oregon	-0.1%	-4,239	-6,051	4,304
Pennsylvania	-0.1%	-11,079	-24,825	25,776
Rhode Island	0.2%	-428	-3,224	5,777
South Carolina	1.7%	-1,271	82,562	9,291
South Dakota	1.0%	2,813	4,812	1,788
Tennessee	1.1%	1,028	63,417	13,054
Texas	1.6%	158,253	186,767	128,534
Utah	1.1%	24,796	1,338	10,285
Vermont	0.1%	-1,804	844	1,312
Virginia	0.4%	15,689	-6,985	28,117
Washington	0.4%	14,860	-15,276	28,919
West Virginia	-0.2%	-8,666	3,595	1,101
Wisconsin	0.3%	1,147	5,648	13,653
Wyoming	0.4%	103	2,016	322

Source: Census Bureau

How have the age of the population and types of households in the United States changed over time?

The proportion of people ages 65 and older in the population is rising, while the proportion of people younger than 18 is falling. The elderly population's share has risen 6 percentage points since 1980, up to 18% in 2023. The share of children in the population decreased by 6 points to 22%. Meanwhile, the composition of US households also shifted. Married-parent households have fallen from 31% of US households in 1980 to 18% in 2023, while the share of households comprised of adults living alone without children increased.

SHARE OF POPULATION
BY AGE GROUP

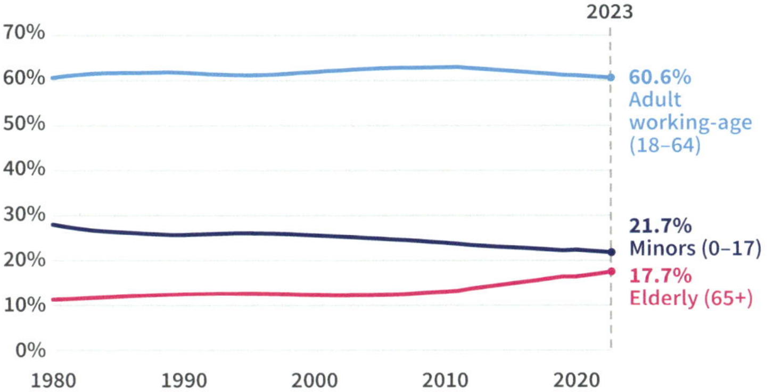

Source: Census Bureau

SHARE OF HOUSEHOLDS
BY HOUSEHOLD TYPE

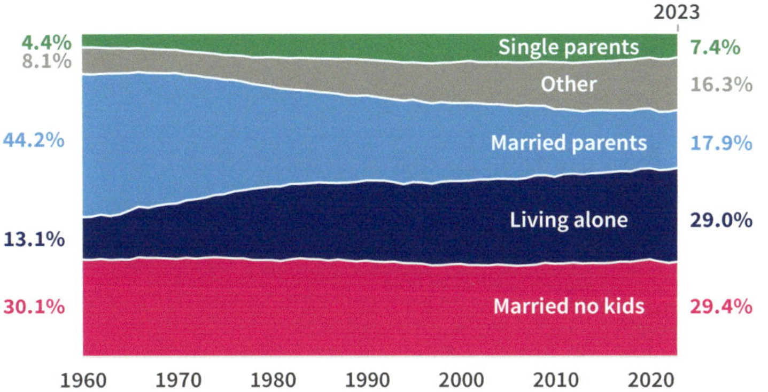

Source: Census Bureau

How is the population's racial and ethnic makeup changing?

In 2022, white non-Hispanic people were 59% of the population, down from 69% in 2000 and 76% in 1990. Hispanic people were 19% of the population and Black people were 13% in 2022. Between 2000 and 2022, the multiracial population increased fastest (up 132%), followed by Asian or Pacific Islander (93%) and Hispanic (79%) people.

SHARE OF POPULATION
BY RACE/ETHNICITY

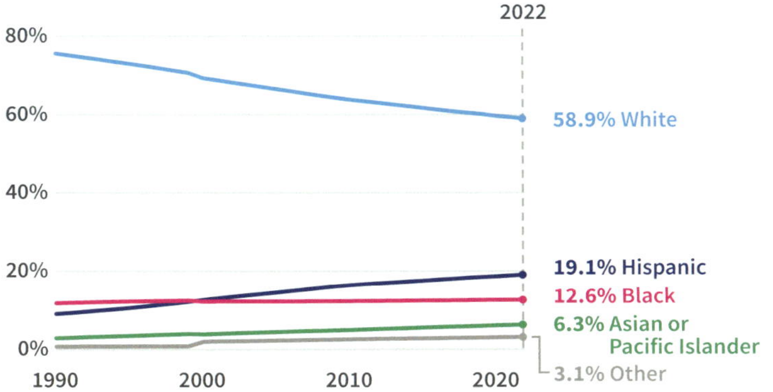

Source: Census Bureau
Note: All groups are non-Hispanic except for Hispanic group. "Other" group includes American Indians and Alaska Natives and people of two or more races.

POPULATION (2000 VS. 2022)
BY RACE/ETHNICITY

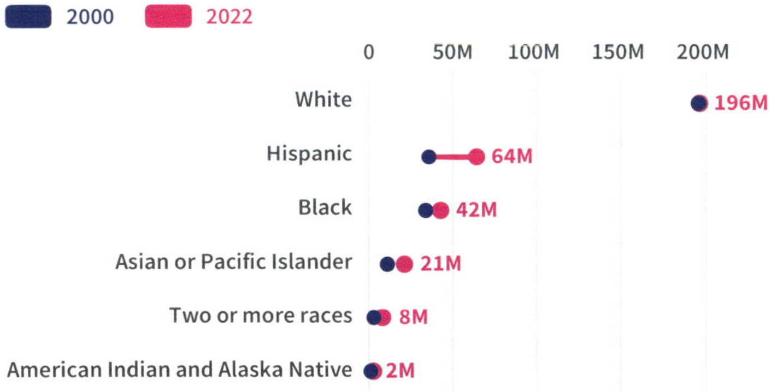

Source: Census Bureau
Note: All groups are non-Hispanic except for Hispanic group.

Immigration & border security

Immigration & border security facts

Incoming authorized immigrants

- About 2.6 million authorized immigrants entered the US in FY 2022, hitting levels above FY 2019 after a 48% dip in FY 2020.
- Work is the most common reason for authorized immigration to the US (41% of immigrants in FY 2022). In FY 2022, 39% of those immigrants came from Mexico. The number of immigrant workers who were Mexican nationals almost quadrupled between FY 2010 and FY 2022.
- About half of immigrants coming to be with family or for school are from Asian countries, with Indians comprising the largest share of both.
- There were about 492,000 asylum applications in FY 2022, more than three times higher than in FY 2015. About 16% of asylum application decisions were approvals in FY 2022.
- Admissions of both refugees and asylees have risen after dips in FY 2020 and FY 2021 but are still below highs set in the 2010s.

Immigrants in the US

- About 46 million foreign-born individuals lived in the US as of 2022, representing 13.9% of the population. More than half were naturalized US citizens, while an estimated 24% were unauthorized immigrants.

Immigration enforcement and courts

- Border enforcement actions, which are when people are deemed inadmissible at a port of entry or apprehended after crossing the border illegally, reached a record 3.2 million in FY 2023, up 16% from FY 2022.
- The US removed about 109,000 people in FY 2022, up 27% from FY 2021 but still 75% lower than the FY 2013 peak.
- Returns, a voluntary alternative for some immigrants subject to being removed that does not carry the same legal penalties as deportation, increased 47% in FY 2022 to 261,000, but remain 84% below the peak in FY 2000.
- The number of immigration court cases pending at the end of each year has been increasing since at least 2009, reaching 2.5 million at the end of 2023.

Immigrants in the workforce

- The foreign-born labor force is at the highest level since at least 2007.
- Foreign-born workers are most prevalent in the construction industry (29%) and the other services industry (23%).
- Work visas issued fell in FY 2020 but reached a 25-year peak in FY 2023. Around 27% were for agricultural (H-2A) workers, and 23% were for specialty occupations (H-1B).

About the data

What are the primary sources of data on this topic?

- Department of Homeland Security (DHS)
- Refugee Processing Center
- Department of State
- Customs and Border Protection
- Census Bureau
- Bureau of Labor Statistics

Other things to know about the data

- Refugee data from the State Department's Refugee Processing Center and DHS doesn't always match exactly, so numbers in some charts showing new refugee arrivals or total arrivals may not match.

GOVERNMENT SPENDING 1980–2023
IMMIGRATION & BORDER SECURITY

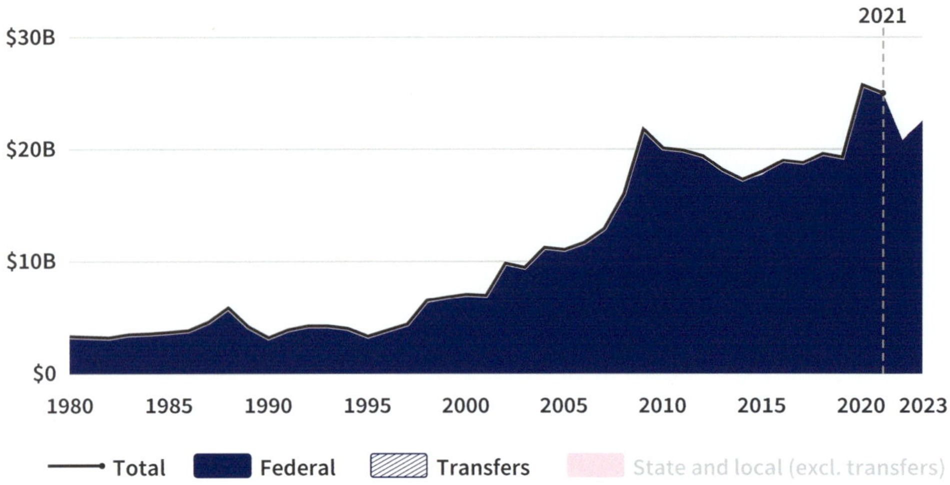

2023 FEDERAL SPENDING*

$23 billion

PERCENT OF FEDERAL SPENDING

0.1% **0.4%**

Source: USAFacts aggregation of data from the Office of Management and Budget (OMB), the Census Bureau, and the Bureau of Economic Analysis (BEA)
Adjusted for inflation (FY 2023 dollars)
Note: *Includes direct spending and transfers.

Federal agencies spending: Immigration & border security

Federal agency	Net spending in FY 2023*	Share of spending transferred to state and local governments	Share of spending that was mandatory
Department of Homeland Security	$23.0 billion	0%	**
Department of State	-$438 million	0%	***

Source: USAFacts calculations based on the Public Budget Database from the Office of Management and Budget
*Because of budgetary rules pertaining to offsetting receipts and offsetting collections, agencies can have negative net outlays, negative net transfers, or negative net mandatory spending. This happens when money agencies receive from certain sources exceeds the amount they spend, resulting in a surplus. For more information on this issue, see here: https://www.whitehouse.gov/wp-content/uploads/2023/03/ap_18_offsetting_fy2024.pdf.
**The Department of Homeland Security received $3.2 billion more than it spent on mandatory immigration and border security.
***The Department of State received $480 million more than it spent on immigration and border security in FY 2023 because of fees such as visa fees, immigrant lottery fees, and passport fees.

How many authorized immigrants come to the US and what pathways do they use?

About 2.6 million new authorized immigrants entered the US in FY 2022, rising above FY 2019 levels after a 48% dip in FY 2020 and an 18% increase in FY 2021. Immigrants can be authorized to enter the US through a green card, a temporary visa, or through the refugee or asylee process. Temporary visas (excluding tourism visas) account for about 75% of all new authorized immigrant entries since FY 1997.

NEW IMMIGRANT ARRIVALS

TOTAL

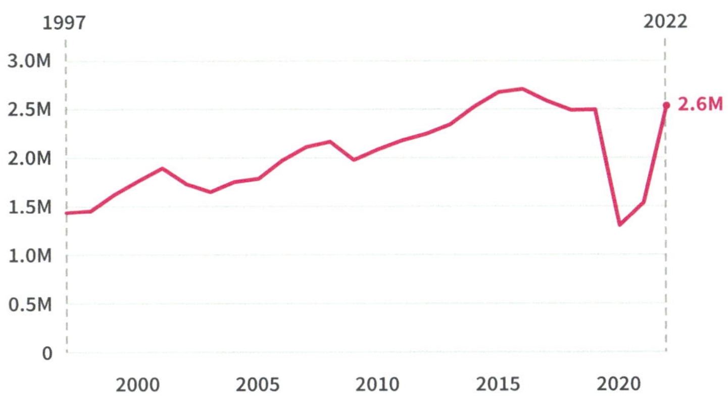

BY TYPE

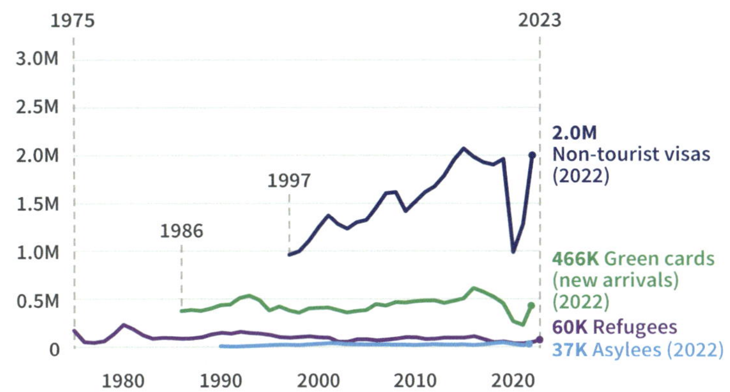

Source: Department of Homeland Security, Department of State, Refugee Processing Center

From what regions and for what reasons do immigrants come to the US?

A plurality of new authorized immigrants in FY 2022 came to the US for work, accounting for 41% of new immigrant arrivals that year. Mexico and India accounted for 40% of all immigrants, outnumbering immigrants from Africa, Europe, and South America combined.

NEW IMMIGRANT ARRIVALS (FY 2022)

BY REGION OF BIRTH/NATIONALITY

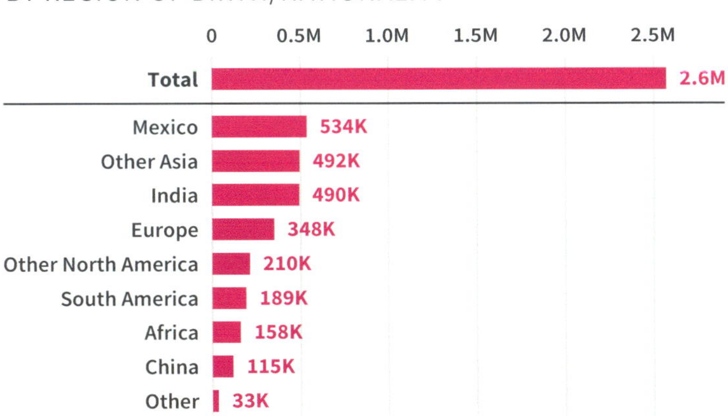

BY REASON FOR GRANTED ENTRY

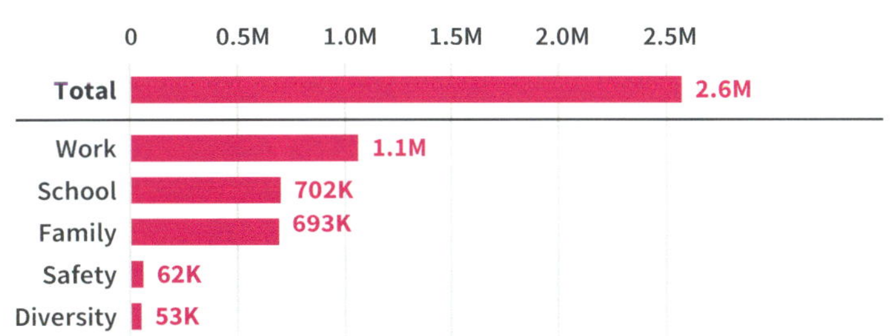

Source: Department of Homeland Security, Department of State, and Refugee Processing Center
Note: Data for safety and diversity may sometimes be an underestimate as some countries' data is suppressed. Data includes non-tourist visas, new arrival green cards, refugees, and asylees.

Where do immigrant workers and students come from?

A plurality of immigrants coming to the US for work are of Mexican nationality, accounting for 39% of this group in FY 2022.[i] The number of workers coming from Mexico almost quadrupled between FY 2010, when they hit a low, and FY 2022 compared to 39% growth in workers coming from all other countries.

Most student visas were issued to people from Asia, accounting for 52% of students entering the US in FY 2022. A majority of these used to be issued to Chinese students, however, the number issued to Chinese students fell 78% from its FY 2015 peak by FY 2022. This coincided with a change in policy in 2014 that made Chinese students eligible for five-year student visas rather than one.[ii] Meanwhile, visas issued to students coming from India increased 51%.

NEW IMMIGRANT ARRIVALS, BY COUNTRY OF BIRTH/NATIONALITY

Mexico · Other North America · South America · Africa · Europe · India · China · Other Asia · Other

IMMIGRANTS COMING FOR **WORK**

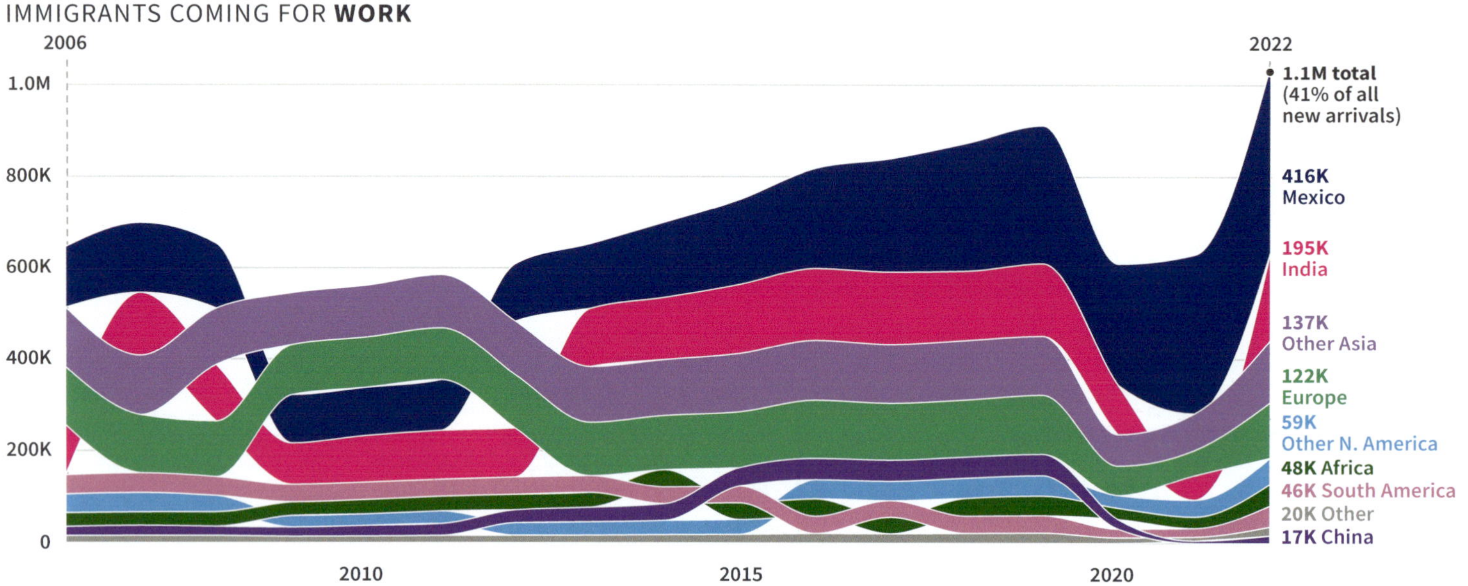

IMMIGRANTS COMING FOR **SCHOOL**

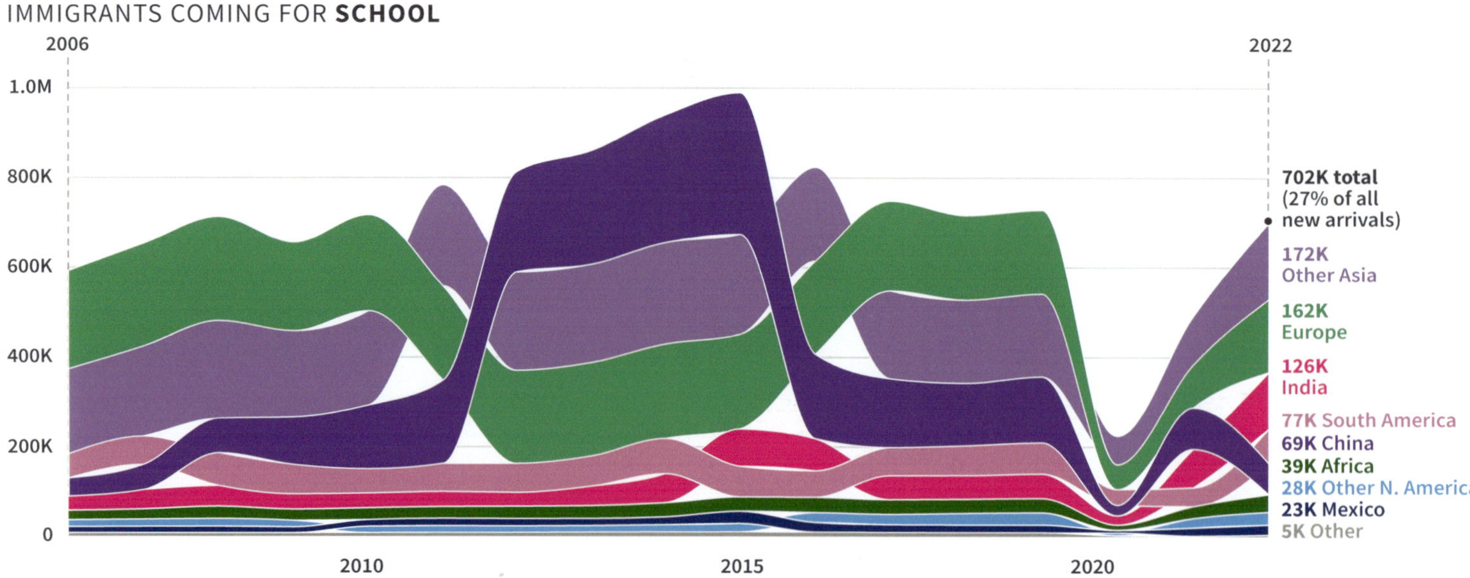

Source: Department of Homeland Security and Department of State

Note: Data for safety and diversity (included in reasons for immigration other than work, family , or school) may sometimes be an underestimate as some countries' data is suppressed. Data includes non-tourist visas, new arrival green cards, refugees, and asylees.

How has family immigration changed over time?

Why else do people immigrate to the United States, and where do they come from?

In FY 2022, Indians accounted for about 24% of immigrants coming to the US to be with their families, the most of any nationality. Many people also came to be with family from Mexico (14%), Asian countries besides India and China (20%), and North/Central American countries besides Mexico (16%).

People from Asian countries other than China and India have typically been the largest category of people who come to the US for reasons other than work, family, or school since FY 2006. Almost two-thirds of these Asian immigrants are refugees or asylees. Asian countries (besides China and India) accounted for 39% of immigrants coming for safety, on diversity visas, or for reasons besides work or family in FY 2022. Africa accounted for another 25% of such immigrants in FY 2022, with about half coming on diversity visas, and the other half coming as refugees or asylees.

IMMIGRANTS COMING FOR **FAMILY**

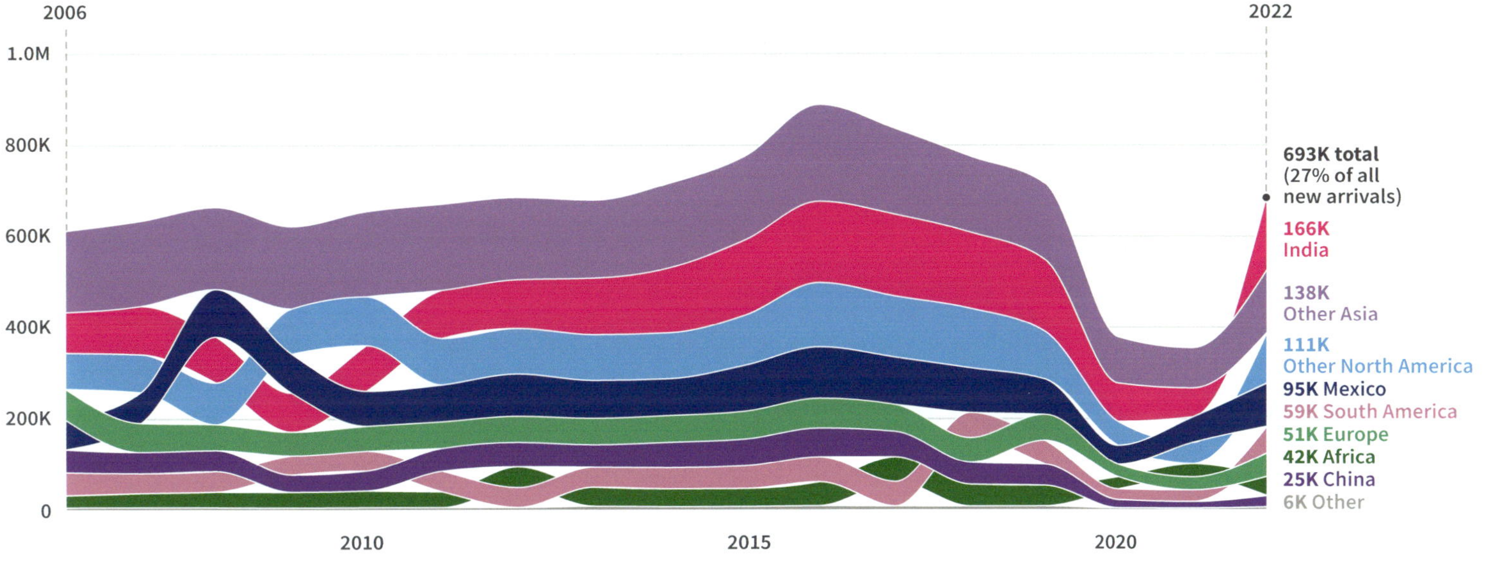

IMMIGRANTS COMING FOR REASONS **OTHER** THAN WORK, FAMILY, OR SCHOOL

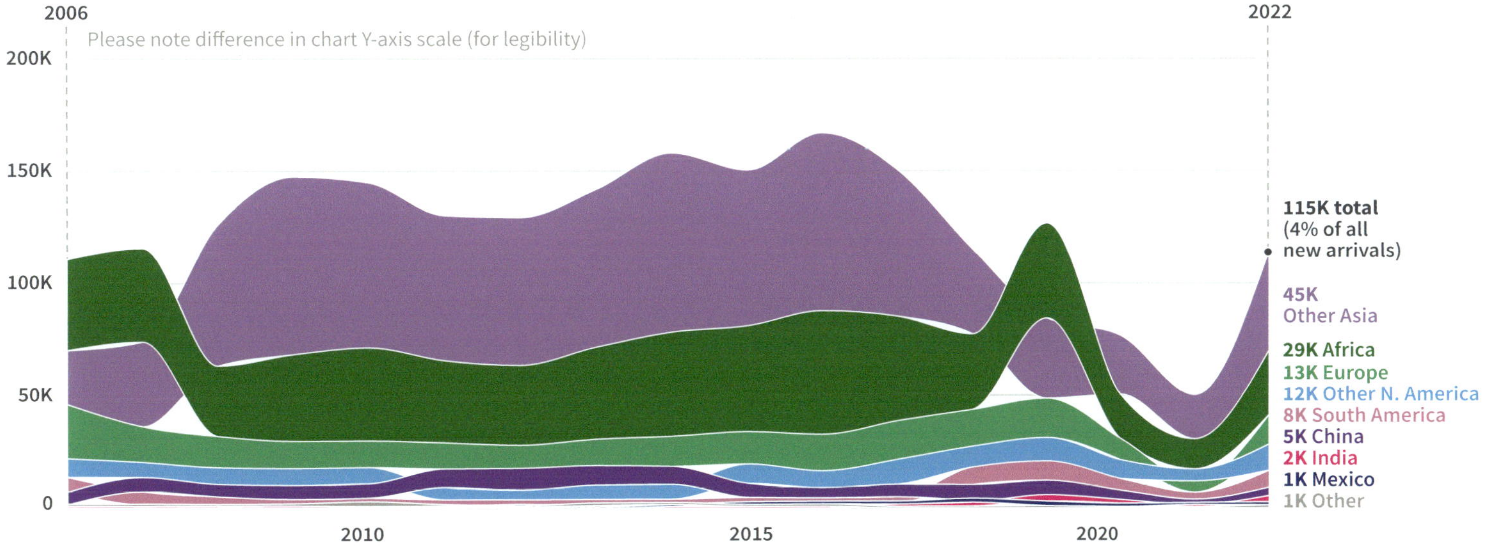

How many people are denied entry at US borders?

Border enforcement actions reached a record high of 3.2 million in FY 2023. These actions take place when individuals are deemed "inadmissible" at ports of entry or are apprehended after crossing the border between legal ports of entry. Between 2020 and 2023, it also included people expelled under a pandemic-era law. The number of people deemed inadmissible increased fourfold from FY 2019 to FY 2023, reaching 1.1 million. Those deemed inadmissible may be allowed into the US for humanitarian or emergency reasons, and in other specific cases.

ANNUAL BORDER ENFORCEMENT ACTIONS

BY AGENCY

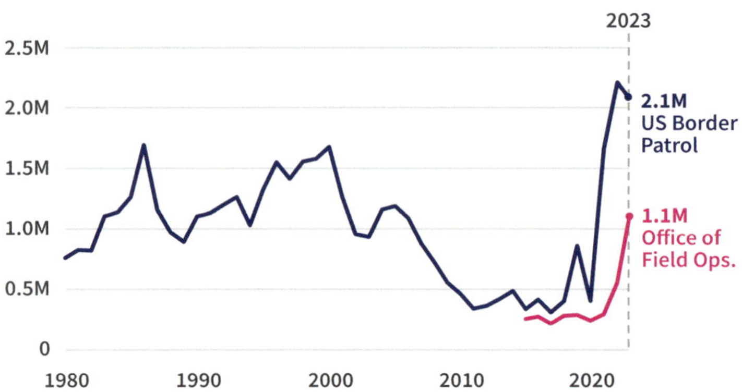

Source: US Customs and Border Protection

Note: Office of Field Operations actions include encounters with people deemed inadmissible at ports of entry. USBP actions include people apprehended while illegally entering the US between ports of entry. Both include people expelled under Title 42.

MONTHLY BORDER ENFORCEMENT ACTIONS

BY AGENCY (RECENT MONTHS)

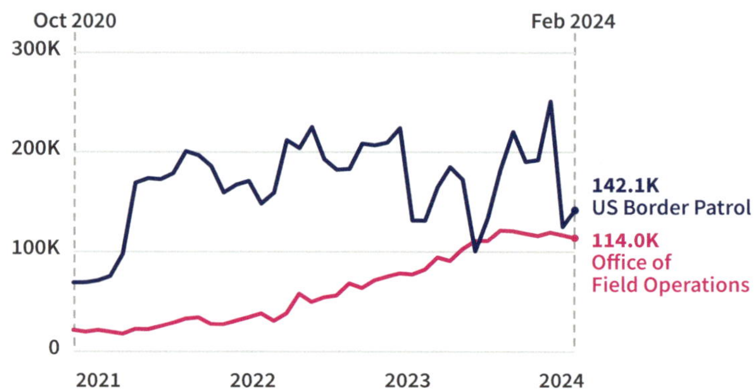

Source: US Customs and Border Protection

Note: Office of Field Operations actions include encounters with people deemed inadmissible at ports of entry. USBP actions include people apprehended while illegally entering the US between ports of entry. Both include people expelled under Title 42.

How many immigrants are asylum seekers?

FY 2022 asylum applications totaled about 492,000, more than three times higher than in FY 2015, the earliest data available from DHS. There are two types of asylum applications. One, defensive asylum, occurs when a person applies for asylum during deportation proceedings (including those apprehended by Border Patrol or deemed inadmissible by the Office of Field Operations at a port of entry).[iii] The other, affirmative asylum, occurs when people apply for asylum proactively without being in immigration proceedings. It can include people who are in the country legally and illegally.

ASYLUM APPLICATION CASES RECEIVED

BY TYPE

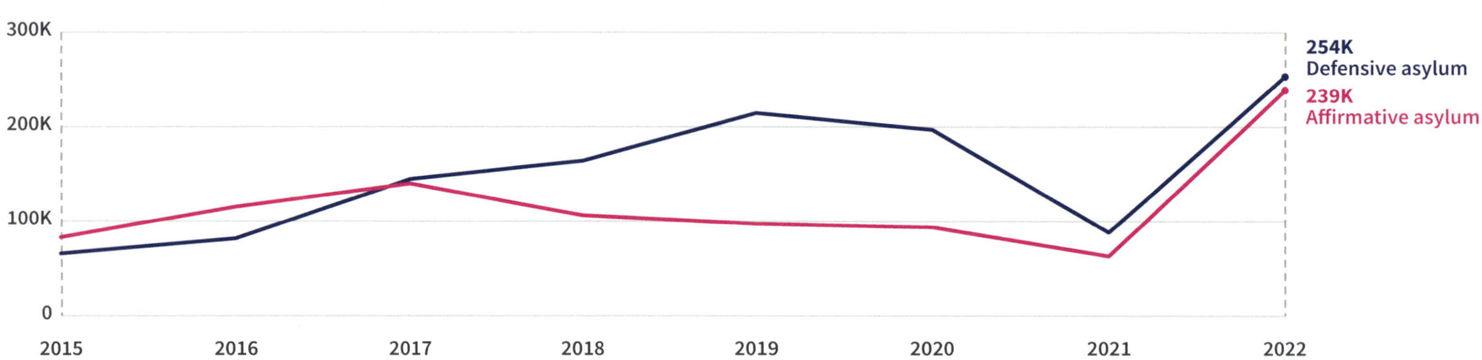

Source: Department of Homeland Security

How many people are granted asylum?

More than 36,000 people were granted asylum in the US in FY 2022. Asylee admissions more than doubled in FY 2022 after falling in FY 2020 and FY 2021. About 40% of asylees were from Asia, and 26% were from North America. Although more asylees were admitted in FY 2022 than in any year between FY 2006 and FY 2017, the percentage of asylum applications granted fell from 28% of 65,000 decided cases in FY 2014 to 16% of 198,000 in FY 2022. Outcomes vary for people whose cases are not granted, with some able to stay in the US and others ordered to be removed.[iv]

DECISIONS FOR ASYLUM CASES
AMONG AFFIRMATIVE OR DEFENSIVE ASYLUM CASES CLOSED EACH YEAR

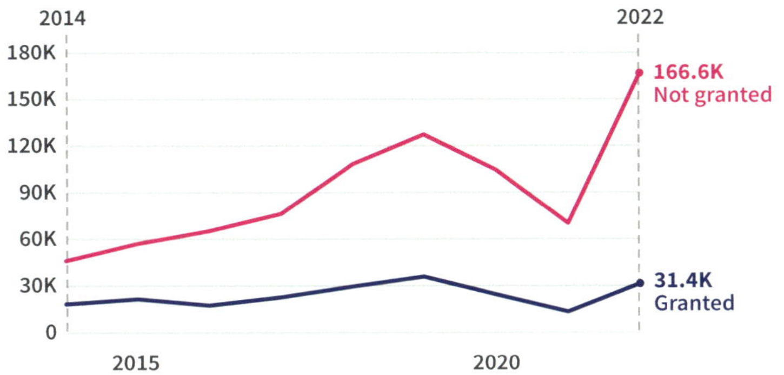

Source: Executive Office for Immigration Review and Department of Homeland Security
Note: Some cases may represent multiple individuals. Initial case completions only. Cases not granted can include denials, administrative closures, or cases with a closed status of "Other."

INDIVIDUALS GRANTED AFFIRMATIVE OR DEFENSIVE ASYLUM
BY REGION

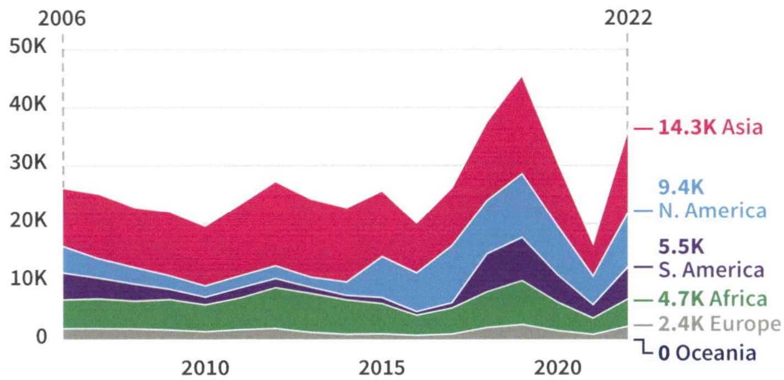

Source: Department of Homeland Security
Note: Excludes 896 asylees between 2007 and 2021 whose region was unknown.

How many refugees come to the US each year?

Both refugees and asylees have left their homes due to fear or persecution and are seeking safety elsewhere, but refugees apply before coming to the US.[v] The president sets the limit for the number of refugees that can enter the US. The US admitted about 25,000 refugees in FY 2022, with 45% coming from Africa and 37% from Asia. The US admitted 60,000 refugees in fiscal year 2023, the most since FY 2016.

REFUGEE CEILINGS AND ADMISSIONS

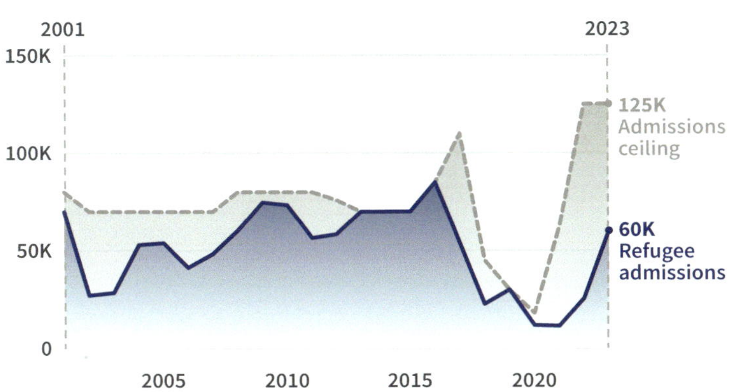

Source: Refugee Processing Center

REFUGEES ADMITTED
BY REGION

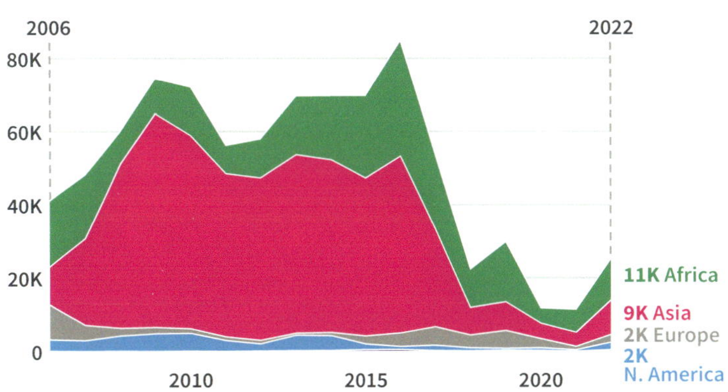

Source: Department of Homeland Security
Note: Due to the scale, 1,527 refugee arrivals between 2009 and 2022 whose region of origin is unknown are excluded from this chart, as are 15 refugees from Oceania between 2018 and 2022, and 3,542 from South America between 2006 and 2022.

How many immigrants are removed or returned from the US?

Removal proceedings (also called "deportation") can occur when a noncitizen in the US violates immigration law and receives a removal order from an immigration judge. About 109,000 people were removed from the US in FY 2022, up 27% from 2021 but still 75% lower than the 2013 peak of 432,000. About 58% of FY 2022 removals were due to the individual having a prior criminal conviction. The most common crimes associated with criminal removals in FY 2022 were immigration (15% of criminal removals), drug (14%), and assault (9%) offenses. On the other hand, returns don't have a formal removal order and are voluntary; they can include people apprehended near the border but do not include the same legal penalties as removals. Returns increased 47% in FY 2022 to 261,000, but remain 84% below the 2000 peak.

NONCITIZEN REMOVALS

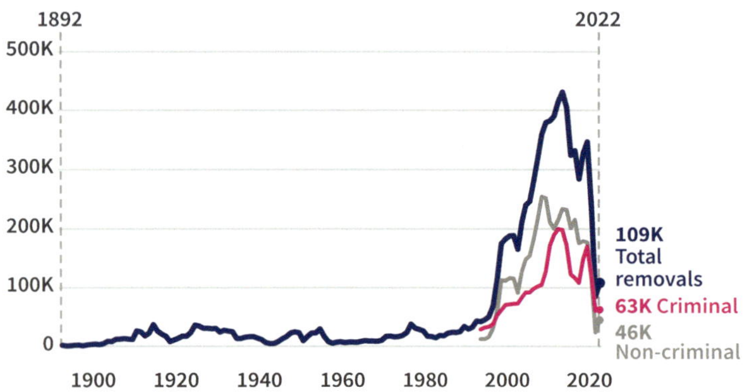

Source: Department of Homeland Security
Note: Removals are based on an order of removal, and have administrative or criminal consequences placed on subsequent reentry.

NONCITIZEN RETURNS

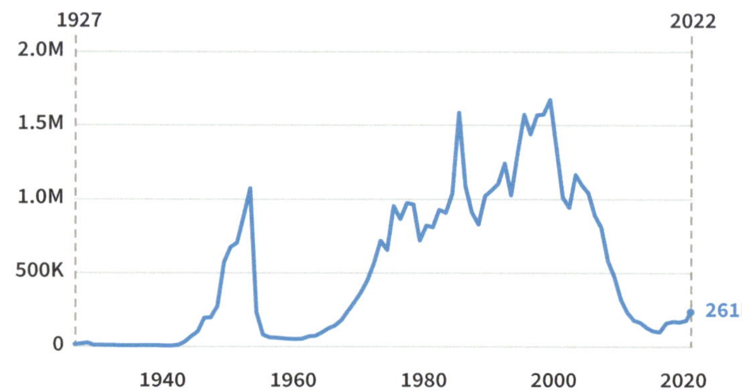

Source: Department of Homeland Security

Are immigration courts keeping up with their caseload?

Since 2009, there have been more new immigration cases than cases completed. The gap was highest in FY 2023, reaching a record of about 674,000 more cases received than completed. This has led to a growing number of pending cases at the end of each fiscal year, with about 2.5 million cases pending at the end of FY 2023.

IMMIGRATION COURTS CASELOAD

NEW CASE RECEIPTS AND TOTAL CASE COMPLETIONS

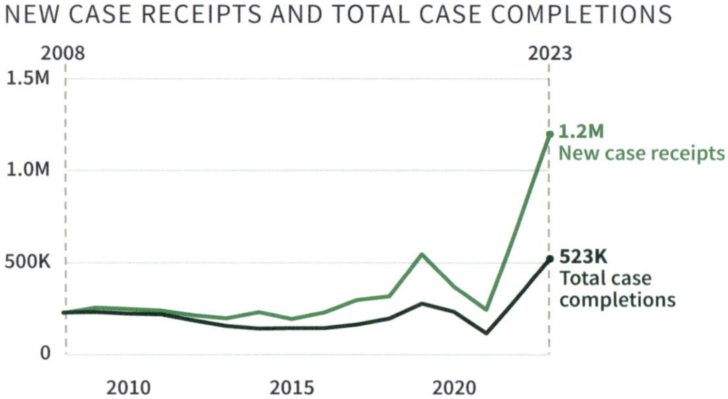

Source: Executive Office for Immigration Review

PENDING CASES AT END OF FISCAL YEAR

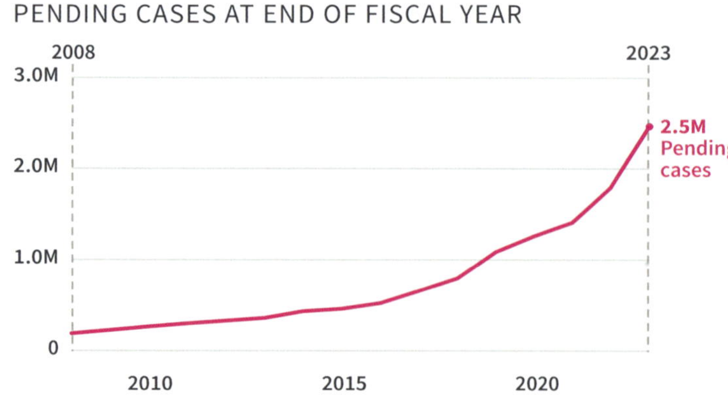

How many immigrants live in the US?

As of 2022, about 46 million people living in the US were born in another country. Of these, more than half were naturalized citizens. The Department of Homeland Security estimated there were 11.0 million unauthorized immigrants in the US in 2022.

FOREIGN-BORN POPULATION

BY NATURALIZATION STATUS

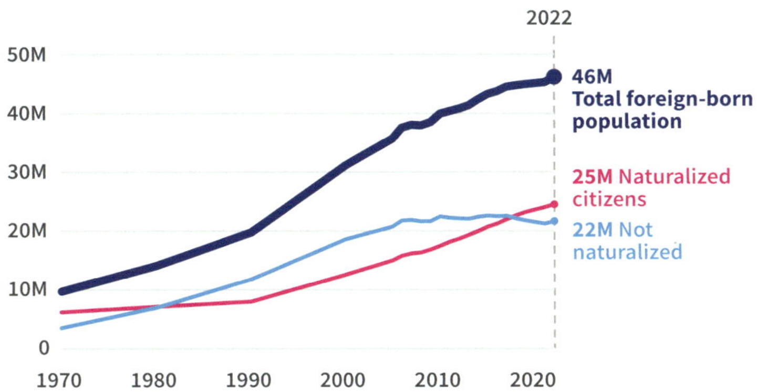

Source: Census Bureau

ESTIMATED UNAUTHORIZED IMMIGRANT POPULATION

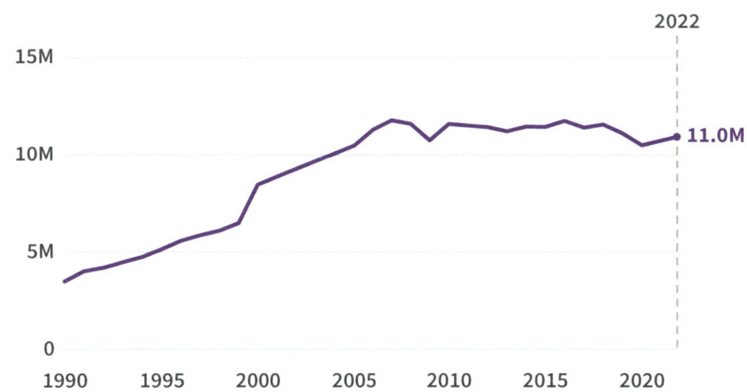

Source: Department of Homeland Security

What share of the population are immigrants, and how do they differ from the native-born population?

Immigrants are 13.9% of the population. They are more likely to be in the labor force and in a married-couple household than people born in the US. They are more likely to be female, more likely to be prime working age (25–54), and less likely to have a bachelor's degree compared to native-born Americans.

FOREIGN-BORN RESIDENTS

AS A SHARE OF THE POPULATION

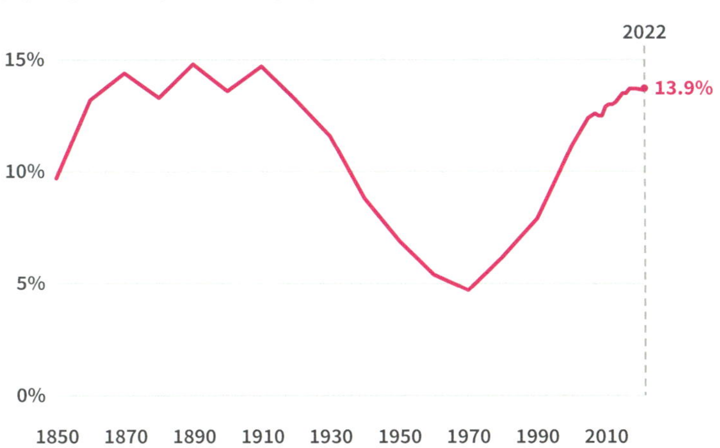

Source: Census Bureau

SELECTED CHARACTERISTICS OF FOREIGN- AND NATIVE-BORN POPULATIONS (2022)

SHARE OF POPULATION WITH EACH CHARACTERISTIC

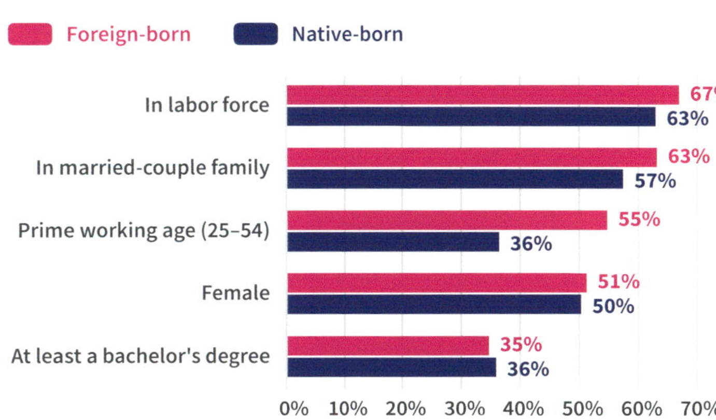

Source: Census Bureau

Note: Data for those with at least a bachelor's degree counts adults ages 25 and older. Data for those in the labor force counts people ages 16 and older.

How does workforce participation compare between native-born and foreign-born people?

The labor force participation rate (the share of the group that are employed or looking for work) averaged 66.6% for foreign-born people in 2023, compared to 61.8% for native-born people. Meanwhile, these groups historically have similar unemployment rates — an average of 3.7% for native-born people and 3.6% for foreign-born people in 2023.

LABOR FORCE PARTICIPATION RATE
BY NATIVITY

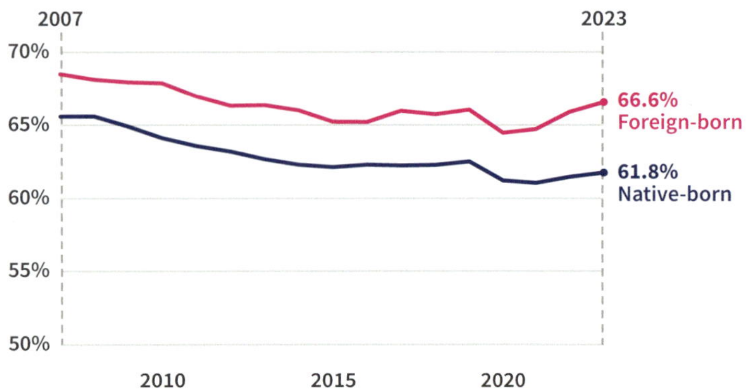

Source: Bureau of Labor Statistics
Note: Among population 16 years and older.

UNEMPLOYMENT RATE
BY NATIVITY

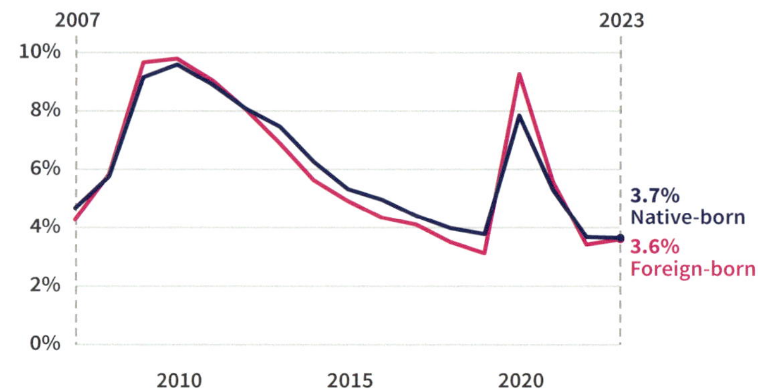

Source: Bureau of Labor Statistics
Note: Among population 16 years and older.

How many foreign-born workers are there?

The US had about 31 million foreign-born workers in 2023, 18.6% of the total labor force. This was a record size (in number and share). The foreign-born labor force share varies across states, from a low of 2.4% in West Virginia to 32.2% in California in 2022.

CIVILIAN LABOR FORCE LEVEL
TOTAL AND FOREIGN-BORN

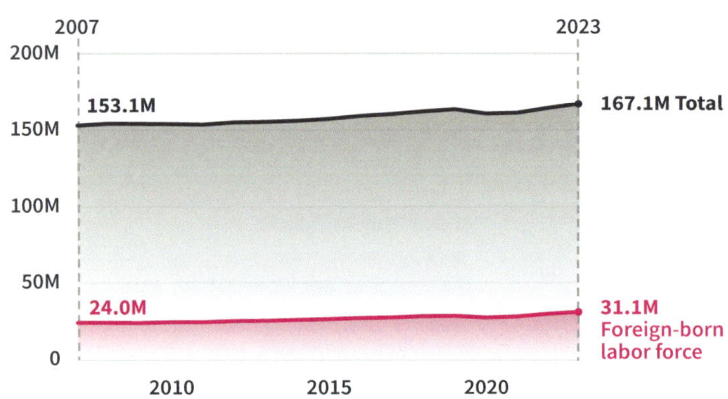

Source: Bureau of Labor Statistics

PERCENT OF THE CIVILIAN LABOR FORCE THAT IS FOREIGN-BORN (2022)
BY STATE

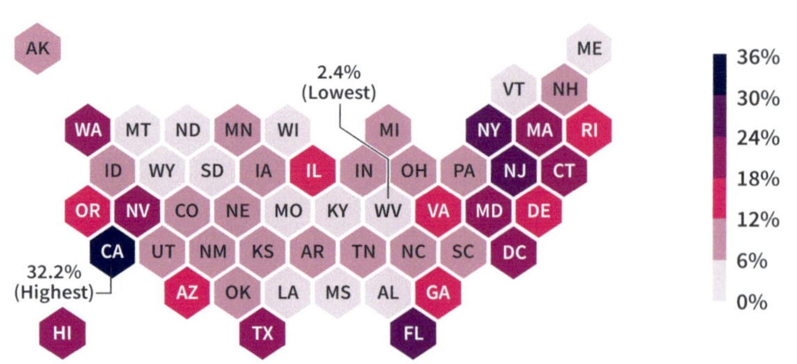

Source: Census Bureau
Note: Comparisons between some estimates may not be statistically significant.

Which industries rely the most on foreign-born workers?

Educational and health services employed the most foreign-born workers: 5.2 million in 2022. However, after accounting for the size of each industry, foreign-born workers were most prevalent in construction (29.2% of all workers), the other services industry (which includes activities such as dry cleaning, religious ministry, grantmaking, and equipment and machinery repair[vi]) (22.8%), and professional and business services (21.3%). They were least prevalent in public administration (9.2%).

FOREIGN-BORN EMPLOYMENT LEVEL (2022)

BY INDUSTRY

Source: Census Bureau

SHARE OF WORKERS THAT ARE FOREIGN-BORN (2022)

BY INDUSTRY

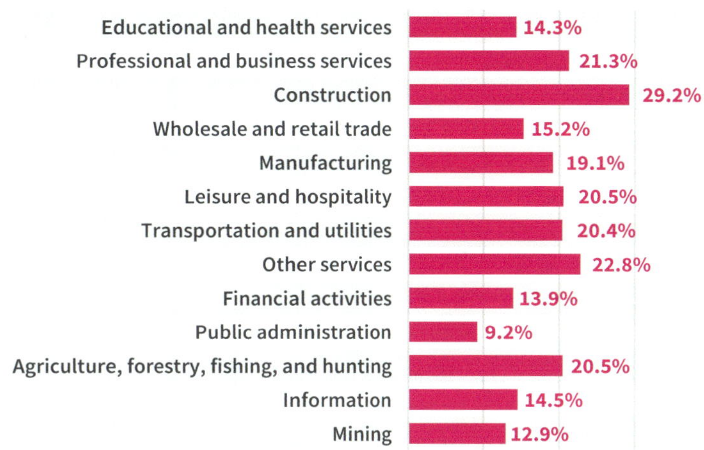

Source: Census Bureau

How many work visas does the US give and for what types of occupations?

Awarded work visas dipped in FY 2020 but increased after that. In FY 2023, they reached their highest level since at least 1997. Around 27% of FY 2023 work visas were for agricultural (H-2A) workers. About 23% were for workers in specialty occupations, with 266,000 H-1B visas awarded that year at a record high.

WORK VISAS GRANTED

BY TYPE

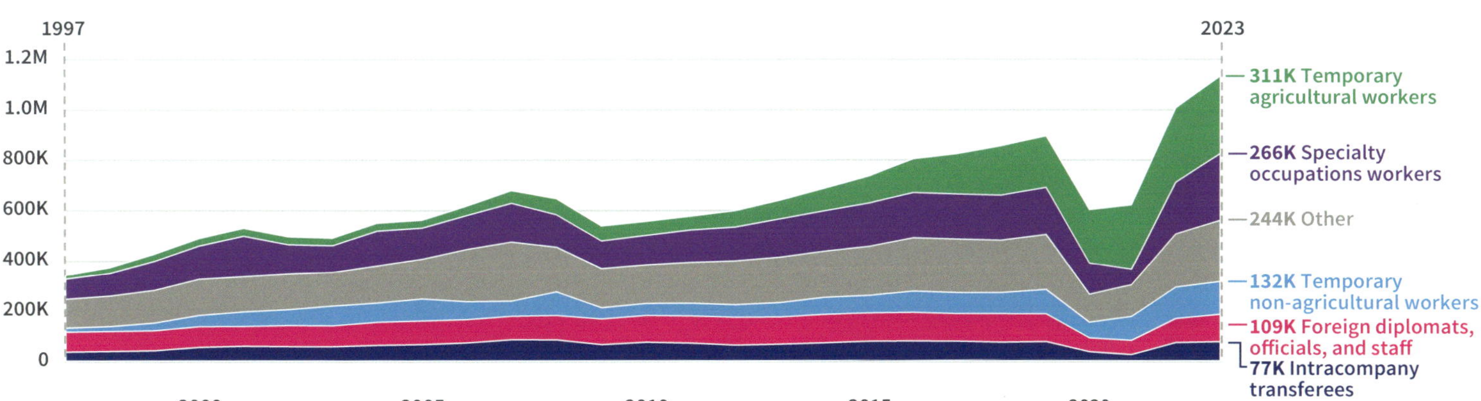

Source: Department of State

Note: Some green cards are also awarded each year for employment reasons. In 2022, about 49,000 new arrival green cards were given for work, about 4.8% of the number of total work visas granted that year.

Economy

Economy facts

Inflation

- The Consumer Price Index (CPI) 12-month inflation rate peaked at 9.0% in June 2022, the highest since the early 1980s. It cooled to below 4% from June to December 2023.
- Consumers faced prices in December 2023 that were 20.4% higher for food, 18.7% higher for shelter, and 33.5% higher for energy than in January 2021.
- To combat inflation, the Federal Reserve increased interest rates seven times in 2022 and four times in 2023, reaching a target range of 5.25% to 5.50% by late July 2023.
- The Personal Consumption Expenditures Index (PCE) 12-month inflation rate inched towards the Federal Reserve's target rate of 2% year-over-year inflation in 2023 and the beginning of 2024.

US trade

- The US trade deficit decreased by 22% from 2022 to 2023, from $990.3 billion to $773.4 billion.
- The services trade surplus increased to $288.2 billion in 2023, reversing a four-year downward trend.
- Canada remained the nation's top trading partner in 2023, followed by Mexico and China, marking the first time in 20 years that the US imported more from Mexico than China.
- The country's largest trade deficit was with China, totaling $253.4 billion.

Economic growth

- In 2023, real GDP (GDP adjusted for inflation) increased 2.5%, which is above the average annual rate of 2.1% from 2000 through 2022.
- From 2022 to 2023, real GDP decreased in one state, Delaware, and increased by more than 5.5% in North Dakota and Texas.
- In 2023, US employers added approximately 3.1 million jobs, indicating growth but at a slower pace than in 2021 and 2022. Florida, Nevada, Texas, and Alaska saw job increases of 3% or more.

Labor market

- The unemployment rate remained steady at 3.6% in 2023, matching the previous year. These were the lowest levels since 1969. Rates varied across states, from a 1.9% low in North Dakota to a 5.1% high in Nevada.
- The 2023 job openings rate averaged 5.7%, or about 9.35 million job openings. This is down 1.1 percentage points from the 2022 peak, but higher than any other year prior to 2021.
- The labor force participation rate was 62.6% in 2023, slightly below the 2019 level. State participation rates varied, with Mississippi at the low end and Utah at the high end.

About the data

What are the primary sources of data on this topic?

- Bureau of Labor Statistics (BLS)
- Bureau of Economic Analysis (BEA)
- Federal Reserve of St. Louis (FRED) gathers and publishes data from BLS and BEA. USAFacts often accesses economic data through FRED's website.

What adjustments did USAFacts make to this data?

- Trade balance was adjusted for inflation using the Consumer Price Index for All Urban Consumers (not seasonally adjusted).

Other things to know about the data

- The Bureau of Labor Statistics and Bureau of Economic Analysis update many economic indicators monthly, including data about inflation, employment, job openings, unemployment, and labor force participation.

GOVERNMENT SPENDING 1980–2023

ECONOMY

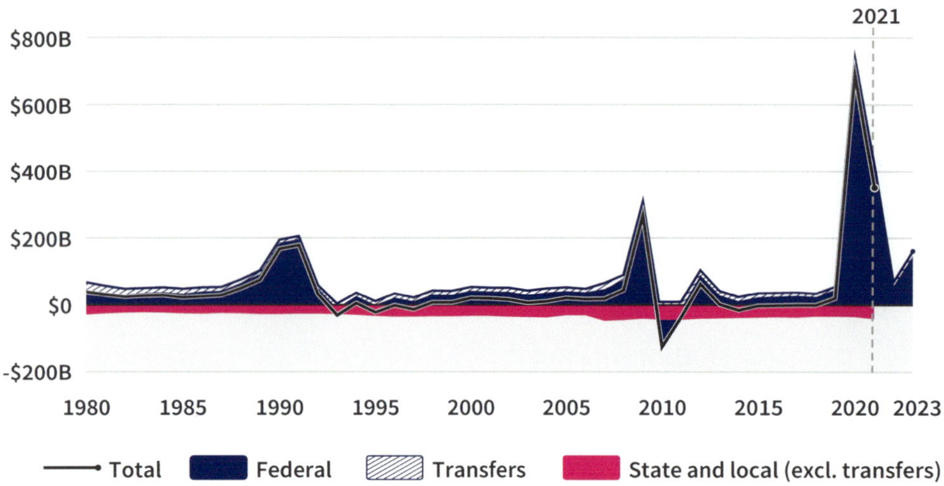

2023 FEDERAL SPENDING*

$161 billion

PERCENT OF FEDERAL SPENDING

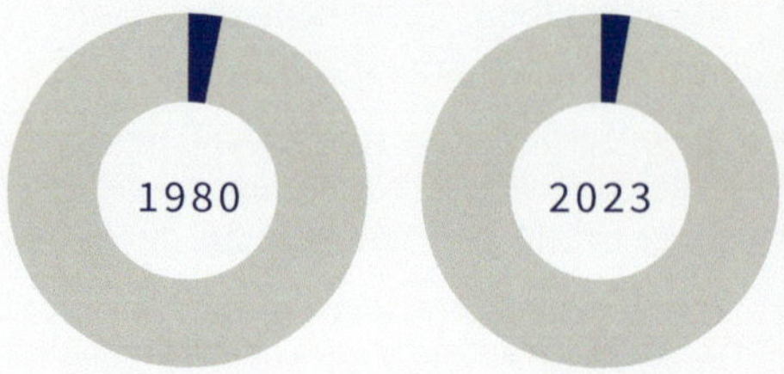

3% **3%**

Source: USAFacts aggregation of data from the Office of Management and Budget (OMB), the Census Bureau, and the Bureau of Economic Analysis (BEA)
Adjusted for inflation (FY 2023 dollars)
Note: *Includes direct spending and transfers. Federal spending, transfers, and state and local spending data capture net expenditures. In some cases, this results in negative net spending.

Federal agencies spending: Economy

Federal agency	Net spending in FY 2023	Share of spending transferred to state and local governments	Share of spending that was mandatory
Federal Deposit Insurance Corporation	$91.7 billion	0%	100%
National Aeronautics and Space Administration	$24.5 billion	0%	0%
Department of Housing and Urban Development	$9.8 billion	91%	0%
National Science Foundation	$8.9 billion	0%	4%
Other agencies	$26.7 billion	14%	36%

Source: USAFacts calculations based on the Public Budget Database from the Office of Management and Budget

How quickly are prices increasing?

The CPI is a common measure of price inflation. The 12-month percent change in CPI began rising in early 2021, peaking at 9.0% in June 2022 — the highest 12-month inflation rate since the early 1980s. Inflation has cooled since then, eventually falling and remaining below 4% from July 2023 through December 2023. Still, food prices were 20.4% higher in December 2023 than in January 2021. Shelter prices were 18.7% higher. Energy prices were highest in June 2022 compared to January 2021. They've since fallen, but remained 33.5% higher in December 2023 than in January 2021.

CONSUMER PRICE INDEX

12-MONTH PERCENT CHANGE

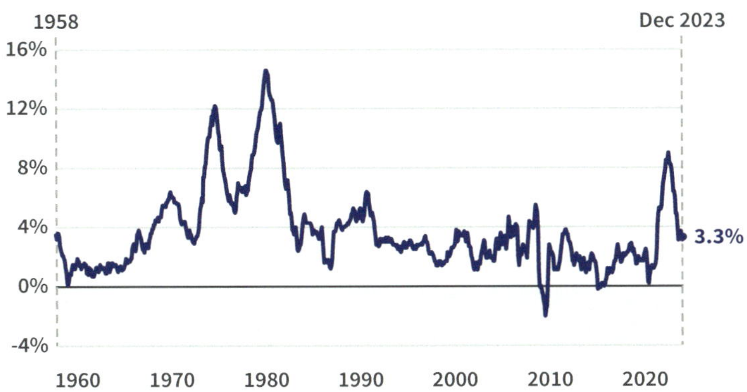

Source: Bureau of Labor Statistics
Note: Seasonally adjusted.

PERCENT CHANGE IN CONSUMER PRICE INDEX FROM JANUARY 2021

BY SELECT CATEGORIES

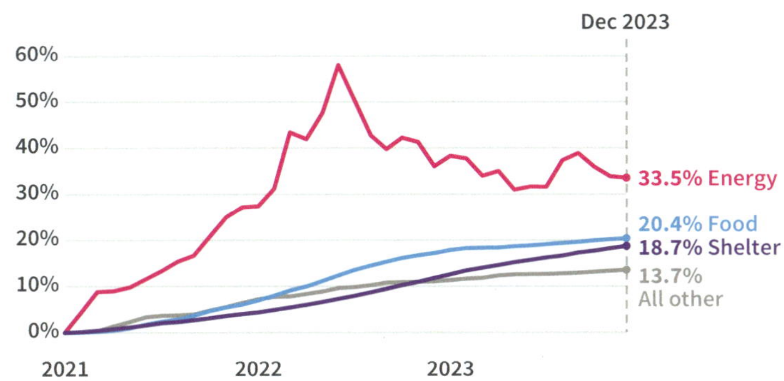

Source: Bureau of Labor Statistics
Note: Seasonally adjusted.

How does the Federal Reserve aim to influence inflation?

The Federal Reserve raised interest rates seven times in 2022 and four times in 2023 to slow inflation. It raised the federal funds interest rate to between 5.25% and 5.50% in late July 2023 and has left rates unchanged since. The PCE price index measures the prices of goods and services consumers purchase and is the Federal Reserve's preferred inflation measure. Inflation inched towards the Fed's target rate of 2% year-over-year in 2023 and the beginning of 2024.

PERSONAL CONSUMPTION EXPENDITURES PRICE INDEX

12-MONTH PERCENT CHANGE

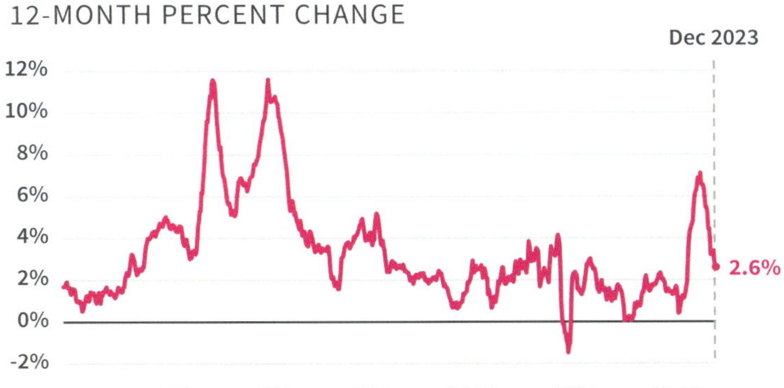

Source: Bureau of Labor Statistics
Note: Seasonally adjusted.

FEDERAL FUNDS RATE

Source: Board of Governors of the Federal Reserve System

Is the US economy growing?

In 2023, US GDP reached $27.4 trillion. Real GDP, which accounts for inflation, increased 2.5%, which was above the 2000–2022 average annual rate of 2.1%. From 2022 to 2023, real GDP decreased in one state, Delaware, and increased by less than 1% in Georgia, Mississippi, New York, and Wisconsin. It increased by more than 5.5% in North Dakota and Texas.

ANNUAL PERCENT CHANGE IN REAL GROSS DOMESTIC PRODUCT (GDP)

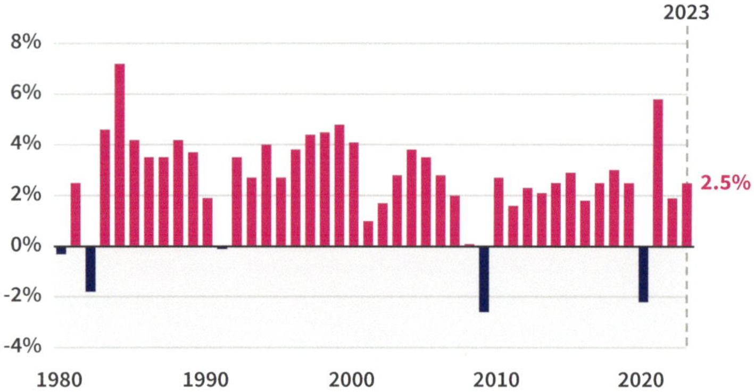

Source: Bureau of Economic Analysis

PERCENT CHANGE IN REAL GDP (2022 VS. 2023)

BY STATE

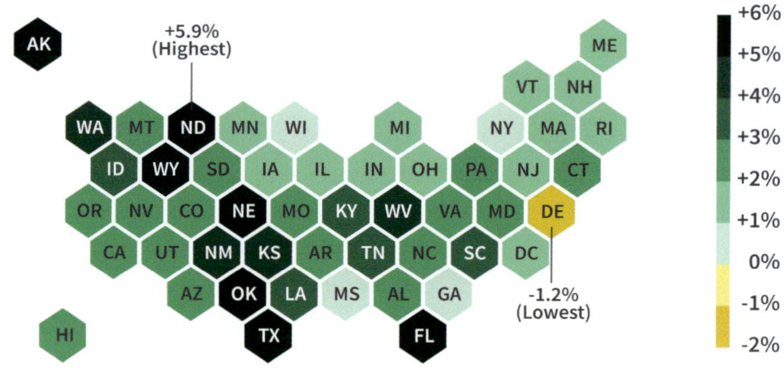

Source: Bureau of Economic Analysis

How many more people are employed compared to 2022?

US employers added about 3.1 million jobs in 2023. This was fewer than in 2021 and 2022, but more than any other year since 1999. From 2022 to 2023, four states had job increases of 3% or more: Nevada, Florida, Texas, and Alaska. Washington, DC, and California had the smallest increases, at 0.9% each.

NET CHANGE IN EMPLOYMENT (JOBS)

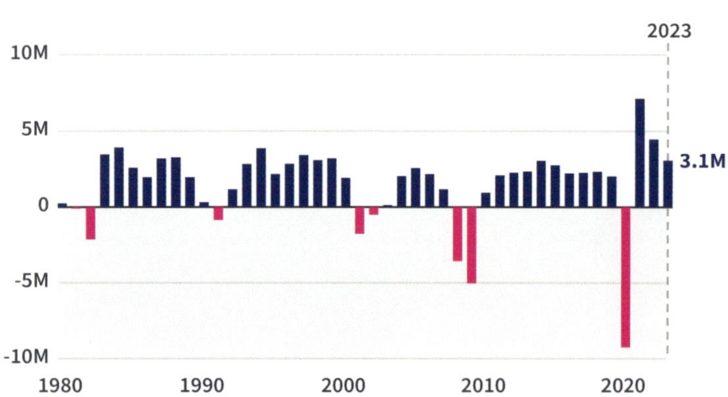

Source: Bureau of Labor Statistics

PERCENT CHANGE IN ANNUAL AVERAGE EMPLOYMENT (2022 VS. 2023)

BY STATE

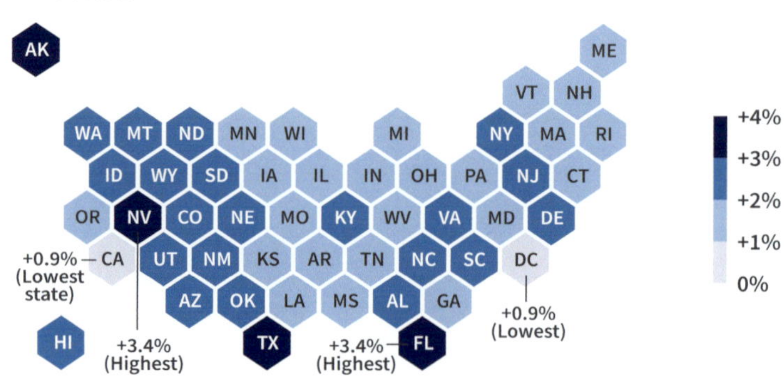

Source: Bureau of Labor Statistics

What is the unemployment rate and how does it vary by state?

The average unemployment rate was 3.6% in 2023, unchanged from 2022 and lower than any other year since 1969. At the state level, rates ranged from a low of 1.9% in North Dakota to a high of 5.1% in Nevada.

UNEMPLOYMENT RATE
ANNUAL AVERAGE

Source: Bureau of Labor Statistics

UNEMPLOYMENT RATE (2023 AVERAGE)
BY STATE

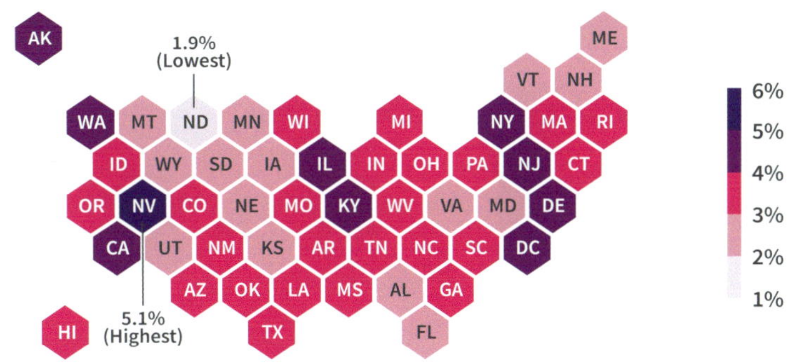

Source: Bureau of Labor Statistics

Are employers hiring?

The average job openings rate in 2023 was 5.7%, equal to 9.35 million job openings. This is down 1.1 percentage points from the 2022 peak of 6.8%, but higher than any other year prior to 2021. The number of open jobs exceeded the number of people looking for work in the last eight months of 2021, and all of 2022 and 2023. The job openings rate ranged from 4.4% in New York to 8.1% in Alaska.

JOB OPENINGS RATE
ANNUAL AVERAGE

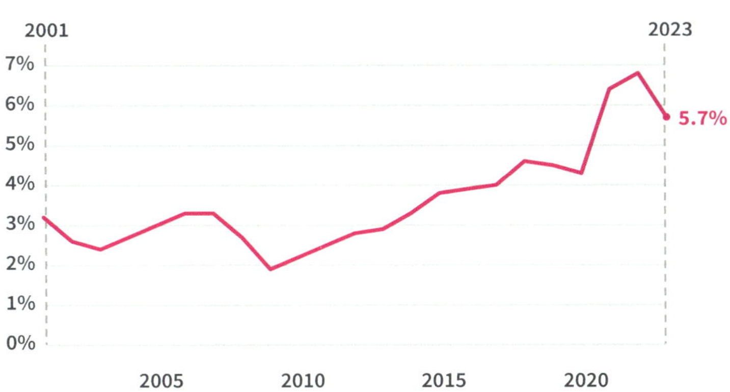

Source: Bureau of Labor Statistics

JOB OPENINGS RATE (2023 AVERAGE)
BY STATE

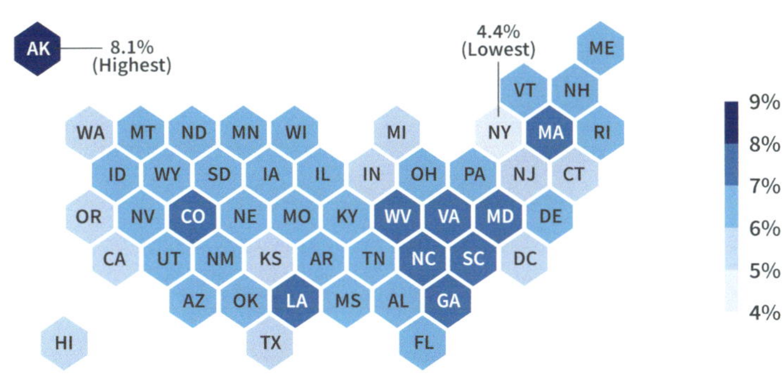

Source: Bureau of Labor Statistics

What is the labor force participation rate in the US, and how has it changed?

The labor force participation rate, the share of the population ages 16 and older that is either employed or looking for work, peaked between 1997 and 2000. Since then, it mostly declined through 2015 before increasing in 2019 to 63.1%. It hit a low of 61.7% during the pandemic but reached 62.6% in 2023, remaining 0.5 percentage points below 2019. The Bureau of Labor Statistics expects the labor force participation rate to continue declining as the share of Americans who are older grows.[vii] Although the labor force participation rate for those 55 and older has increased since 2000, they participate in the workforce at much lower rates than 20- to 54-year-olds.

LABOR FORCE PARTICIPATION RATE
ANNUAL AVERAGE

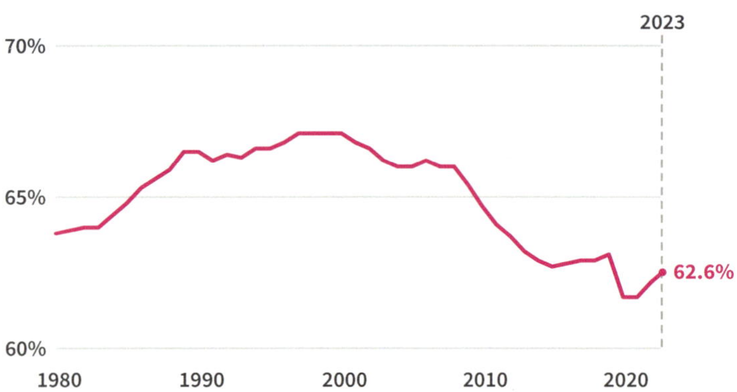

Source: Bureau of Labor Statistics

LABOR FORCE PARTICIPATION RATE
ANNUAL AVERAGE, BY AGE GROUP

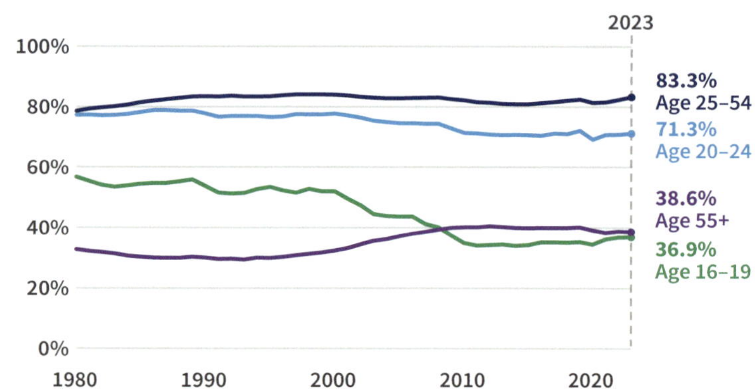

Source: Bureau of Labor Statistics

What is the labor force participation rate by state, and how has it changed?

In 2023, the labor force participation rate ranged from a low of 54.0% in Mississippi to highs of 69.5% in Utah and 71.7% in Washington, DC. The South had eight of the 10 states with the lowest participation rates. Thirty-five states had labor force participation rates lower in 2023 than in 2019. Labor force participation rates decreased the most in Maryland and New Hampshire, by 4.2 percentage points.

LABOR FORCE PARTICIPATION RATE (2023 AVERAGE)
BY STATE

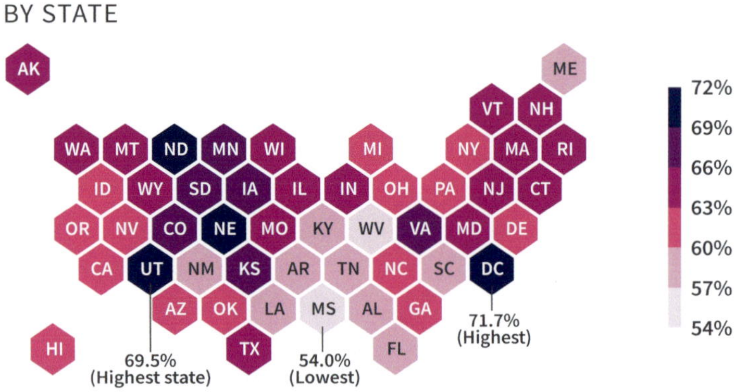

Source: Bureau of Labor Statistics

PERCENTAGE POINT CHANGE IN THE LABOR FORCE PARTICIPATION RATE (2019 VS. 2023)
ANNUAL AVERAGE, BY STATE

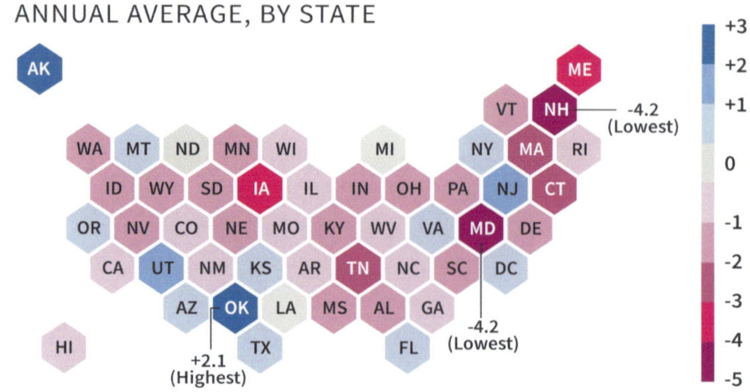

Source: Bureau of Labor Statistics

What is the trade balance in the US?

The US continued to import more than it exported in 2023; however, the trade deficit fell 22% from $990.3 billion in 2022 to $773.4 billion in 2023. The services trade surplus increased to $288.2 billion, following four consecutive years of decline.

NET TRADE BALANCE

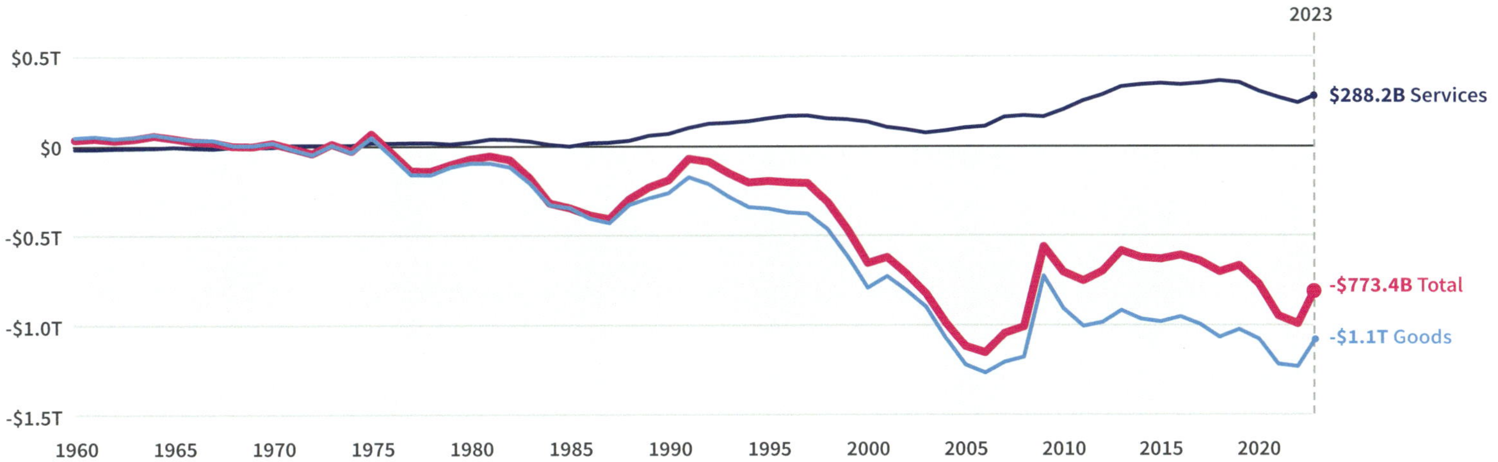

Source: Bureau of Economic Analysis
Adjusted for inflation (2023 dollars)

Who are the country's top trading partners?

Canada was the nation's top trading partner when combining the value of imports and exports. For the first time in 20 years, the US imported more goods and services from Mexico than China in 2023. However, the largest trade deficit was with China, at $253.4 billion.

NET TRADE BALANCE WITH TOP TRADING PARTNERS

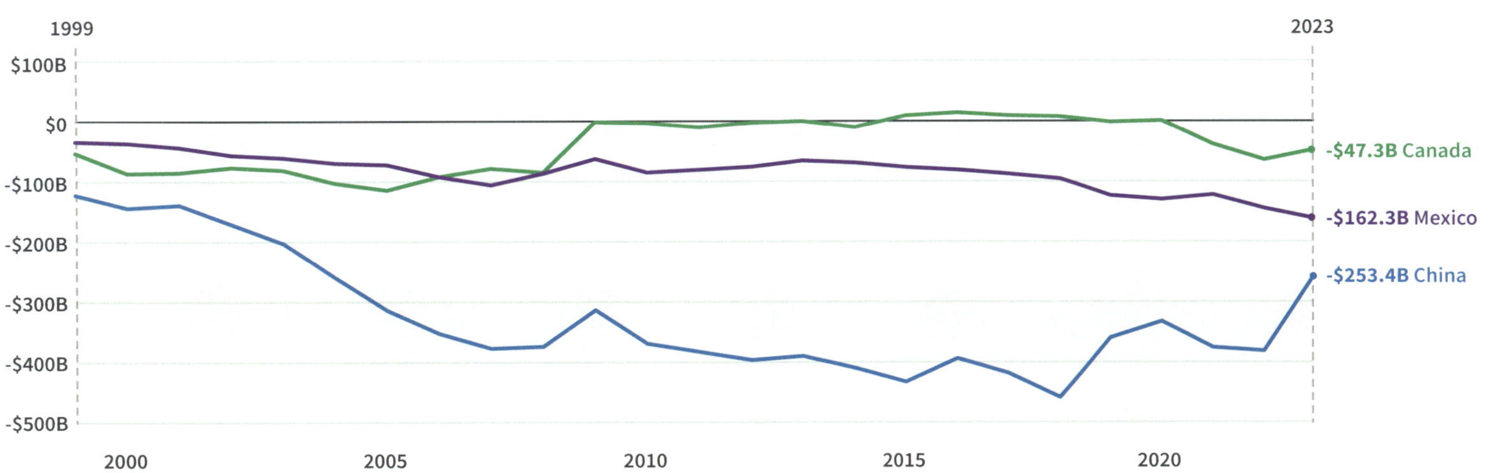

Source: Bureau of Economic Analysis
Adjusted for inflation (2023 dollars)

Standard of living

Standard of living facts

Gross domestic product (GDP) per person

- In 2023, real gross domestic product (rGDP, or GDP adjusted for inflation) per person in the US reached an all-time high of $66,749, up 2.0% from 2022.
- 2023 rGDP per person exceeded $85,000 in New York, Massachusetts, and Washington state, while it was below $46,000 in Mississippi, West Virginia, and Arkansas.
- The change in rGDP per person from 2022 to 2023 varied by state, decreasing most in Delaware (-2.4%) and increasing most in Alaska (5.3%).

Family income, taxes, and transfers

- In 2022, the average middle-class family made about $64,420 in market income, paid $21,620 in taxes, and received $25,780 in government assistance.
- Between 2000 and 2022, average tax payments increased for all families except the bottom 20% of earners (adjusted for inflation) and government assistance increased for all income quintiles.
- The Mortgage Interest Deduction and Charitable Contribution Deduction benefit higher-earning families more than lower-earning families, while the Earned Income Tax Credit most benefits the 20th-40th percentile of earners. In 2022 the expanded Child Tax Credit average benefits were highest among families in the 60th-80th percentile of earners.

Poverty

- The US poverty rate was 11.5% in 2022, but 15% among children.
- In 2022, nine out of the 10 states with the highest poverty rates were in the South. New Mexico had the highest poverty rate, with one in five people living in poverty.

Housing

- Nearly 52% of renters and almost 23% of homeowners spent 30% or more of their income on housing in 2022.
- The United States had 15.3 subsidized housing units available per 1,000 people in 2023, a figure that has been relatively stable since 2016.
- Per 1,000 people, Washington, DC, plus Rhode Island and New York, had the most subsidized units. Arizona, Utah, and Idaho had the fewest.
- In 2023, the average wait time for subsidized housing was 25 months, consistent with 2022 and slightly shorter than 2021 and 2020.

Food insecurity

- In 2022, 12.8% of US households experienced food insecurity. Households with children faced nearly a 5 percentage point rise in food insecurity rates compared to the previous year.
- An average of 42.1 million people received SNAP benefits each month in FY 2023, up 18% from FY 2019. The average per-person benefit surged to $211.93 a month due to COVID-19 relief efforts, despite emergency allotments ending in March 2023.

Median annual wages

- The nation's median annual wage was $48,151 in 2023, down 0.3% from 2022 after adjusting for inflation.
- Massachusetts, Washington, and New York had the highest median wages, each with wages above $56,500. Median wages were under $40,000 in three states: Mississippi, Arkansas, and West Virginia.

About the data

What are the primary sources of data on this topic?

- Census Bureau
- Internal Revenue Service
- Bureau of Economic Analysis
- Bureau of Labor Statistics
- Department of Housing and Urban Development
- Department of Agriculture

What adjustments did USAFacts make to this data?

- There are many ways to define middle class. USAFacts defines the middle class as those in the middle fifth of the family market income distribution — or the 40th–60th percentile. Families are defined in this analysis as tax filing units and can consist of one or more individuals.
- USAFacts combines IRS, Census, and some other government sources to provide a closer look at how certain economic and demographic characteristics differ among family types and across the income spectrum. Charts in this section showing market income, taxes, transfers, tax savings, and tax credits rely upon this combined data. USAFacts uses a procedure similar to that used by the Congressional Budget Office and others, as explained in the families and individuals methodology here: https://usafacts.org/methodology/.

GOVERNMENT SPENDING 1980–2023

STANDARD OF LIVING

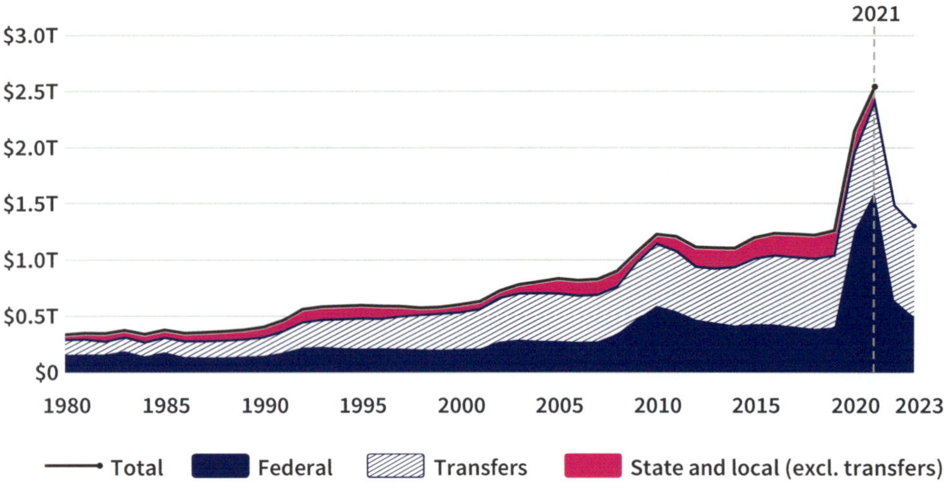

2023 FEDERAL SPENDING*

$1.3 trillion

PERCENT OF FEDERAL SPENDING

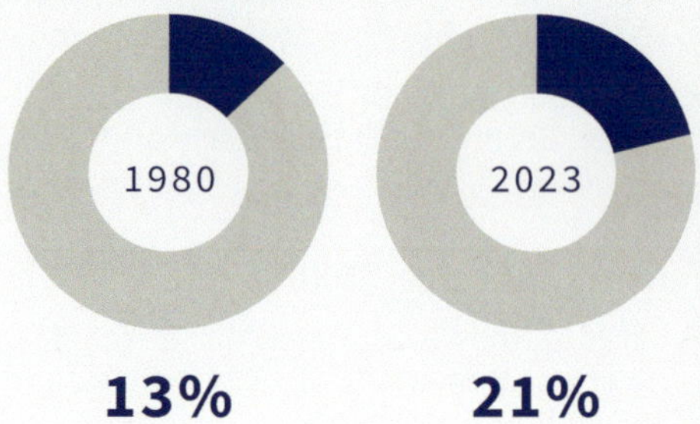

Source: USAFacts aggregation of data from the Office of Management and Budget (OMB), the Census Bureau, and the Bureau of Economic Analysis (BEA)
Adjusted for inflation (FY 2023 dollars)
Note: *Includes direct spending and transfers.

Federal agencies spending: Standard of living

Federal agency	Net spending in FY 2023	Share of spending transferred to state and local governments	Share of spending that was mandatory
Department of Health and Human Services	$706.7 billion	97%	96%
Department of the Treasury	$224.1 billion	8%	100%
Department of Agriculture	$174.2 billion	28%	95%
Social Security Administration	$62.0 billion	0%	93%
Other agencies	$134.5 billion	39%	29%

Source: USAFacts calculations based on the Public Budget Database from the Office of Management and Budget

How has the standard of living changed over time?

GDP per person is often used as a proxy for a country's standard of living.[viii] Real gross domestic product per person was $66,749 in 2023, an all-time high. It increased 2.0% from 2022, higher than the average annual change from 2000 through 2022 of 1.3%.

REAL GROSS DOMESTIC PRODUCT (GDP)

PER CAPITA

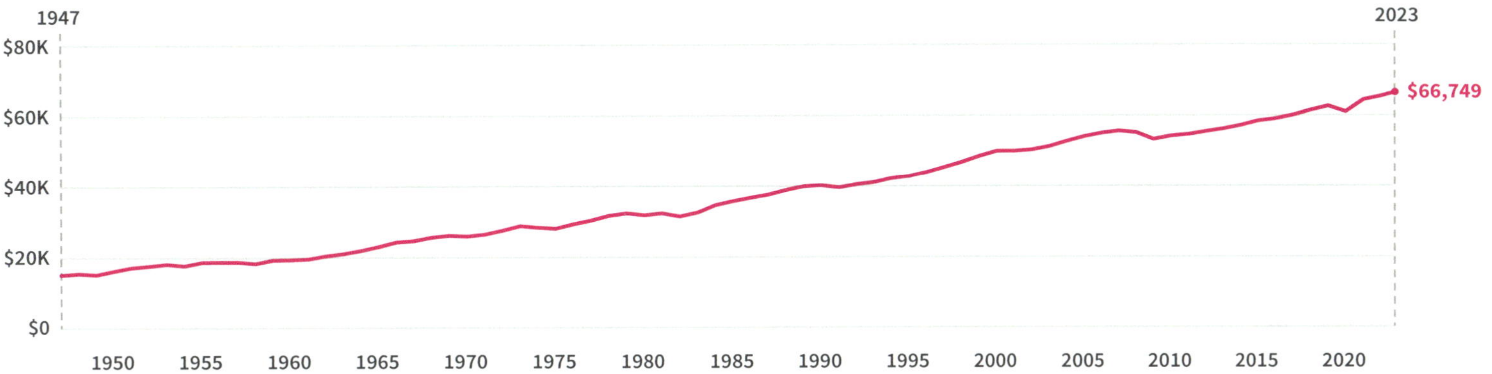

Source: Bureau of Economic Analysis

How does the standard of living vary by state?

In 2023, rGDP per person exceeded $85,000 in three states — New York, Massachusetts, and Washington — and was less than $46,000 in three states — Mississippi, West Virginia, and Arkansas. From 2022 to 2023, the change in GDP per capita ranged from -2.4% in Delaware to 5.3% in Alaska.

REAL GDP PER CAPITA (2023)

BY STATE

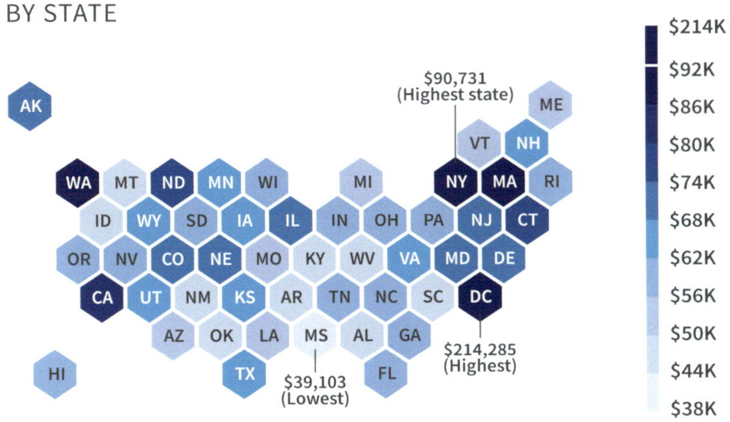

Source: Bureau of Economic Analysis

PERCENT CHANGE IN REAL GDP PER CAPITA (2022 VS. 2023)

BY STATE

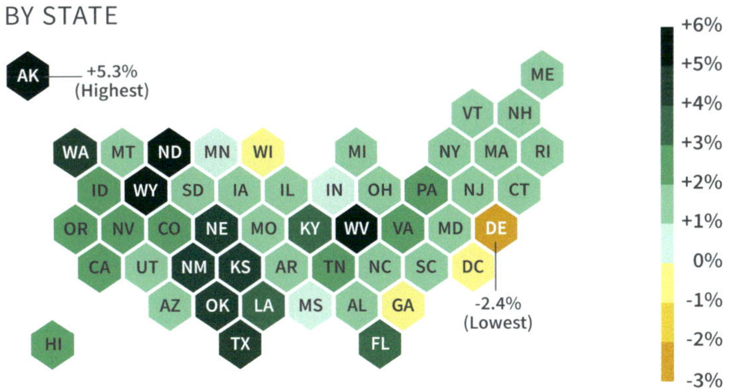

Source: Bureau of Economic Analysis

How much do people in the US make and how has that changed?

In 2022, the average middle-class family (the middle 20% of income earners) earned about $64,420 in market income. That is down 1% from 2000 after adjusting for inflation. Income for the bottom 20% and second 20% also decreased. The largest percent decrease was among the bottom 20%, with their average market income falling 48% to $2,804. Income for the top 1% rose most — 19% — to over $2.9 million.

AVERAGE TOTAL MARKET INCOME (2000 AND 2022)
BY INCOME GROUP

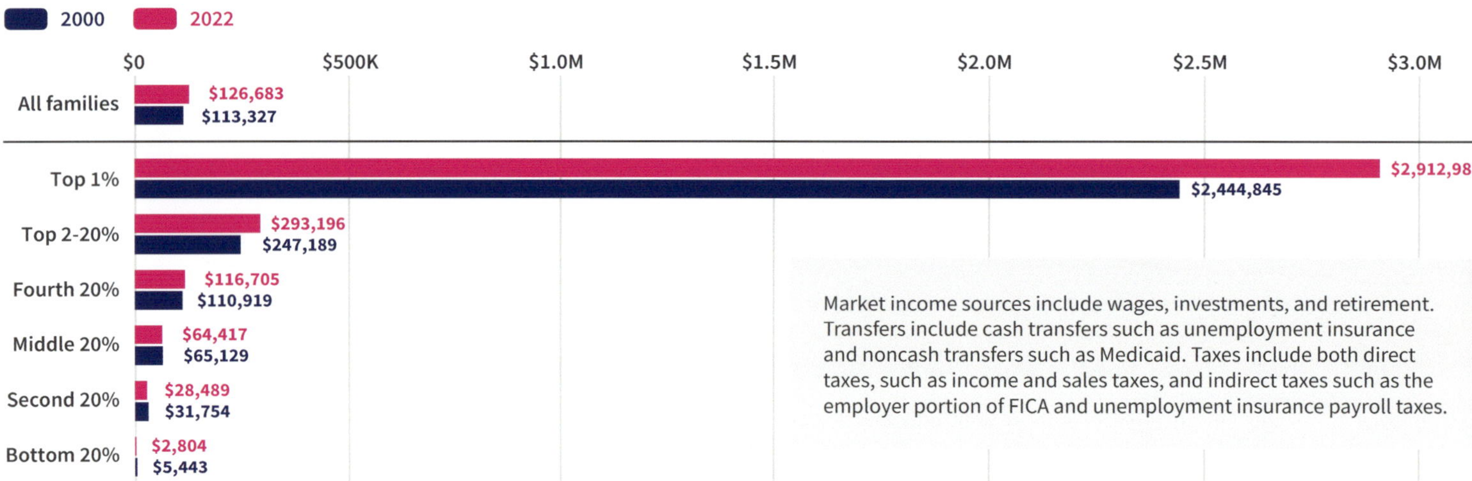

Market income sources include wages, investments, and retirement. Transfers include cash transfers such as unemployment insurance and noncash transfers such as Medicaid. Taxes include both direct taxes, such as income and sales taxes, and indirect taxes such as the employer portion of FICA and unemployment insurance payroll taxes.

Source: USAFacts calculations using data from the Internal Revenue Service and Census Bureau
Adjusted for inflation (2023 dollars)

How much do Americans pay in taxes and how much do they receive from the government?

The average middle-class family paid $21,620 in taxes and received $25,778 in government assistance in 2022. The average family in each percentile, except those in the bottom 20%, paid more in taxes compared to 2000 after adjusting for inflation. Average government assistance to families increased across all income percentiles. It increased more than 50% for all groups, except for the bottom 20%. Part of the increase between 2000 and 2022 was due to temporary COVID-19 programs that sent more money to individuals and families (i.e., expanded Child Tax Credit, SNAP).

AVERAGE TAXES PAID (2000 AND 2022)
BY INCOME GROUP

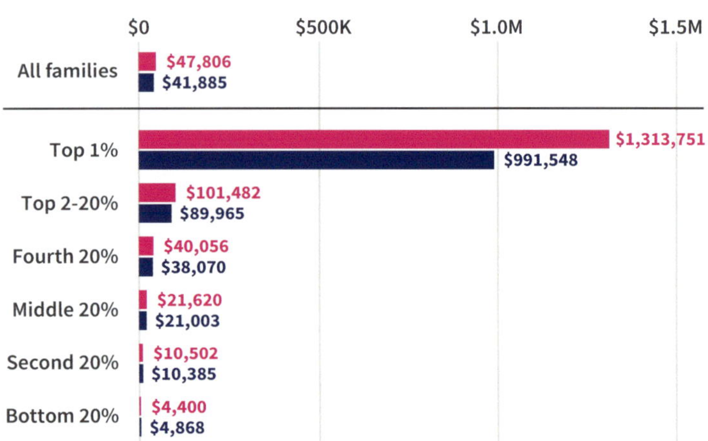

AVERAGE TRANSFERS RECEIVED (2000 AND 2022)
BY INCOME GROUP

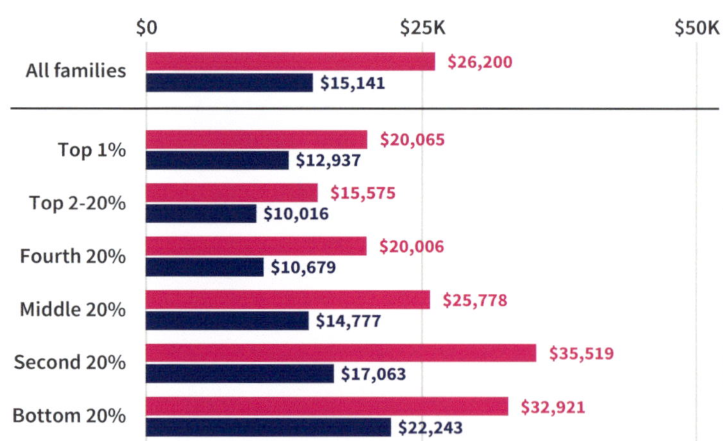

Source: USAFacts calculations using data from the Internal Revenue Service and Census Bureau
Adjusted for inflation (2023 dollars)

How much tax savings do families achieve through credits and deductions?

Tax deductions and credits can reduce people's tax liability and government revenue. **Deductions** lower a person's taxable income, which means they owe less money. Two of the costliest deductions for the federal government are the Charitable Contribution Deduction and the Mortgage Interest Deduction. In 2022, the top 20% saved more money in taxes from the Charitable Contribution Deduction and from the Mortgage Interest Deduction than lower-earning income percentiles.

The government provides tax **credits** to encourage certain behaviors and reduce how much taxpayers owe. The Earned Income Tax Credit (EITC) and Child Tax Credit (CTC) are the costliest tax credits for the federal government. Both support families with children but have different eligibility rules. The EITC primarily targets lower-income families; the second 20% of earners received the highest average EITC benefit. The 2017 Tax Cuts and Jobs Act (TCJA) extended the CTC to higher-earning families (married couples earning up to $400,000 are eligible for at least a partial benefit). In 2022, families in the fourth 20% of earners received the highest average credit. The CTC provision of the TCJA, along with changes to the standard deduction, marginal tax rates, itemized deductions, and some other provisions will expire at the end of 2025 without new legislation from Congress.

AVERAGE SAVINGS FROM CHARITABLE CONTRIBUTION DEDUCTION (2022)

BY INCOME GROUP

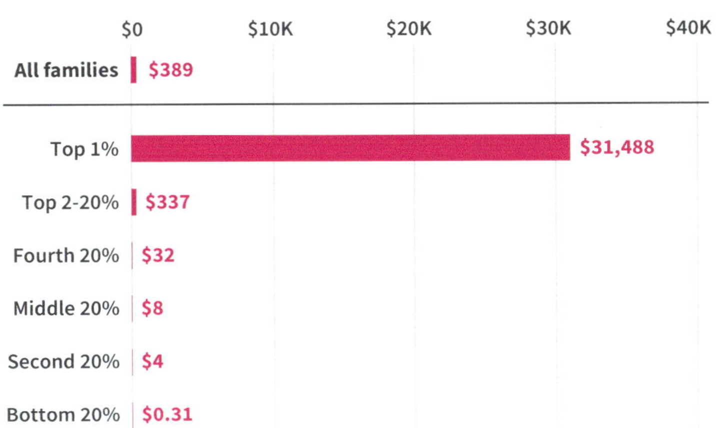

AVERAGE SAVINGS FROM MORTGAGE INTEREST DEDUCTION (2022)

BY INCOME GROUP

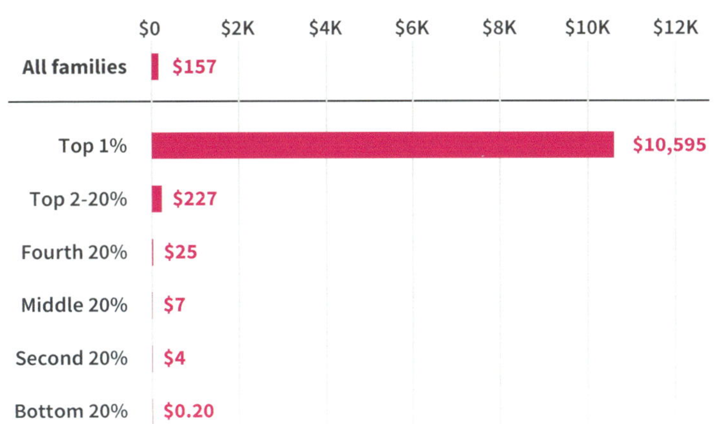

AVERAGE CREDIT FROM CHILD TAX CREDIT (2022)

BY INCOME GROUP

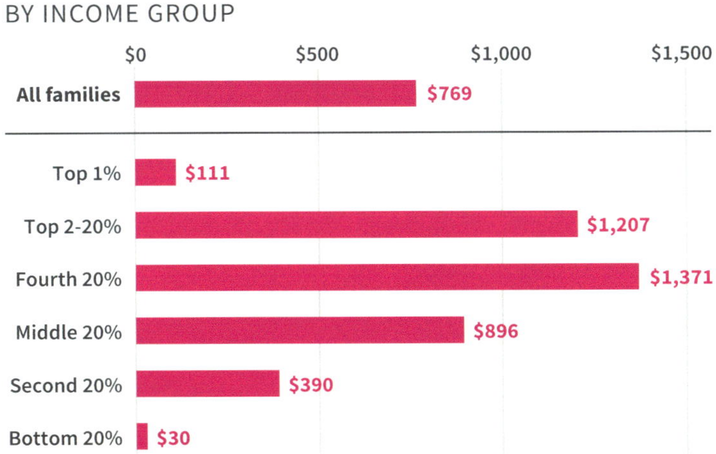

AVERAGE CREDIT FROM EARNED INCOME TAX CREDIT (2022)

BY INCOME GROUP

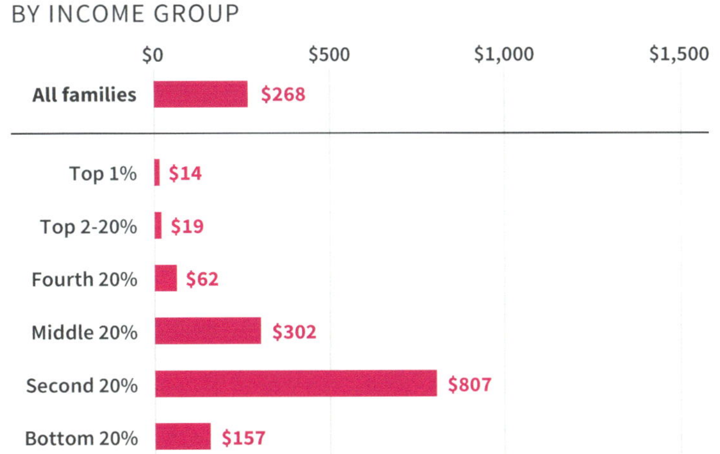

Source: USAFacts calculations using data from the Internal Revenue Service and Census Bureau
Adjusted for inflation (2023 dollars)

How much do workers in the US earn?

The nation's median annual wage was $48,151 in 2023. After adjusting for inflation, this was down 0.3% from 2022. Massachusetts, Washington, and New York had the highest median wages, all over $56,500. Three states had median wages under $40,000: Mississippi, Arkansas, and West Virginia.

MEDIAN ANNUAL WAGES

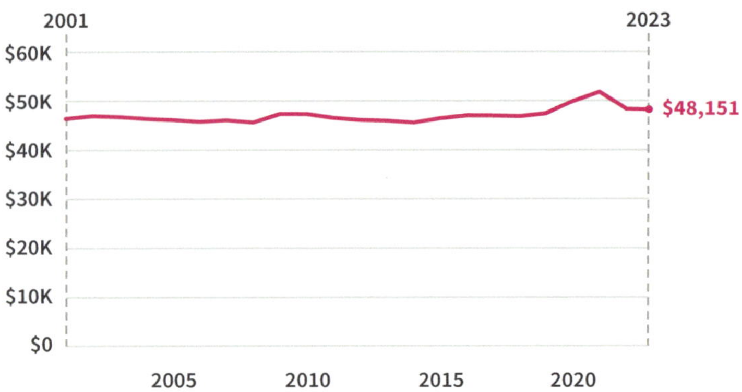

Source: Bureau of Labor Statistics
Adjusted for inflation (2023 dollars)

MEDIAN ANNUAL WAGES (2023)
BY STATE

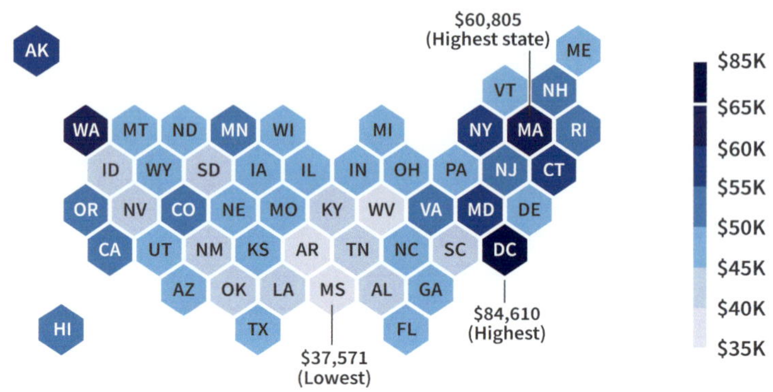

Source: Bureau of Labor Statistics
Adjusted for inflation (2023 dollars)

What is the US poverty rate?

The overall poverty rate was 11.5% in 2022 and 15.0% among children. Both remain above their pre-pandemic levels in 2019. The overall poverty rate has only been lower than its current rate in two of the last 44 years (2019 and 2000) and the child poverty rate has only been lower in one (2019). In 2022, nine out of the 10 states with the highest poverty rate were in the South. In New Mexico, the state with the highest poverty rate, 1 in 5 people were in poverty.

POVERTY RATE
SHARE OF PEOPLE IN POVERTY

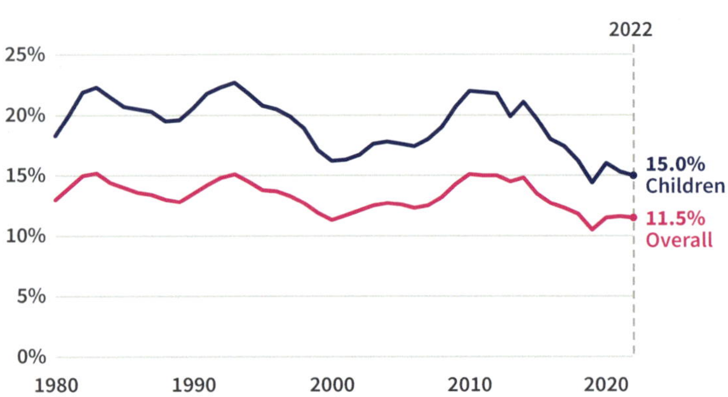

Source: Census Bureau
Note: Children include those under 18.

OVERALL POVERTY RATE (2022)
BY STATE

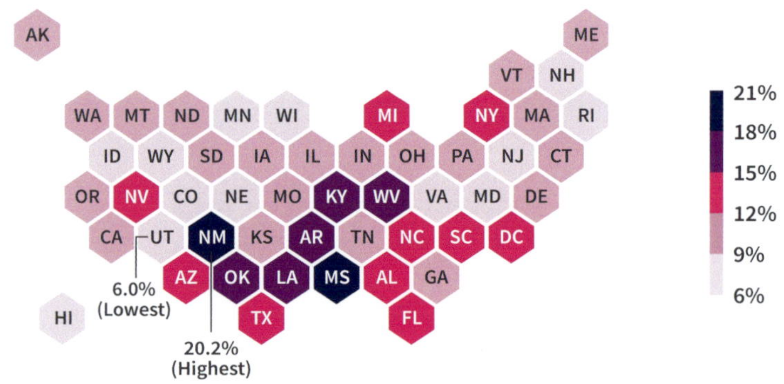

Source: Census Bureau

What share of people pay too much for housing?

The Department of Housing and Urban Development (HUD) says households should spend less than 30% of their income on housing to have enough money for other needs. Households spending more than this threshold are considered housing burdened. Nearly 52% of renters were housing burdened in 2022, while almost 23% of homeowners were. Both rates are down compared to 2010, but rose in both 2021 and 2022.

SHARE OF HOUSEHOLDS THAT ARE HOUSING BURDENED

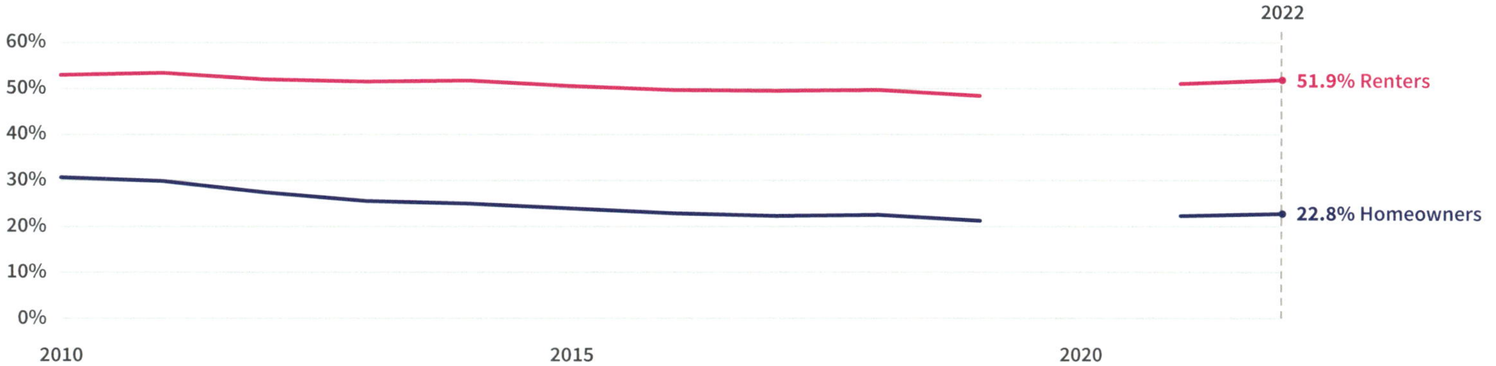

Source: Census Bureau
Note: The Department of Housing and Urban Development defines housing-burdened families as those who pay more than 30% of their income for housing. Data for 2020 is not available.

Where do people pay too much for housing?

In 2022, every state had a higher share of housing-burdened renters than homeowners. The share of renters that spent more than 30% of their income on housing was the highest in Florida, Hawaii, and Nevada. Three-fifths of renters in Florida were housing burdened. Meanwhile, the share of homeowners that were housing burdened ranged from 31% in California to 14% in West Virginia.

SHARE OF HOUSEHOLDS THAT ARE HOUSING BURDENED (2022)
BY STATE

RENTERS

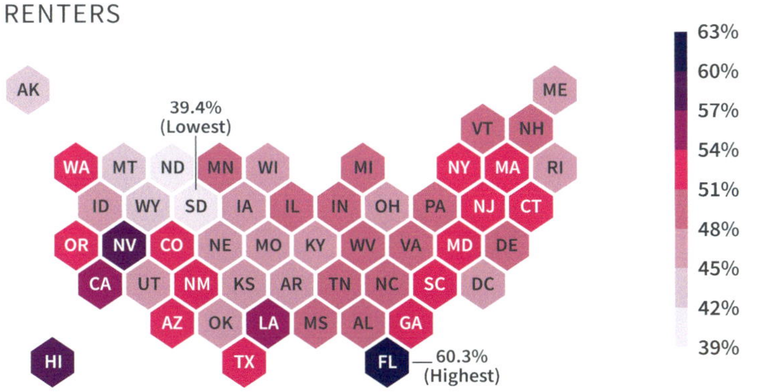

HOMEOWNERS

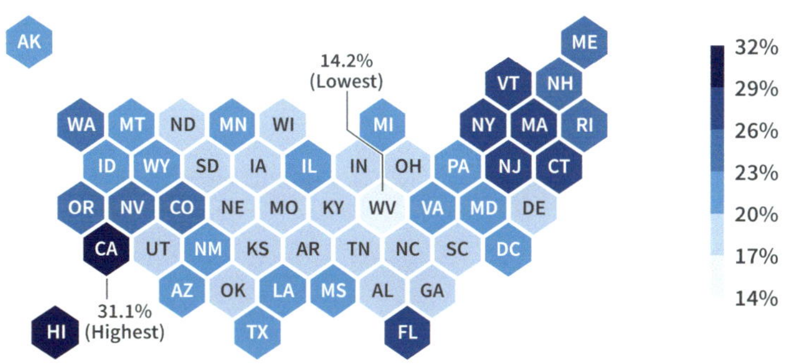

Source: Census Bureau
Note: The Department of Housing and Urban Development defines housing-burdened families as those who pay more than 30% of their income for housing.

How many subsidized housing units are available in the US?

There were 15.3 subsidized housing units available per 1,000 people in 2023. These units housed more than 9 million people and had been occupied by the same individual or family for an average of 10 years. The number of units available has remained at or below 15.5 per 1,000 people since 2016. Washington, DC, Rhode Island, and New York had the highest number of available units per 1,000 people, while Arizona, Utah, and Idaho had the fewest.

SUBSIDIZED HOUSING UNITS AVAILABLE

PER 1,000 PEOPLE

TOTAL

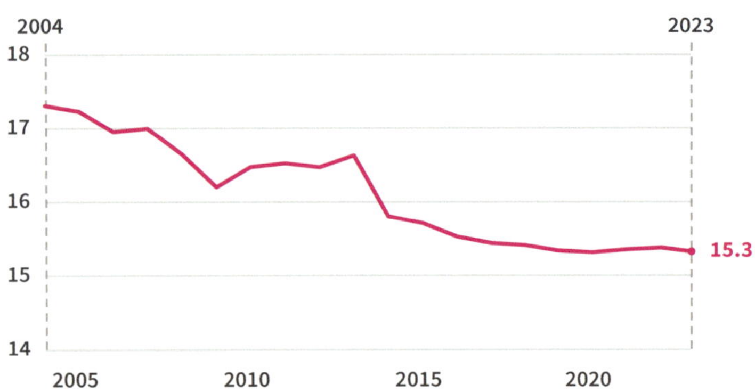

BY STATE (2023)

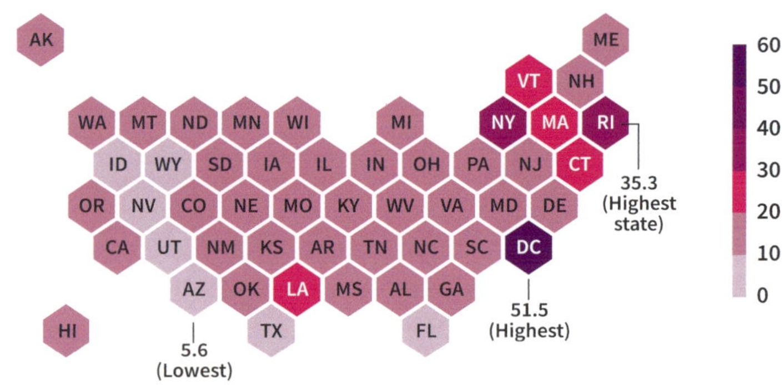

Source: Department of Housing and Urban Development

Note: Data represents the number of units under contract for federal subsidy and available for occupancy, including both occupied and unoccupied units.

How long do people wait for subsidized housing?

On average, those who received subsidized housing in 2023 had waited 25 months. Average wait times did not change from 2022, and were two months shorter than the 2021 and 2020 averages. Massachusetts, Louisiana, Maryland, and Delaware had the longest average wait times, at or above 37 months. Wyoming, North Dakota, and West Virginia had the shortest, under 10 months.[ix]

AVERAGE MONTHS ON SUBSIDIZED HOUSING WAITLIST

TOTAL

BY STATE (2023)

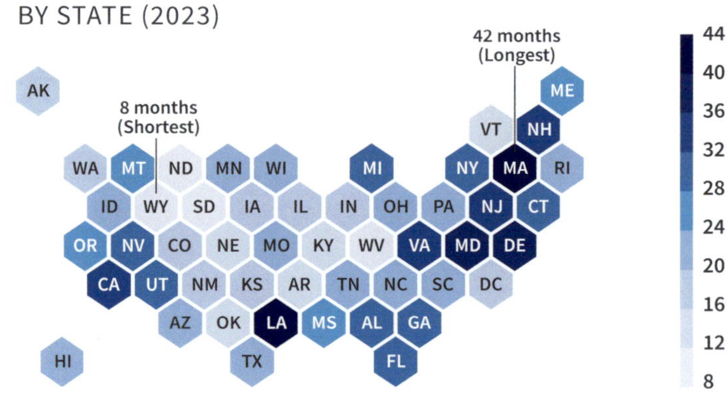

Source: Department of Housing and Urban Development

Note: Among affordable housing program recipients.

What share of households are food insecure?

In 2022, 12.8% of households were food insecure, meaning they were uncertain about having enough food or did not have enough food at some point in the year. This was 2.1 percentage points lower than the peak of 14.9% in 2011, but 2.6 points higher than in 2021. Food insecurity rates for households with children rose nearly 5 percentage points compared to 2021 and are consistently higher than other household types. The six states with food insecurity rates significantly higher than the US average are in the South.

SHARE OF HOUSEHOLDS THAT ARE FOOD INSECURE

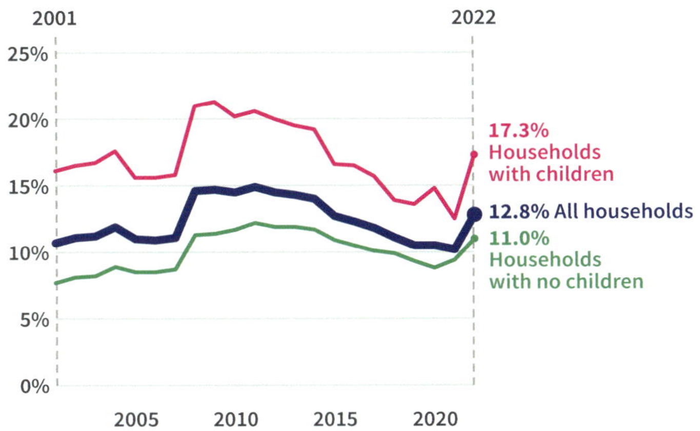

Source: Department of Agriculture

SHARE OF HOUSEHOLDS THAT ARE FOOD INSECURE (2020–2022 AVERAGE)

BY STATE

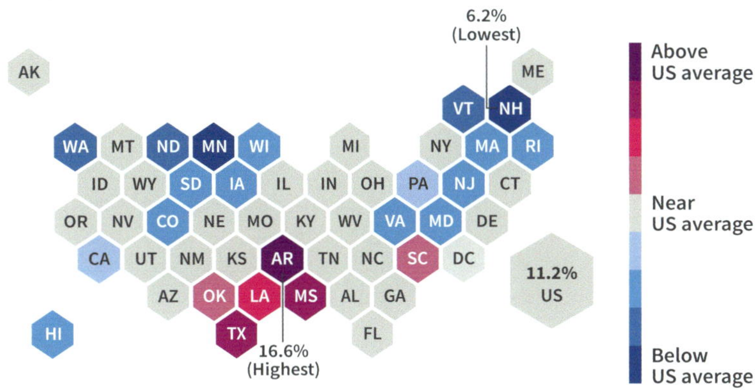

Source: Department of Agriculture
Note: States that are categorized as "Near US average" have rates that are not statistically significantly different from the US average.

How many people receive nutrition assistance (SNAP)?

How much do they receive?

An average of more than 42.1 million people received SNAP benefits each month in FY 2023, 18% more than in FY 2019, but less than the peak of 47.6 million in FY 2013. The average monthly SNAP benefit was $211.93 per person in FY 2023, 37% higher than in FY 2019 but 12% lower than FY 2022. Congress expanded SNAP benefits during the pandemic to combat food insecurity. These emergency allotments ended nationwide in March 2023.[x]

NUTRITION ASSISTANCE (SNAP)

AVERAGE MONTHLY RECIPIENTS

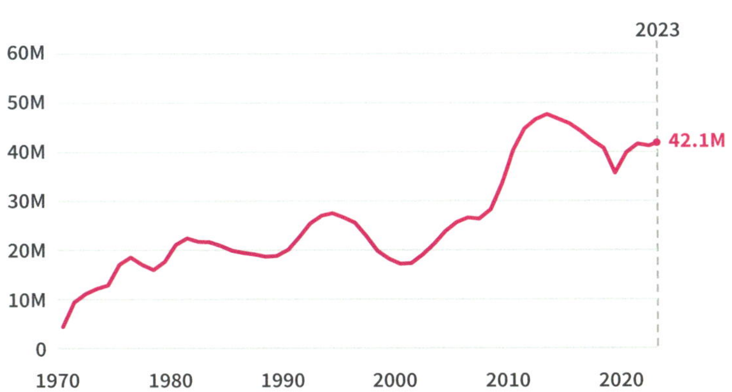

Source: Department of Agriculture

NUTRITION ASSISTANCE (SNAP)

AVERAGE MONTHLY BENEFIT PER PERSON

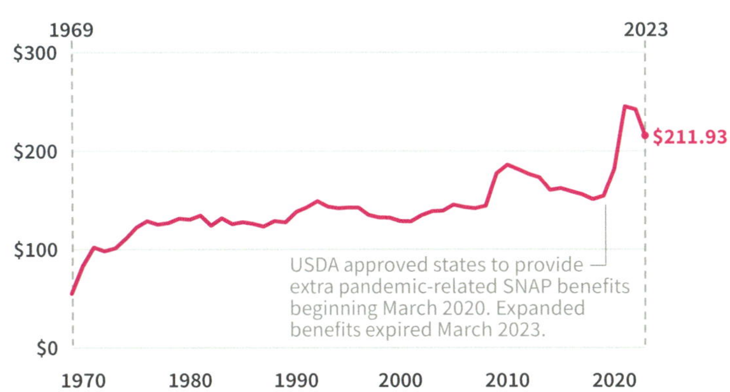

Source: Department of Agriculture
Adjusted for inflation (FY 2023 dollars)

Wealth & savings

Wealth & savings facts

Wealth distribution

- At the end of 2023, the top 20% income quintile held 71% of the nation's wealth, totaling about $103.0 trillion.
- The middle class (middle 20% of income earners) held about 8% of the national wealth, equivalent to $12.1 trillion.
- Since the fourth quarter of 2019, wealth among the middle class increased by the largest percentage of any income group (up 22%).

Retirement accounts

- The share of families with at least one retirement account steadily increased from 1989 to 2001. Retirement account participation has fluctuated ever since. In 2022, 54% of families had a retirement account.
- Median retirement account savings rose 16% between 2013 and 2022, after accounting for inflation.
- Among those with retirement accounts, median savings for families in the 0–20% income percentile increased by the highest percentage between 2013 and 2022. This group is the least likely to have a retirement account.

Individual savings

- The average personal savings rate was 4.5% in 2023. This was higher than 2022's average, but lower than any year except 2005–2008.

Homeownership

- The US homeownership rate, which is the share of homes occupied by owners rather than renters, has risen annually since 2016. It hit 65.8% in 2022. The rate remains 3 percentage points below the 2004 record.
- Median net housing wealth among families who own their primary residence increased from $139,105 to $200,000 between 2019 and 2022.

Social Security and Disability Insurance

- There were 58.2 million Social Security recipients in 2023 and they received an average monthly benefit of $1,742. This was a 2% increase in recipients and a 6% increase in average benefits from 2022, after adjusting for inflation.
- The number of Disability Insurance recipients decreased to 8.6 million in 2023, down 4% from 2022. They received an average monthly benefit of $1,336, up 6% from the previous year.

Medicare programs

- Sixty-five million people were enrolled in Medicare in 2022, 2% more than in 2021. The average cost of Medicare per beneficiary was $16,374, down from the previous year's high of $17,024, after adjusting for inflation.

About the data

What are the primary sources of data on this topic?

- Federal Reserve Board
- Bureau of Labor Statistics
- Social Security Administration
- Centers for Medicare and Medicaid Services
- Bureau of Economic Analysis

What adjustments did USAFacts make to the data?

- Finance data is adjusted for inflation so comparisons can be made over time.
- USAFacts used the Consumer Price Index for All Urban Consumers (not seasonally adjusted) when making inflation adjustments.

GOVERNMENT SPENDING 1980–2023

WEALTH & SAVINGS

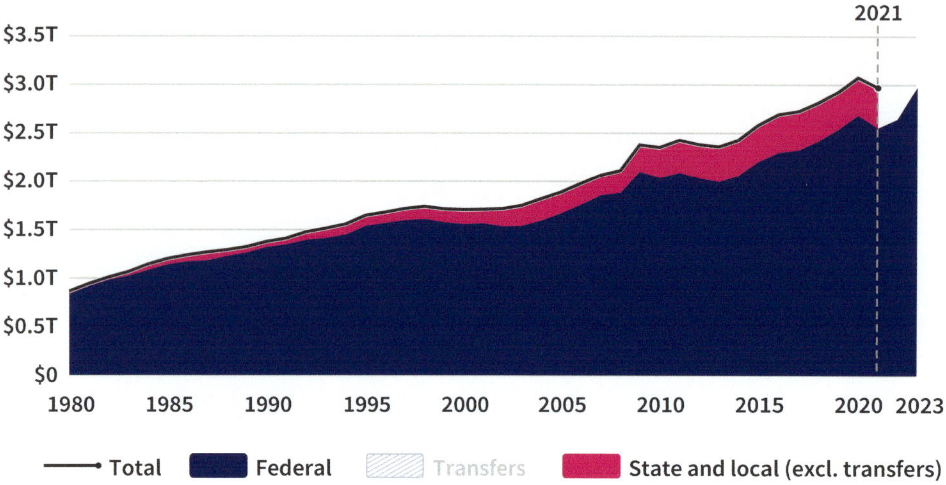

2023 FEDERAL SPENDING

$3.0 trillion

PERCENT OF FEDERAL SPENDING

38% **49%**

Source: USAFacts aggregation of data from the Office of Management and Budget (OMB), the Census Bureau, and the Bureau of Economic Analysis (BEA)
Adjusted for inflation (FY 2023 dollars)

Federal agencies spending: Wealth and savings

Federal agency	Net spending in FY 2023*	Share of spending transferred to state and local governments	Share of spending that was mandatory
Social Security Administration	$1.4 trillion	0%	100%
Department of Health and Human Services	$847.4 billion	0%	99%
Department of the Treasury	$846.6 billion	0%	**
Office of Personnel Management	$115.5 billion	0%	***
Other agencies	-$168.0 billion	0%	****

Source: USAFacts calculations based on the Public Budget Database from the Office of Management and Budget

*Because of budgetary rules pertaining to offsetting receipts and offsetting collections, agencies can have negative net outlays, negative net transfers, or negative net mandatory spending. This happens when money agencies receive from certain sources exceeds the amount they spend, resulting in a surplus. For more information on this issue, see here: https://www.whitehouse.gov/wp-content/uploads/2023/03/ap_18_offsetting_fy2024.pdf.

**The Department of the Treasury received $6.8 billion more than it spent on mandatory wealth and savings programs.

***The Office of Personnel Management spent $116.2 billion on mandatory wealth and savings programs, but received more than it spent on discretionary programs to reduce its net spending.

****Combined, other agencies spent $31.0 billion on mandatory wealth and savings programs, but this was more than offset by receipts from discretionary programs.

How is wealth distributed in the United States?

The top 20% income percentile held about 71% of the nation's wealth — that's $103.0 trillion — in the last three months of 2023. Their total wealth was up 11% compared to 2019. Meanwhile, the middle class (middle 20%) held about 8% of wealth. This was equal to $12.1 trillion, up 22% from before the pandemic. Real estate was the largest category of assets held by the bottom (43%), second (42%), middle (38%), and fourth (34%) income percentiles. Meanwhile, stocks and mutual funds made up 25% of wealth among the top 20% (excluding the top 1%) and 42% among the top 1%. Stocks and mutual funds comprised less than 15% of wealth for other income percentiles.

WEALTH, BY INCOME PERCENTILE

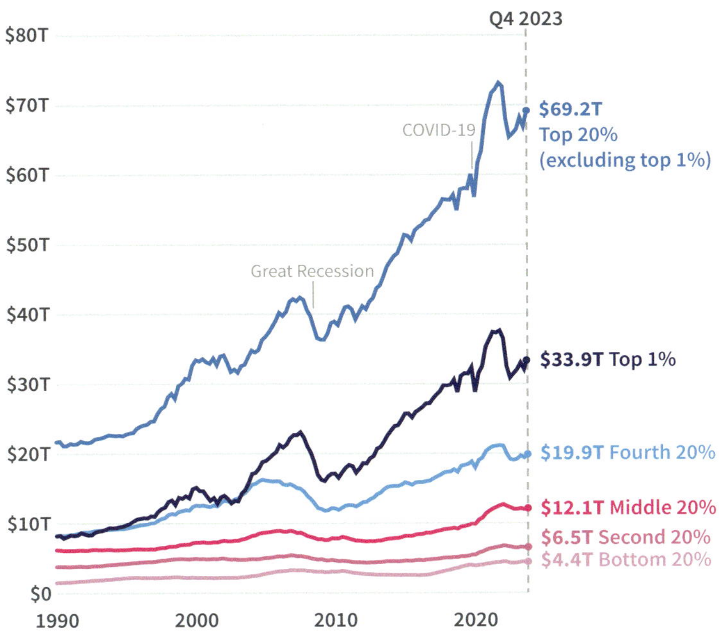

Source: Federal Reserve
Adjusted for inflation (2023 dollars)

SHARE OF WEALTH, BY INCOME PERCENTILE

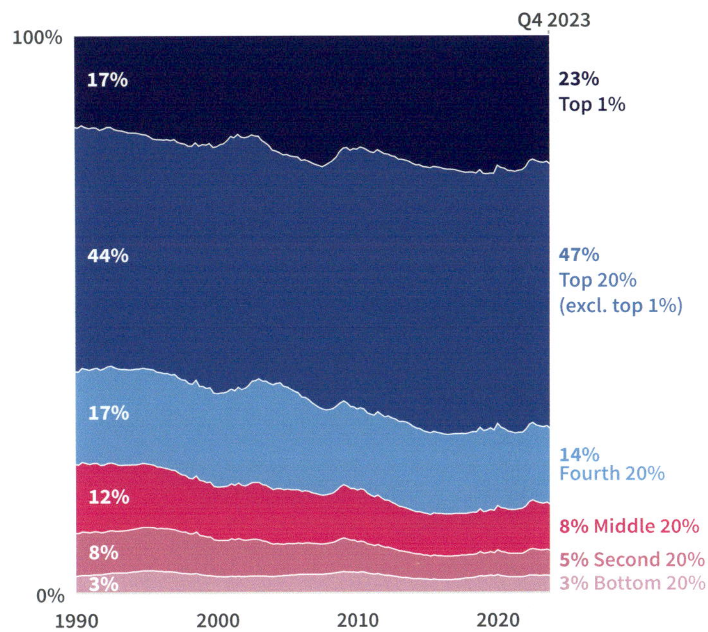

Source: Federal Reserve

What percentage of disposable income do people save?

In 2023, the average personal savings rate was 4.5%. This was higher than 2022's average of 3.3%, but lower than any other years except 2005–2008.

PERSONAL SAVINGS RATE

Source: Bureau of Economic Analysis
Note: Seasonally adjusted. The Bureau of Economic Analysis periodically updates historical data.

Who in the US has retirement accounts?

The share of families with at least one retirement account increased from 37% to 53% between 1989 and 2001. Since then, growth in retirement account participation has been uneven. Participation reached 54% in 2022, slightly above the previous highs of 53% in 2007 and 2001. Fifty-six percent of middle-class families had a retirement account in 2022, slightly higher than the 54% of all families.

SHARE OF FAMILIES WITH RETIREMENT ACCOUNTS

ALL FAMILIES

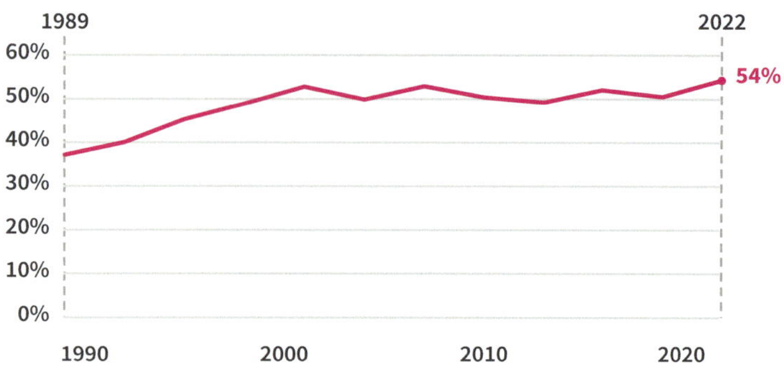

Source: Board of Governors of the Federal Reserve
Note: Survey is conducted every three years.

BY INCOME PERCENTILE (2022)

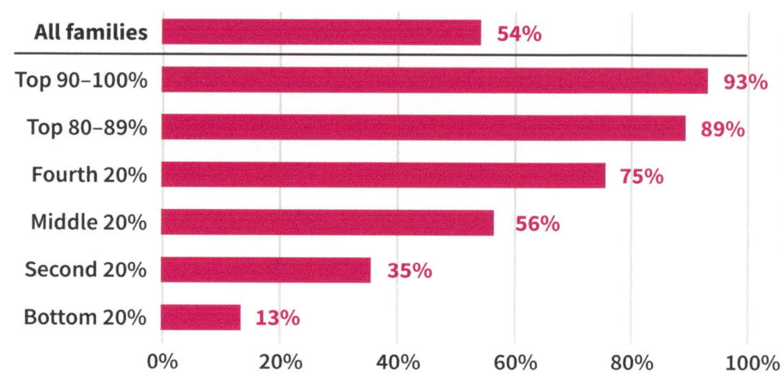

How much do Americans save for retirement?

Among families with retirement accounts, the median amount saved in these accounts changed little between 2013, 2016, and 2019, staying around $75,000 (adjusted for inflation). The median value reached $87,000 in 2022, a 16% increase from 2013. The bottom 20% of families by income more than doubled their retirement account savings to $17,500. Families in the top 80–89% and top 90–100% percentiles increased their retirement savings by 49% and 56%. Middle-class median retirement savings grew at a slower pace, from $31,821 to $39,000 (up 23%).

MEDIAN VALUE OF RETIREMENT ACCOUNTS

ALL FAMILIES

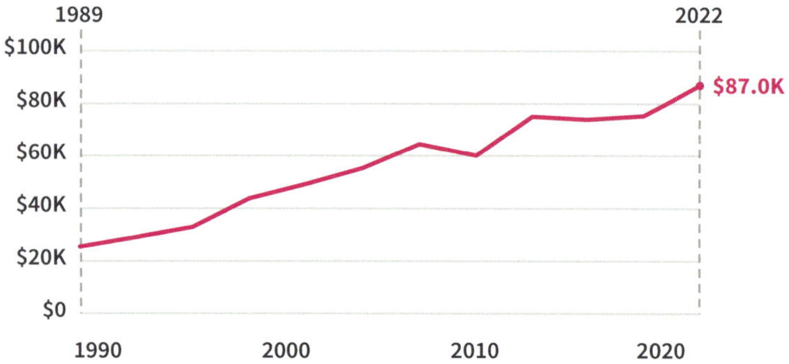

BY INCOME PERCENTILE (2013 VS. 2022)

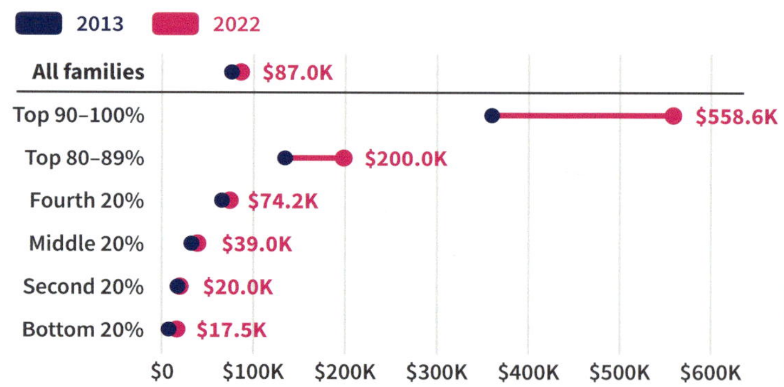

Source: Board of Governors of the Federal Reserve
Note: Inflated by the source to 2022 dollars. Median is calculated among families that have at least one retirement account. Survey is conducted every three years.

Is homeownership increasing or decreasing in the United States?

In 2022, the share of residences occupied by homeowners — called the homeownership rate — was 65.8%. The rate hit an all-time high of 69.0% in 2004. By 2016, the rate had fallen to 63.4%. It's since increased each year. It increased most among people younger than 35. This group's homeownership rates remain the lowest of any age group, however, at 39.0%.

HOMEOWNERSHIP RATES

NATIONAL

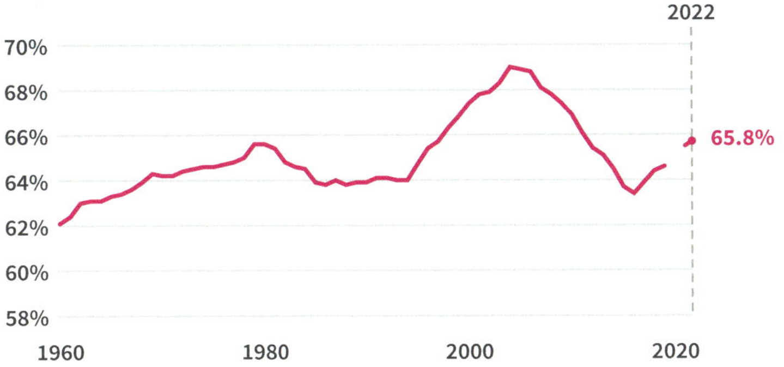

BY AGE OF HOUSEHOLDER

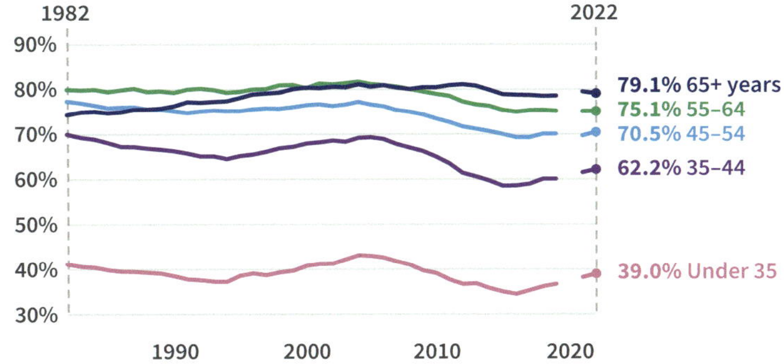

Source: Census Bureau
Note: Data for 2020 is excluded due to pandemic-related survey issues. Age groups are defined by the age of the head of household.

How much wealth do people hold in their homes?

Net housing wealth is the value of a home, minus a mortgage or other debt associated with that home. Median net housing wealth for families who owned their primary residence increased from $139,105 in 2019 to $200,000 in 2022, up 44%. According to the Federal Reserve, this housing wealth growth occurred as rising housing prices exceeded inflation. It also means housing affordability declined over the period. The average home is worth 4.6 times more than median income — the highest ratio in any year of the source survey — up from 3.8 in 2019.

MEDIAN NET HOUSING VALUE

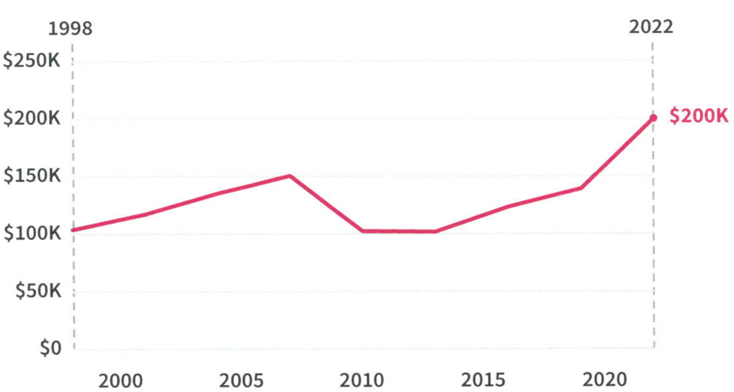

Source: Board of Governors of the Federal Reserve
Note: Inflated by the source to 2022 dollars. Median is calculated among families that own their primary residence. Net housing value is equal to a home's value minus associated mortgages, and home equity loans or lines of credit.

HOUSING AFFORDABILITY

RATIO OF MEDIAN HOUSING VALUE TO MEDIAN INCOME

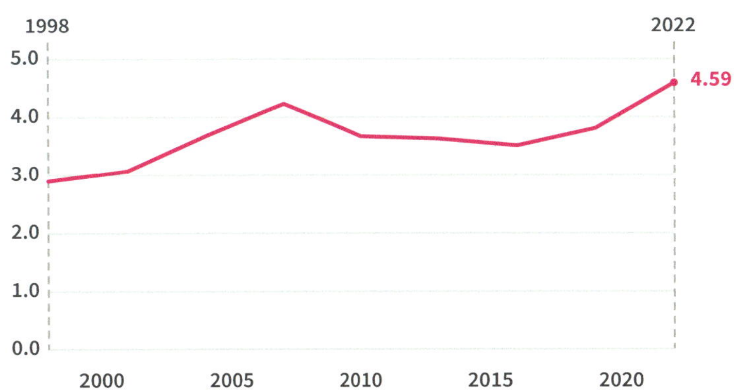

Source: Board of Governors of the Federal Reserve
Note: Survey is conducted every 3 years.

How many people collect Social Security and Disability Insurance?

How much do they receive?

There were 58.2 million Social Security recipients in September 2023, receiving an average benefit of $1,742 a month. The number of recipients increased 2% and average benefits increased 6% over 2022, after adjusting for inflation. Total Disability Insurance recipients decreased 4% to 8.6 million people in 2023. Their average monthly benefit was $1,336, up 6% from the previous year.

SOCIAL SECURITY RETIREMENT AND DISABILITY INSURANCE RECIPIENTS

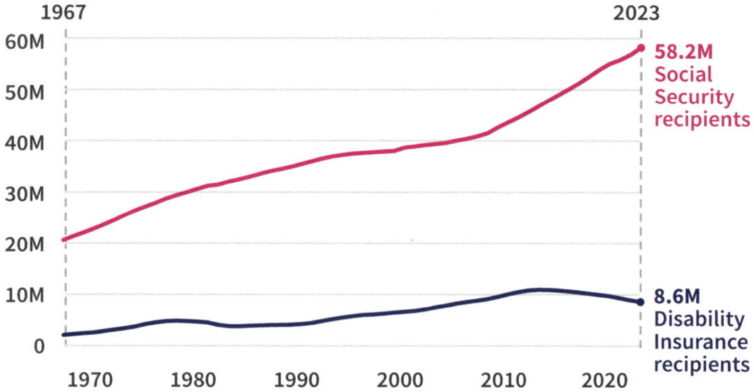

Source: Social Security Administration
Note: Recipients shown here are for September of each year.

SOCIAL SECURITY AND DISABILITY INSURANCE
AVERAGE MONTHLY BENEFIT

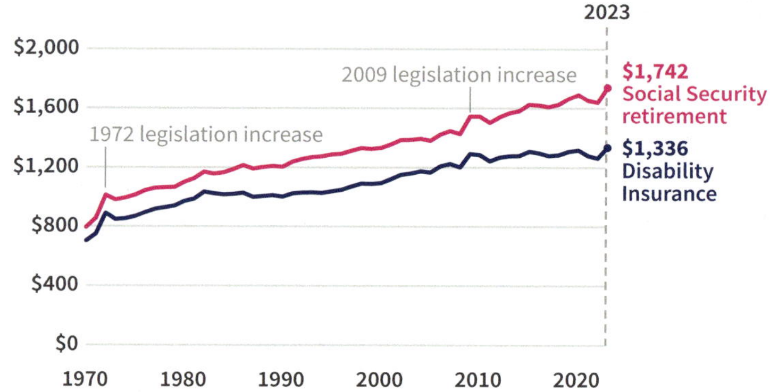

Source: Social Security Administration
Adjusted for inflation (2023 dollars)
Note: Average monthly benefits shown here are for September of each year.

How many people are enrolled in Medicare programs?

How much do those programs cost per beneficiary?

Sixty-five million people were enrolled in Medicare in 2022, 2% more than in 2021. The average cost of Medicare per beneficiary was $16,374, down from a high of $17,024 the previous year (after adjusting for inflation). Nearly half of this cost was for Part B, which supports medical and preventative care.

MEDICARE ENROLLMENT
BY TYPE

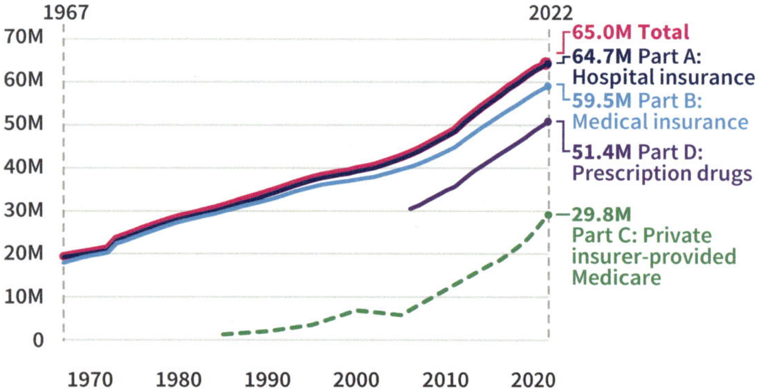

Source: Centers for Medicare and Medicaid Services
Note: Total enrollment includes the number of beneficiaries with hospital insurance (Part A) and/or supplementary medical coverage (Parts B or D). Part C is the Medicare policy that allows for Medicare benefits to be provided by private health insurance companies and is not included in the total enrollment.

AVERAGE MEDICARE COST PER BENEFICIARY
BY TYPE

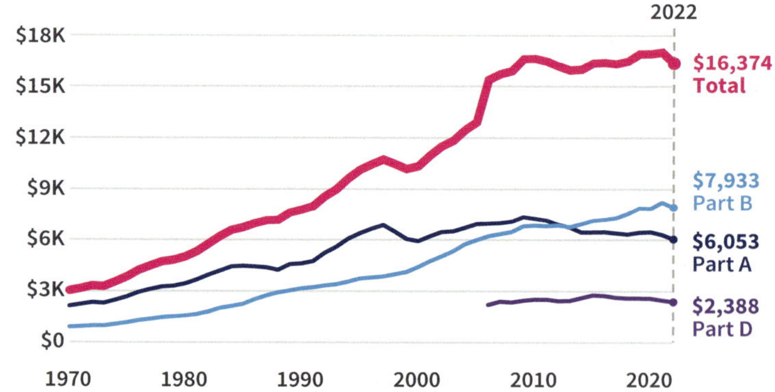

Source: Centers for Medicare and Medicaid Services
Adjusted for inflation (2023 dollars)

Health

Health facts

Health risk factors

- The share of adults who smoke or are obese decreased from 2021 to 2022, but the share who binge drink increased.
- The obesity rate is six percentage points higher than it was in 2011.

Mortality and causes of death

- Life expectancy at birth increased in 2022 to 77.5 years, primarily due to lower COVID-19 death rates.
- Heart disease and cancer have been the two leading causes of death since 1950.
- Accidents were the third-leading cause of death in 2022, driven by drug overdose deaths and other accidental poisonings, the rate of which was seven times what it was in 1999.
- The number of fentanyl deaths increased from just over 3,000 in 2010 to over 74,000 in 2022. It has been involved in more overdose deaths than any other drug annually since 2016.

Mental health

- As of 2021–2022, about 35% of adults ages 18–25 and 21% of adults ages 26 or older had a mental illness in the past year.
- In 2022, about 20% of children ages 12–17, 20% of adults ages 18–25, and 7% of adults ages 26 or older had a major depressive episode in the past year.
- Adults ages 18–25 experienced mental illness in 2018–2019 at a rate nearly 10 percentage points higher than in 2008–2009. It increased less than one percentage point for people 26 and older.

Health insurance coverage and spending

- In 2022, 7.9% of the population (25.9 million people) did not have health insurance, matching the lowest rate last experienced in 2017.
- Per-enrollee spending fell across Medicare, Medicaid, CHIP, and private insurance plans in 2022, after accounting for inflation.

About the data

What are the primary sources of data on this topic?

- Centers for Disease Control and Prevention
- Census Bureau
- Centers for Medicare and Medicaid Services
- Substance Abuse and Mental Health Services Administration (SAMHSA)

Other things to know about the data

- Mental health data in this report is sourced from SAMHSA's National Survey on Drug Use and Health. The survey changed its collection methods in 2020, changing from in-person interviews to a mix of in-person and web-based. Because of this change, SAMHSA strongly advises against direct comparisons between data from 2019 and earlier with later data.

GOVERNMENT SPENDING 1980–2023
HEALTH

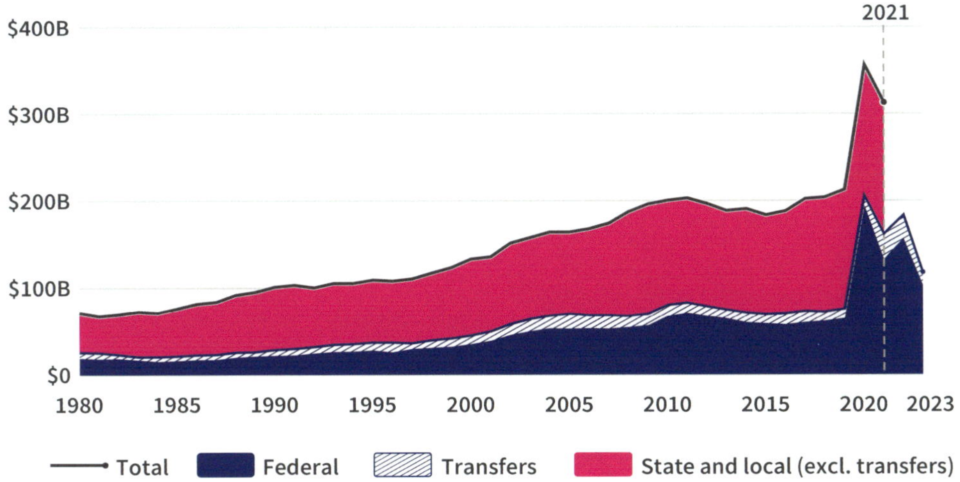

2023 FEDERAL SPENDING*

$118 billion

PERCENT OF FEDERAL SPENDING

1% **2%**

Source: USAFacts aggregation of data from the Office of Management and Budget (OMB), the Census Bureau, and the Bureau of Economic Analysis (BEA)
Adjusted for inflation (FY 2023 dollars)
Note: *Includes direct spending and transfers.

Federal agencies spending: Health

Federal agency	Net spending in FY 2023*	Share of spending transferred to state and local governments	Share of spending that was mandatory
Department of Health and Human Services	$117.3 billion	12%	25%
Patient-Centered Outcomes Research Trust Fund	$689 million	0%	100%
Department of Education	-$1 million	0%	100%
United Mine Workers of America Benefit Funds	-$310 million	0%	100%

Source: USAFacts calculations based on the Public Budget Database from the Office of Management and Budget
*Because of budgetary rules pertaining to offsetting receipts and offsetting collections, agencies can have negative net outlays, negative net transfers, or negative net mandatory spending. This happens when money agencies receive from certain sources exceeds the amount they spend, resulting in a surplus. For more information on this issue, see here: https://www.whitehouse.gov/wp-content/uploads/2023/03/ap_18_offsetting_fy2024.pdf.

What share of adults have common health risks?

Although the share of Americans with obesity decreased slightly to 33.6% in 2022, the share is 6 percentage points higher than it was in 2011. The share of adults who smoke tobacco continued downwards in 2022, falling below 14% for the first time since data collection began, while the share of adults who binge drink increased by 1.6 percentage points (16.9%).

HEALTH RISK FACTORS

% OF ADULTS WITH OBESITY

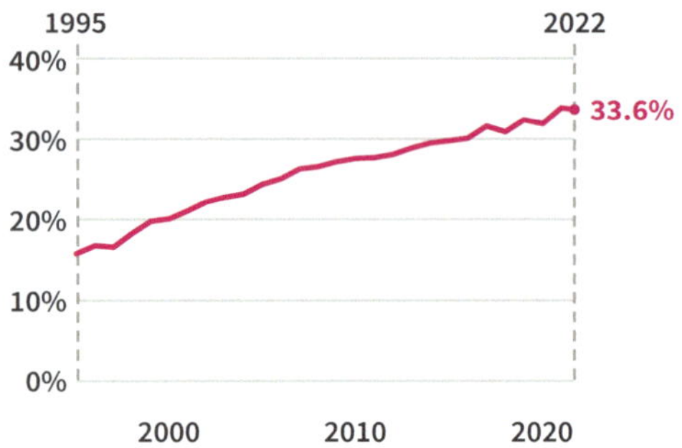

% OF ADULTS WHO SMOKE

% OF ADULTS WHO BINGE DRINK

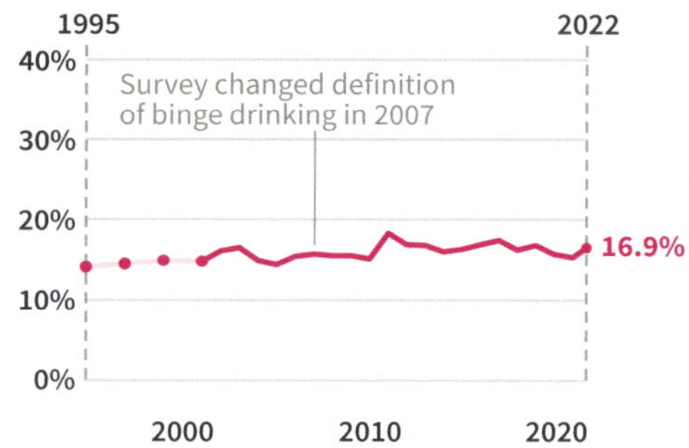

Source: Centers for Disease Control and Prevention
Note: Due to survey changes that occurred in 2011, pre- and post-2011 data is not directly comparable.

What is life expectancy in the US?

Provisional data for 2022 shows that life expectancy at birth increased by 1.1 years to 77.5, after decreasing in 2020 and 2021. It's now 0.5 years higher than in 2020 but 1.3 years lower than in 2019. Waning COVID-19 mortality accounted for approximately 84% of the rise in life expectancy according to the CDC.[xi]

LIFE EXPECTANCY AT BIRTH

Source: Centers for Disease Control and Prevention
Note: Data for 2022 is provisional.

What are the leading causes of death in the US?

Heart disease and cancer have been the two leading causes of death since 1950.[xii] The death rate was 210.9 deaths from heart disease per 100,000 people in 2022 and 182.5 per 100,000 people for cancer. COVID-19 was the only top cause of death whose death rate dropped from 2021 to 2022, decreasing by 55% and dropping from the third-leading cause of death to fourth, behind accidents.

TOP FIVE CAUSES OF DEATH
PER 100,000 PEOPLE

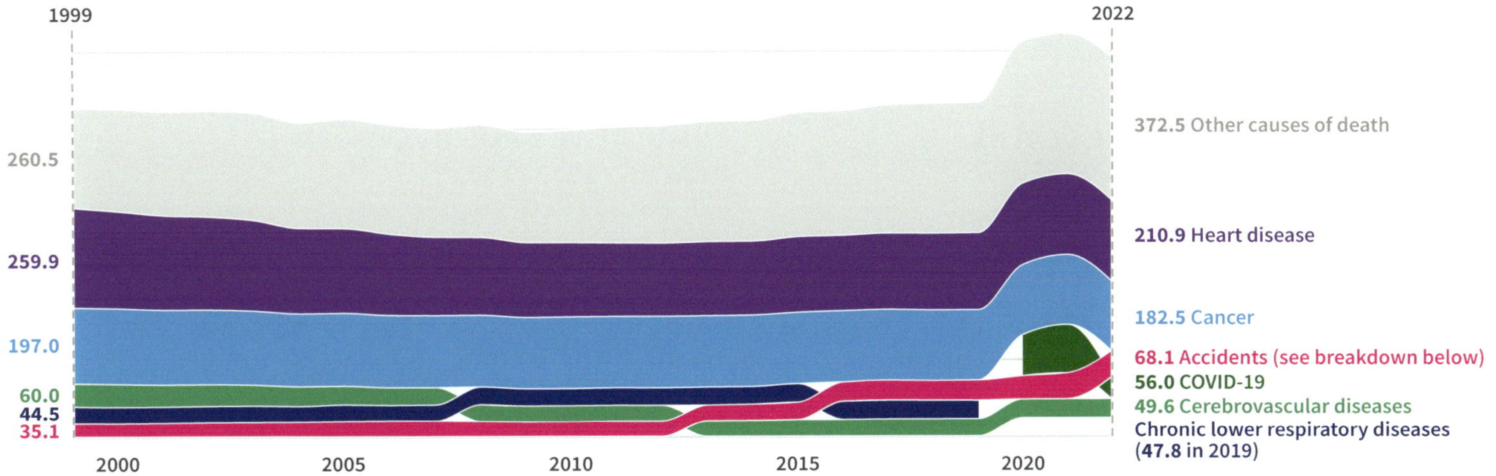

Source: Centers for Disease Control and Prevention
Note: Chronic lower respiratory disease was not a top five cause of death from 2020–2022.

What types of accidental deaths are most prevalent, and what has driven the increase in the death rate from accidents?

In 2011, accidental poisonings (including drug overdoses) overtook motor vehicle accidents as the most common type of accidental death. While the motor vehicle accident death rate decreased for 14 of the last 20 years, the accidental poisoning death rate increased by 164% from 1999 to 2011 and another 166% from 2011 to 2022. Accidental poisonings account for more than three-quarters of the increase in the death rate from accidents since 1999.

ACCIDENTAL DEATHS, BY TYPE OF ACCIDENT
PER 100,000 PEOPLE

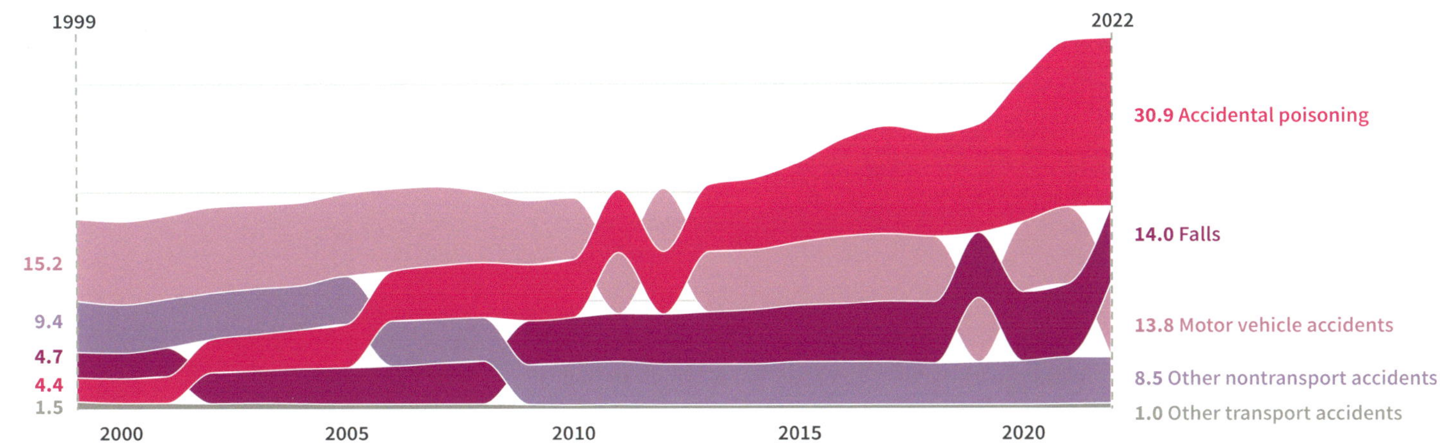

Source: Centers for Disease Control and Prevention

What are trends in drug overdose deaths data?

The rates of drug overdose deaths involving fentanyl and methamphetamine increased 75 and 52 times, respectively, between 1999 and 2022. Fentanyl has been involved in more overdose deaths than any other drug annually since 2016. West Virginia had the last decade's highest cumulative drug overdose death rate among US states, with 538 deaths per 100,000 people from 2013 through 2022. Delaware (363 deaths per 100,000 people), Ohio (358), and Kentucky (354) followed. Between 2013 and 2022, drug overdose deaths were most common among people ages 45 to 64 (345 deaths per 100,000) and 18 to 44 (330). American Indian or Alaska Natives (316) and men (301) have also been especially impacted by rising drug overdose deaths.

DRUG-INVOLVED OVERDOSE DEATHS

AGE-ADJUSTED RATE PER 100,000 PEOPLE

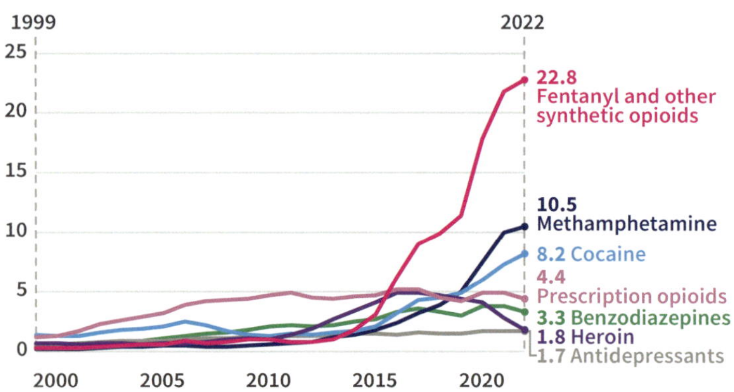

Source: Centers for Disease Control and Prevention

Note: Data for 2022 is preliminary. Data for methamphetamine is classified by the CDC as psychostimulants with abuse potential, although it is primarily methamphetamine.

CUMULATIVE DRUG OVERDOSE DEATHS (2013–2022)

PER 100,000 PEOPLE

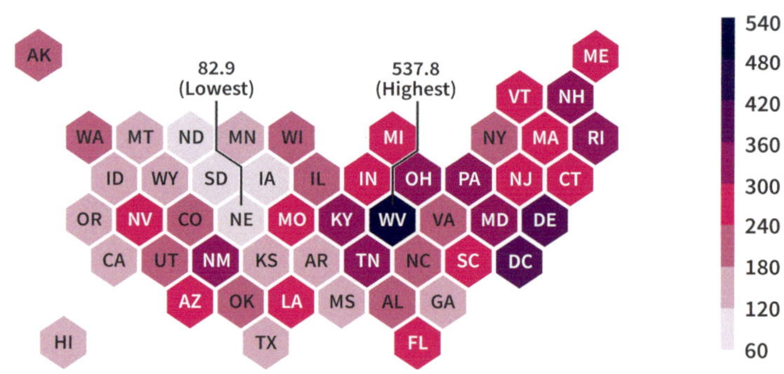

Source: Centers for Disease Control and Prevention

Note: Data for 2022 is preliminary.

CUMULATIVE DRUG OVERDOSE DEATHS (2013–2022)

PER 100,000 PEOPLE

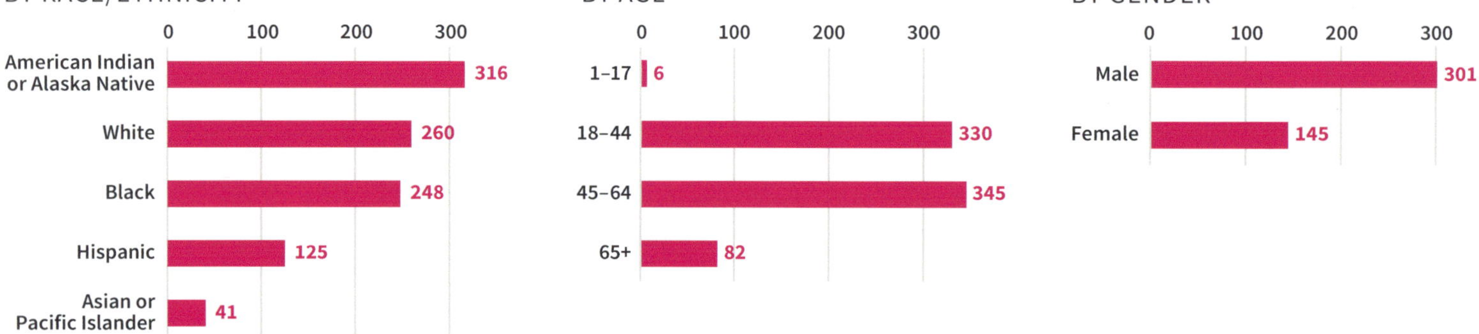

Source: Centers for Disease Control and Prevention

Note: Data for 2022 is preliminary. Definitions of the racial categories changed in 2020. Beginning in that year, the CDC began exclusively providing data that included "More than one race" as a group. Prior to this change, multiracial was not an option and those individuals were captured in a single "primary" race category.

How common is mental illness in the United States?

Similar shares of adults ages 18–25 and 26 or older experienced mental illness across the first several years of the National Survey on Drug Use and Health, but a gap of more than 1 percentage point first appeared in 2011–2012. The gap has since widened, with a growing share of people 18 to 25 experiencing mental illness while rates stayed flat for people 26 and older. As of 2021–2022, about 35% of adults 18–25 and 21% of adults 26 or older had any mental illness in the past year. Oregon had the highest rate of mental illness for people 18–25 in 2021–2022 (44.5%), followed by Montana (44.3%), Washington (41.8%), Idaho (41.7%), New Hampshire (41.2%), and Alaska (40.4%).

SHARE OF PEOPLE THAT HAD ANY MENTAL ILLNESS IN THE PAST YEAR

BY AGE GROUP

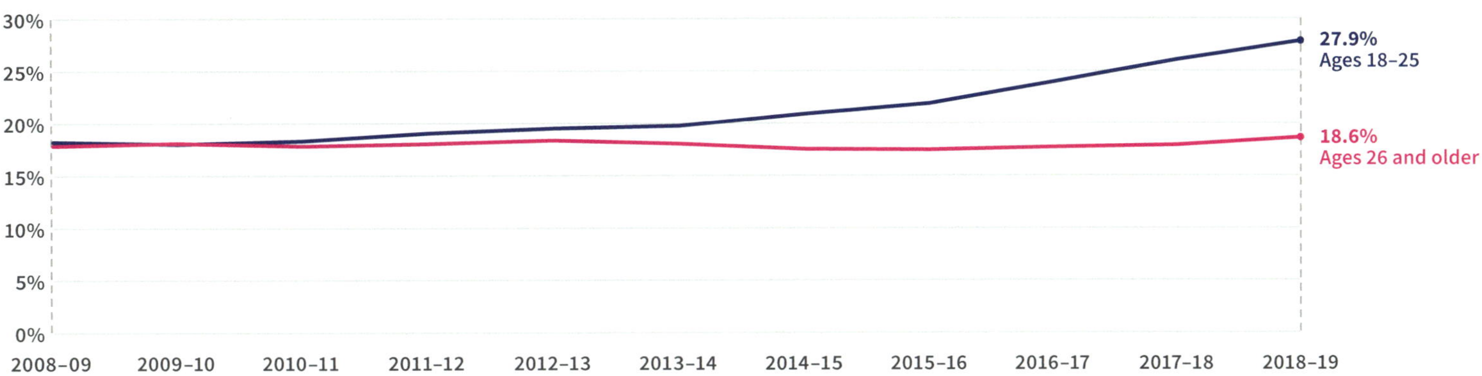

Source: Substance Abuse and Mental Health Services Administration

Note: Each survey year spans 2 consecutive calendar years. The source changed methods in 2020. Data from this chart should not be compared to the source data from 2020 and later.

SHARE OF PEOPLE THAT HAD ANY MENTAL ILLNESS IN THE PAST YEAR (2021–2022)

BY STATE

AGES 18–25

AGES 26 AND OLDER

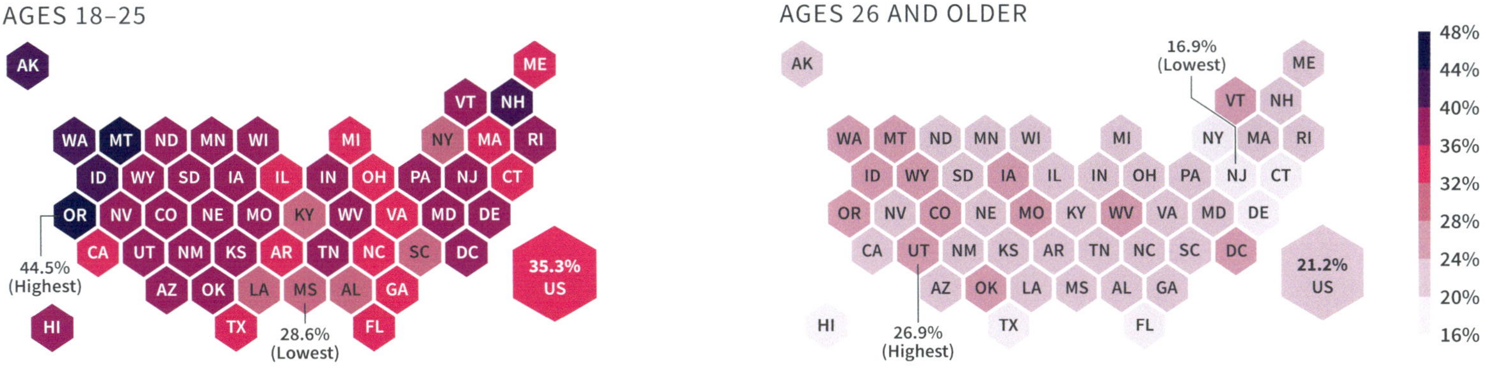

Source: Substance Abuse and Mental Health Services Administration

Note: The source changed methods in 2020. Data from these maps should not be compared to source data from 2019 and earlier.

How common is major depression in the US?

Twenty percent of children ages 12–17, 20% of adults ages 18–25, and 7% of adults ages 26 or older experienced a major depressive episode in 2021–2022. The most recent depression data should not be directly compared to estimates from 2019 or earlier due to changes in the source methodology; however, depression prevalence among people 12–17 and 18–25 increased throughout the 2010s. As much as one-quarter of Oregonians ages 12–17 and 18–25 experienced a depressive episode in 2021–2022, the most of any state.

SHARE OF PEOPLE THAT HAD A MAJOR DEPRESSIVE EPISODE IN THE PAST YEAR

BY AGE GROUP

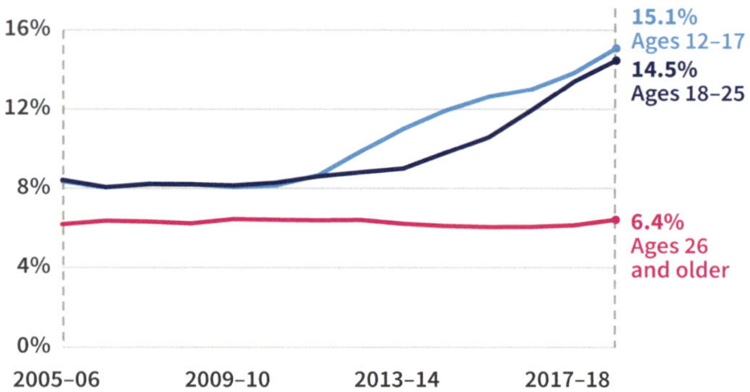

Source: Substance Abuse and Mental Health Services Administration

Note: Each survey year spans 2 consecutive calendar years. The source changed methods in 2020. Data from this chart should not be compared to the source data from 2020 and later.

The Substance Abuse and Mental Health Services Administration defines a major depressive episode as "a period of at least two weeks when an individual experienced a depressed mood or loss of interest or pleasure in daily activities and had a majority of specified depression symptoms." Some depression symptoms include insomnia, fatigue, feelings of worthlessness, and recurrent thoughts of suicide.[xiii]

SHARE OF PEOPLE THAT HAD A MAJOR DEPRESSIVE EPISODE IN THE PAST YEAR (2021–2022)

BY STATE

AGES 12–17

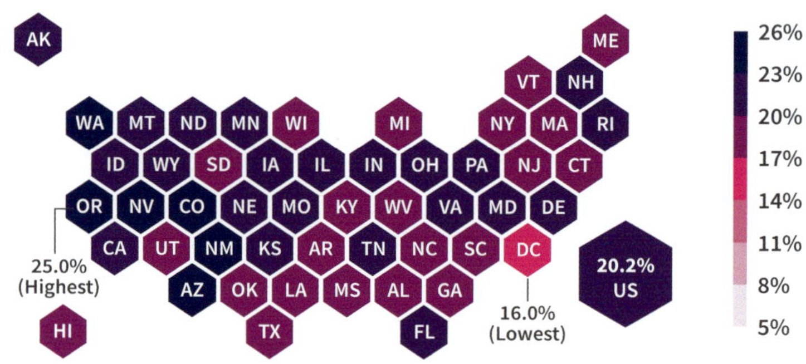

AGES 18–25

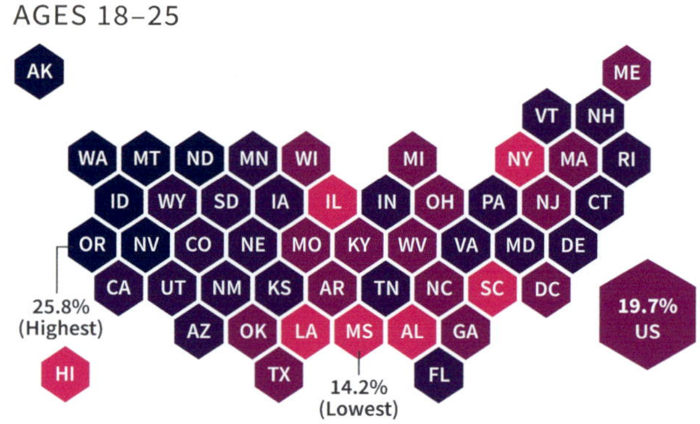

AGES 26 AND OLDER

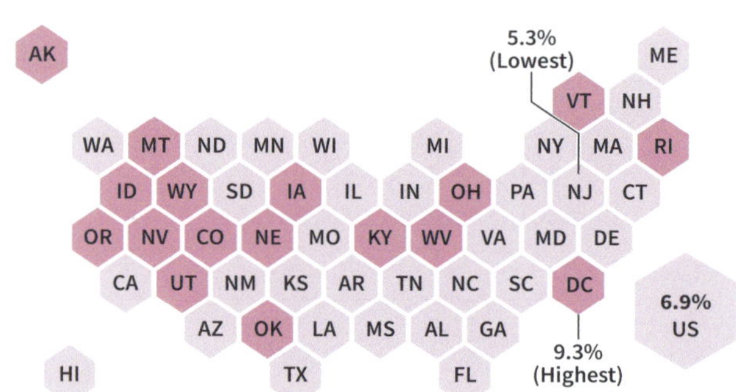

Source: Substance Abuse and Mental Health Services Administration

Note: The source changed methods in 2020. Data from these maps should not be compared to source data from 2019 and earlier.

How many people don't have health insurance?

In 2022, 7.9% of the population, equal to 25.9 million people, did not have health insurance. This is down from 8.3% in 2021 and 8.6% in 2020. Nearly two-thirds of the population — 216.5 million people — were covered by private health insurance. From 2021 to 2022, the share of people enrolled in private insurance and Medicaid decreased while the share covered by Medicare increased.

HEALTH INSURANCE COVERAGE

SHARE OF PEOPLE

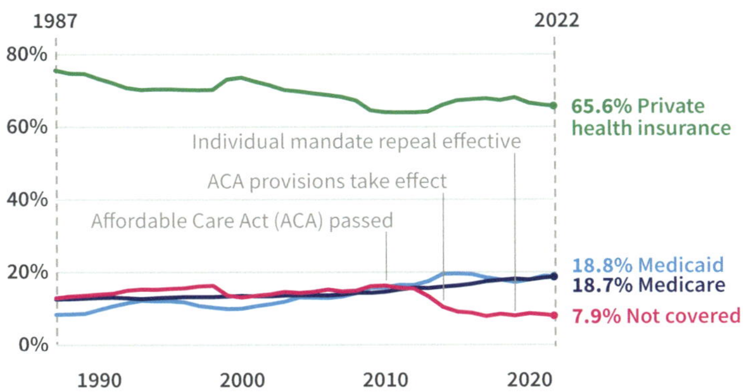

NUMBER OF PEOPLE

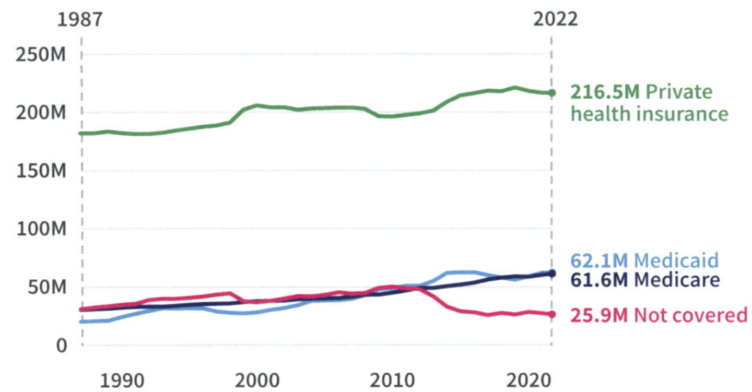

Source: Census Bureau
Note: The types of insurance are not mutually exclusive; people may be covered by more than one during the year.

How much do health insurance providers spend per enrollee?

Per-enrollee spending fell across Medicare, Medicaid, CHIP, and private insurance plans in 2022 when adjusted for inflation. Medicare and Medicaid cover older and low-income populations and spend more per enrollee than private insurance. However, the amount spent per enrollee decreased more for Medicare and Medicaid than private health insurance from 2021 to 2022.

HEALTH INSURANCE SPENDING PER ENROLLEE

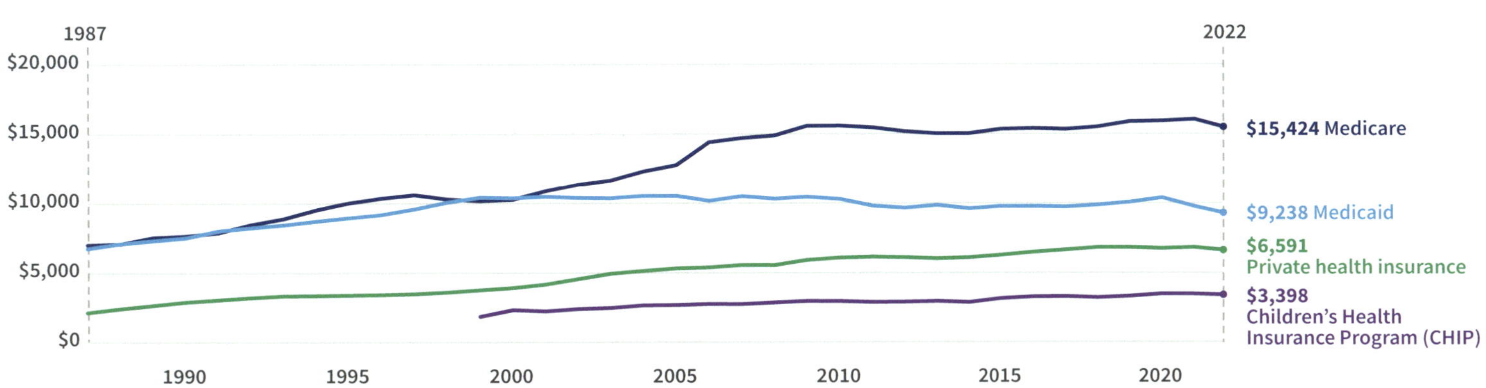

Source: Centers for Medicare and Medicaid Services
Adjusted for inflation (2023 dollars)

Infrastructure

Infrastructure facts

Federal infrastructure and transportation spending

- In FY 2023, the federal government spent $146.2 billion on transportation and infrastructure, with 38% for highways and 20% for air travel.
- The Federal Emergency Management Agency (FEMA) has so far obligated at least $326.3 million to rebuild and repair infrastructure damaged by natural disasters that occurred in 2023.

Condition of American infrastructure

- A higher share of urban roads are in poor condition compared to rural roads, and that's been the case across all years of data. In 2020, the most recent year of complete data, 11% of rural roads and 32% of urban roads were in unsatisfactory condition.
- Since 2012, the share of the nation's highway bridges rated "fair" has increased, while the share in poor or good condition decreased. Fair became the most common bridge rating in 2018, surpassing "good." Forty-nine percent of bridges were rated fair in 2022 and 2023.
- The share of commuter rail and heavy rail tracks in good condition increased between 2018 and 2021. Conditions for light rail tracks were steady.
- In 2023, about 78% of flight departures were on time, up nearly two percentage points from 2022.

Transportation safety

- Traffic injuries per vehicle mile traveled declined between 2016 and 2021. However, fatality rates decreased from 2016 to 2019 before increasing in 2020 and 2021. In 2021, 79.7 people were injured and 1.4 people died per 100 million vehicle miles traveled.
- Between 2013 and 2022, there were 259 accidents on scheduled flights operated by US air carriers. Air carrier accidents can include a variety of incidents where a person onboard is seriously injured or a plane is damaged. Three accidents resulted in fatalities. Turbulence caused more than one-third of accidents but did not result in any fatalities.
- Rail transit accidents are most common on light rail systems. There were 679 accidents per 100 million vehicle miles traveled by light rail in 2022 (up 6% over 2021) compared to 50 on heavy rail (up 14% over 2021).

Broadband use

- In 2022, 20.7% of people did not have a fixed broadband subscription in their home. The share of people without a broadband subscription was highest in Mississippi (33.5%) and Louisiana (29.8%).
- The share of people without broadband subscriptions was highest among the American Indian/Alaska Native population and varied by household income and homeownership.

About the data

What are the primary sources of data on this topic?

- Federal Emergency Management Agency
- Federal Highway Administration
- Federal Transit Administration
- Bureau of Transportation Statistics
- Department of Transportation
- Census Bureau

What adjustments did USAFacts make to this data?

- To focus specifically on the infrastructure costs related to natural disasters, data for FEMA spending excludes funding for emergency work and administrative costs.
- Federal infrastructure and transportation spending and FEMA spending data has been adjusted for inflation using the Consumer Price Index for All Consumers (not seasonally adjusted).
- USAFacts analyzed Census Bureau American Community Survey microdata to produce estimates of broadband subscriptions among states and different populations.

GOVERNMENT SPENDING 1980–2023
INFRASTRUCTURE

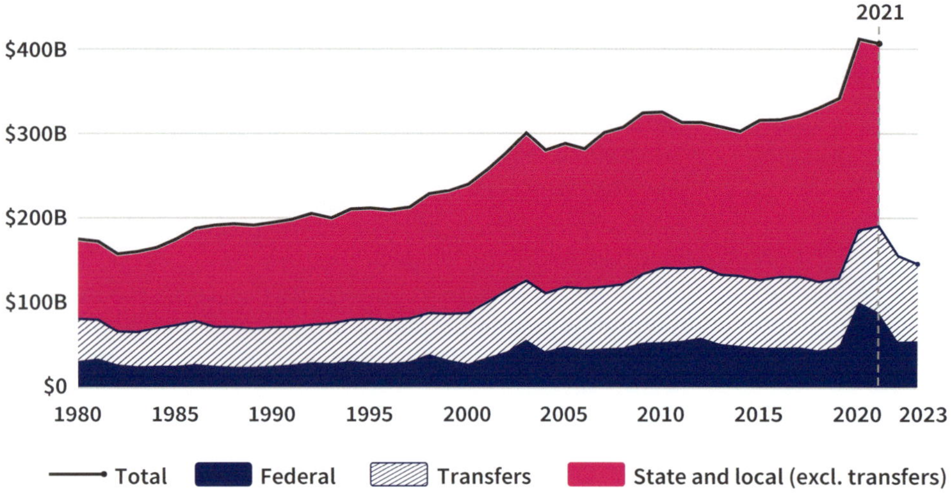

2023 FEDERAL SPENDING*

$146 billion

PERCENT OF FEDERAL SPENDING

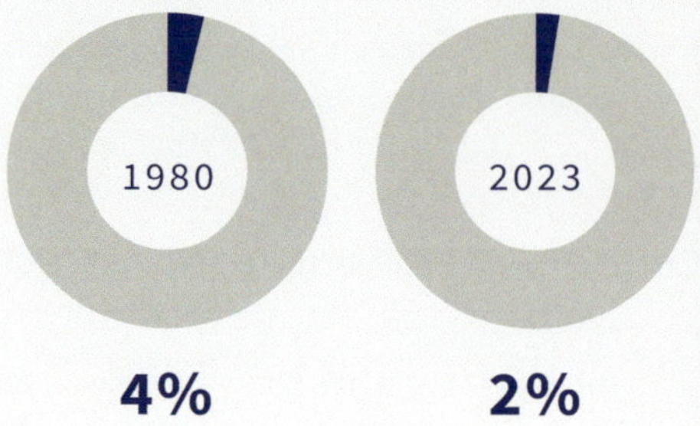

Source: USAFacts aggregation of data from the Office of Management and Budget (OMB), the Census Bureau, and the Bureau of Economic Analysis (BEA)
Adjusted for inflation (FY 2023 dollars)
Note: *Includes direct spending and transfers.

Federal agencies spending: Infrastructure

Federal agency	Net spending in FY 2023*	Share of spending transferred to state and local governments	Share of spending that was mandatory
Department of Transportation	$109.8 billion	80%	11%
Federal Communications Commission	$17.9 billion	14%	65%
Department of Homeland Security	$16.1 billion	1%	**
Department of Commerce	$1.9 billion	12%	22%
Other agencies	$559 million	***	***

Source: USAFacts calculations based on the Public Budget Database from the Office of Management and Budget
*Because of budgetary rules pertaining to offsetting receipts and offsetting collections, agencies can have negative net outlays, negative net transfers, or negative net mandatory spending. This happens when money agencies receive from certain sources exceeds the amount they spend, resulting in a surplus. For more information on this issue, see here: https://www.whitehouse.gov/wp-content/uploads/2023/03/ap_18_offsetting_fy2024.pdf.
**The Department of Homeland Security received $250 million more than it spent on mandatory infrastructure programs.
***Combined, all other agencies received $545 million more than they spent on mandatory infrastructure programs, including $30 million received from the Transportation Services Economic Relief grant program.

How does the federal government spend its infrastructure and transportation dollars?

In FY 2023, the federal government spent $146.2 billion on transportation and infrastructure. About 38% of this spending (including transfers to state and local governments) was for highway transportation and 20% was for air travel. Infrastructure and transportation expenditures fell for the second consecutive year after COVID-19 stimulus spending caused it to hit an all-time high in 2021. However, it remains 13% above 2019 pre-pandemic levels (when adjusted for inflation).

FEDERAL TRANSPORTATION AND INFRASTRUCTURE SPENDING

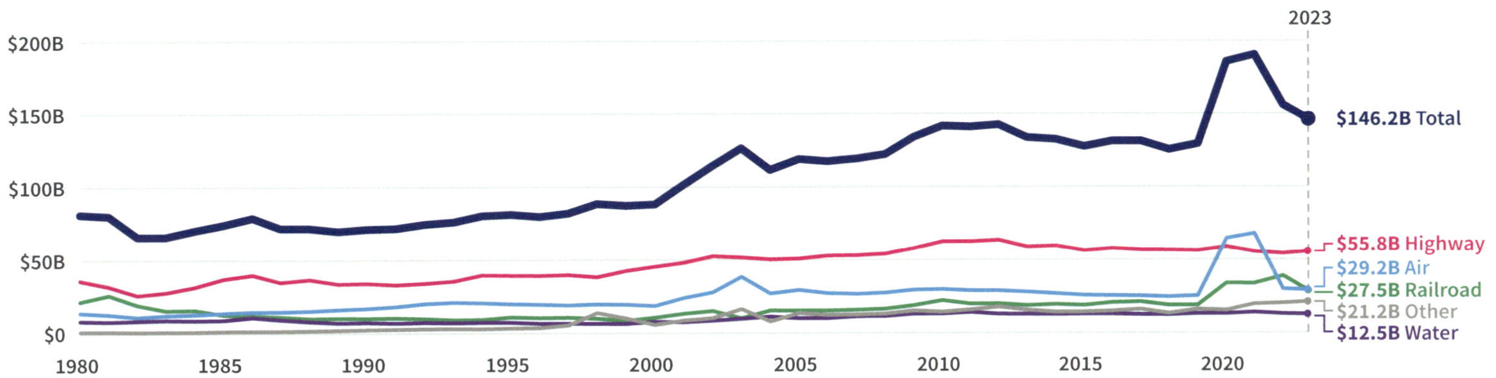

Source: USAFacts aggregation of data from Office of Management and Budget (OMB), the Census Bureau, and the Bureau of Economic Analysis (BEA)
Adjusted for inflation (FY 2023 dollars)
Note: Includes federal transfers to states and local governments.

How much does FEMA spend to rebuild infrastructure after natural disasters?

The Federal Emergency Management Agency (FEMA) has thus far allocated $326.3 million to repair and rebuild infrastructure after natural disasters that occurred in 2023. Most of the funds were designated for rebuilding roads, bridges, and public utilities, such as power lines and water storage facilities.

FEDERAL EMERGENCY MANAGEMENT AGENCY (FEMA) INFRASTRUCTURE SPENDING AFTER NATURAL DISASTERS

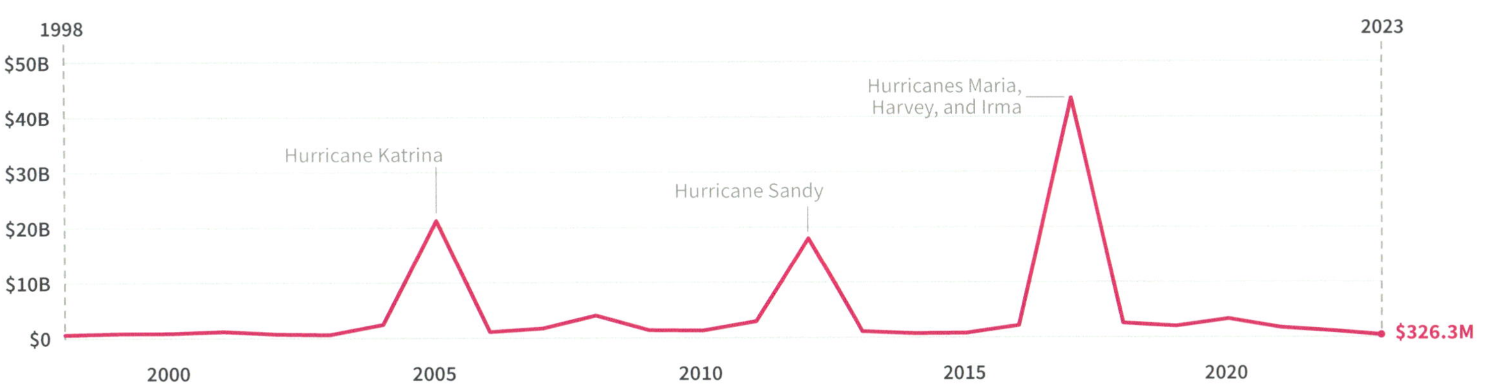

Source: Federal Emergency Management Agency
Adjusted for inflation (2023 dollars)
Note: Data excludes funding for emergency work necessary after a disaster declaration and administrative costs. Data is updated frequently and is correct as of March 25, 2024.

In what condition are the country's roads and bridges?

In 2020, 11% of rural roads and 32% of urban roads were in unsatisfactory condition. Road condition ratings are based on the smoothness of the roadway. The Bureau of Transportation Statistics has not provided complete road data past 2020. About 44% of the nation's highway bridges were in good condition in 2023, down 3 percentage points since 2012. The proportion of bridges rated poor also decreased while an increasing share were rated fair.

SHARE OF ROADS IN UNSATISFACTORY CONDITION
URBAN VS. RURAL ROADS

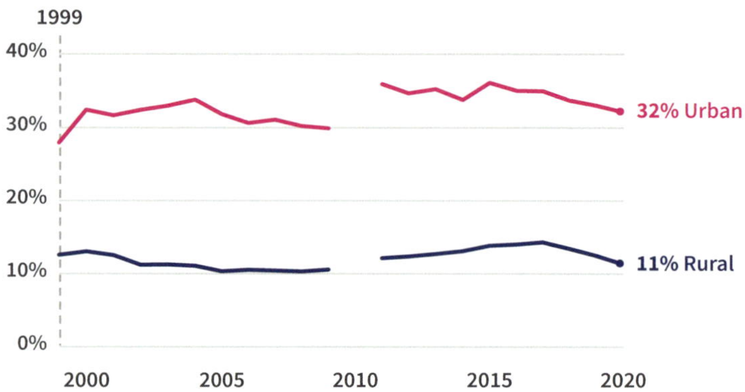

Source: Bureau of Transportation Statistics
Note: Data for 2010 is unavailable.

SHARE OF HIGHWAY BRIDGES
BY CONDITION

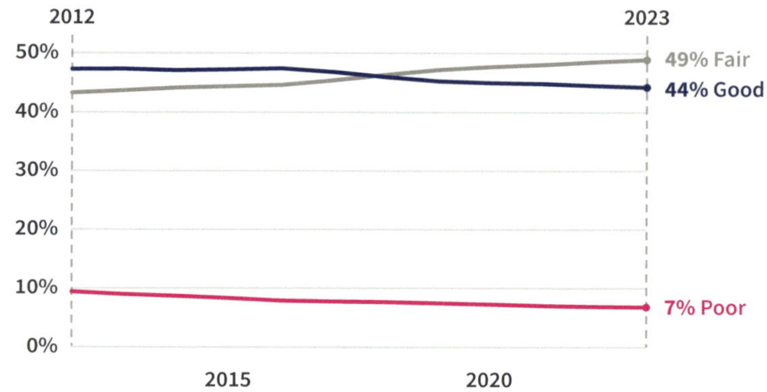

Source: Bureau of Transportation Statistics

Is motor vehicle travel getting safer?

Traffic injuries increased to 79.7 per 100 million vehicle miles traveled in 2021 but remained lower than rates from 2016 through 2019. Injury rates for motor vehicle occupants and other travelers (motorcyclists, pedestrians, and bicyclists) declined between 2016 and 2021. Fatality rates increased 21% in 2020 and 2% in 2021. This erased the progress made reducing the fatality rate over the previous three years. In 2016, 1.2 people died in a motor vehicle accident for every 100 million vehicle miles traveled compared to 1.4 in 2021 — that's more than 5,000 additional deaths in 2021.

TRAFFIC INJURIES
PER 100 MILLION VEHICLE MILES TRAVELED

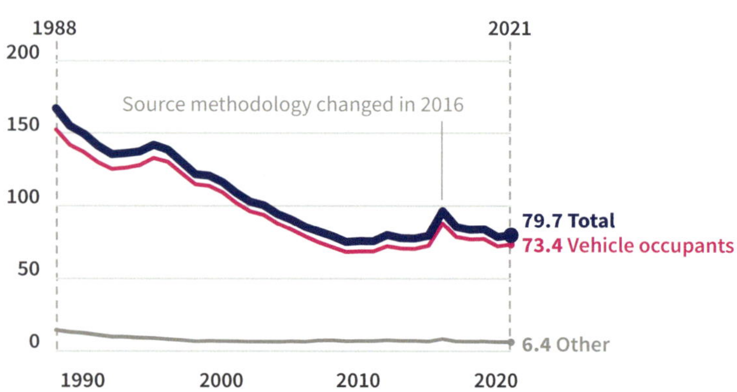

Source: National Highway Traffic Safety Administration
Note: Other includes motorcyclists, pedestrians, and bicyclists. The data collection system changed in 2016. Data for 2016 and later is not comparable to data from 2015 and earlier.

TRAFFIC FATALITIES
PER 100 MILLION VEHICLE MILES TRAVELED

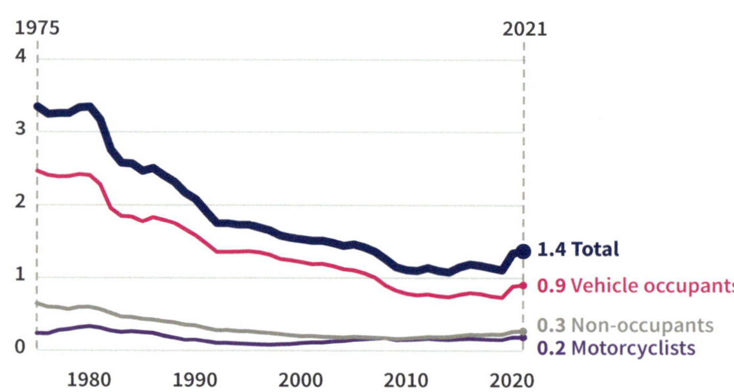

Source: National Highway Traffic Safety Administration
Note: Non-occupants include pedestrians and bicyclists.

Is flight performance improving or declining?

In 2023, about 78% of flight departures were on time, up nearly 2 percentage points from 2022. Air carrier accidents can include events such as ground collisions or cabin incidents where people onboard are injured or killed, or the plane is damaged. There were 259 accidents on scheduled flights in the United States between 2013 and 2022. Turbulence was responsible for 95 of them, or 37%. Ground collisions were responsible for 40 accidents, accounting for 15%. Three accidents resulted in fatalities and 146 resulted in serious injuries.

FLIGHTS ON-TIME PERFORMANCE

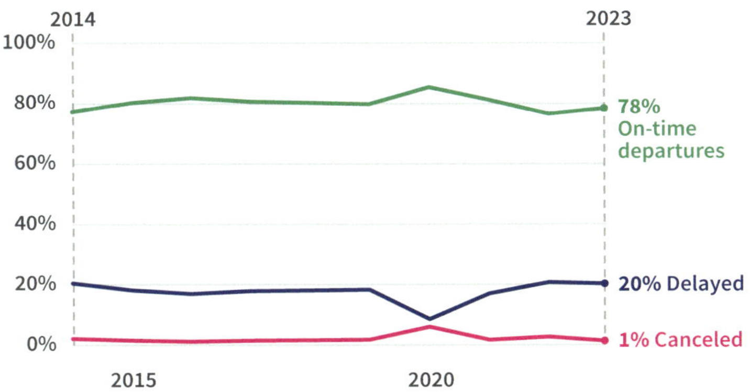

Source: Bureau of Transportation Statistics

NUMBER OF AIR CARRIER ACCIDENTS (2013–2022)

BY ACCIDENT EVENT AND WORST INJURY SEVERITY

Source: National Transportation Safety Board
Note: Accidents occur while any person is on a plane with the intention of flying and a person dies or is seriously injured, or the plane is substantially damaged.

How safe is our nation's rail transportation?

A higher share of commuter rail tracks, heavy rail tracks, and rail vehicles were in a state of good repair in 2021 compared to 2018. Meanwhile, the share of light rail tracks in good repair remained steady. Rail accidents are most common on light rail transit. There were 679 accidents per 100 million vehicle miles on light rail compared to 50 on subways, metros, and other heavy rail in 2022 and 22 on commuter rail in 2019 (the most recent year of data available).

RAIL TRANSIT ASSETS IN A STATE OF GOOD REPAIR (2018 VS. 2021)

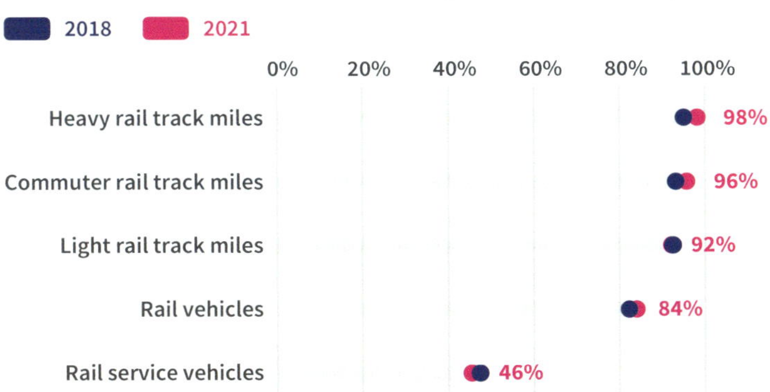

Source: Department of Transportation
Note: Includes only assets which transit agencies own and for which they are responsible for replacing, refurbishing, etc.

RAIL TRANSIT ACCIDENTS

PER 100 MILLION VEHICLE MILES

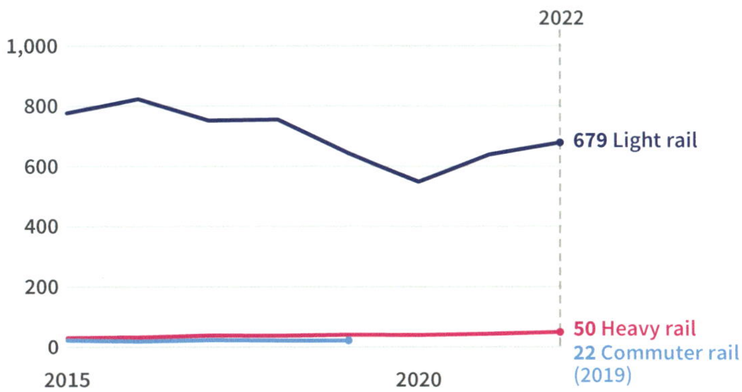

Source: Bureau of Transportation Statistics
Note: Data for 2022 is preliminary. Commuter rail data is unavailable for 2020–2022. Light rail includes streetcar and hybrid rail.

Who doesn't have a broadband subscription?

In 2022, 20.7% of people lived in a home without a fixed broadband subscription. This varied from 12.7% of people in New Hampshire to 33.5% in Mississippi. Broadband subscriptions also varied by race and ethnicity, household income, and homeownership status. American Indian and Alaska Native people were the most likely to lack a broadband subscription in 2022, with 37.8% of their population going without.

SHARE OF PEOPLE WITHOUT A FIXED BROADBAND SUBSCRIPTION (2022)

BY STATE

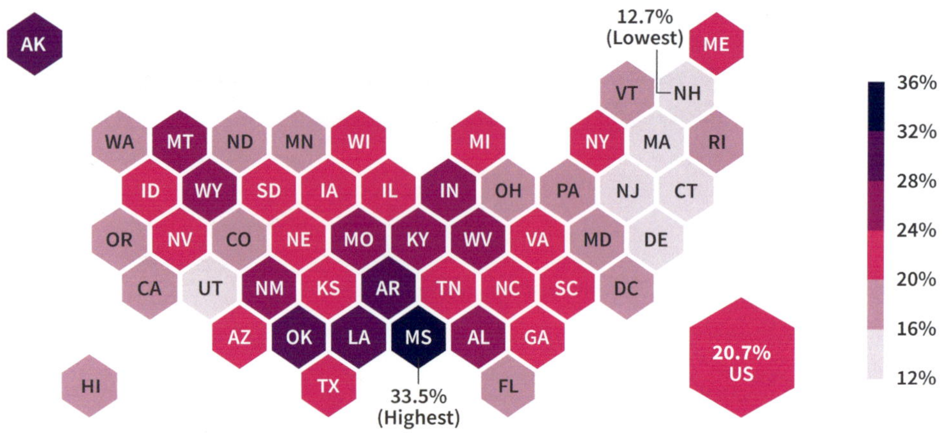

Fixed broadband is a type of high-speed internet connection that uses wires or cables to deliver internet. The Census Bureau asks whether people use broadband, dial-up service (which is slower than broadband), a mobile network, or satellite for their home internet.

Source: USAFacts analysis of Census Bureau data
Note: Fixed broadband includes cable, fiber optic, or DSL.

SHARE OF POPULATION WITHOUT A FIXED BROADBAND SUBSCRIPTION (2022)

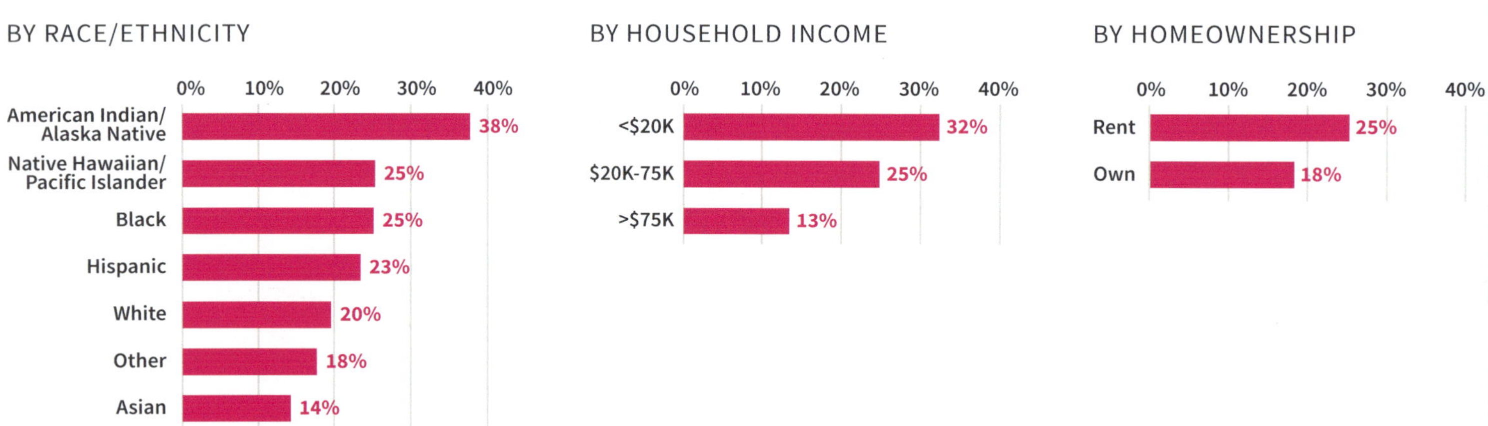

Source: USAFacts analysis of Census Bureau data
Note: Fixed broadband includes cable, fiber optic, or DSL. All races exclude Hispanic. Other includes all other races and multiracial people.

Other key topics

Defense, veterans, & foreign aid

GOVERNMENT SPENDING 1980–2023
DEFENSE, VETERANS SUPPORT, & FOREIGN AID

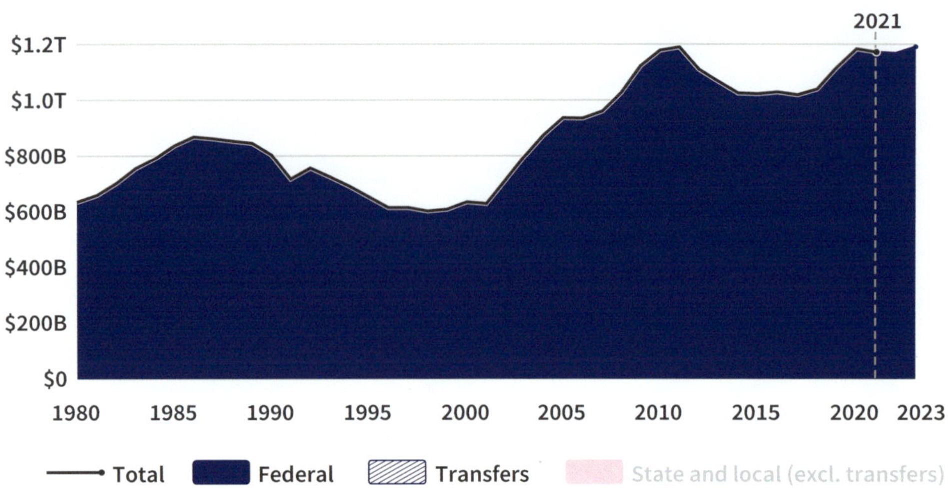

2023 FEDERAL SPENDING*

$1.2 trillion

PERCENT OF FEDERAL SPENDING

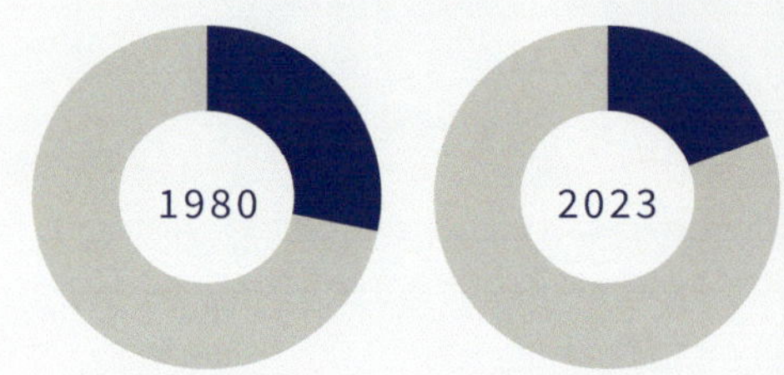

28% **19%**

Source: USAFacts aggregation of data from the Office of Management and Budget (OMB), the Census Bureau, and the Bureau of Economic Analysis (BEA)
Adjusted for inflation (FY 2023 dollars)
Note: *Includes direct spending and transfers.

Federal agencies spending: Defense, veterans, & foreign aid

Federal agency	Net spending in FY 2023	Share of spending transferred to state and local governments	Share of spending that was mandatory
Department of Defense–Military Programs	$775.9 billion	0%	1%
Department of Veterans Affairs	$301.1 billion	1%	57%
International Assistance Programs	$36.1 billion	0%	*
Department of State	$32.0 billion	0%	0%
Other agencies	$46.5 billion	0%	4%

Source: USAFacts calculations based on the Public Budget Database from the Office of Management and Budget
*International Assistance Programs received $12.6 billion more than spent on mandatory defense and foreign aid programs. Because of budgetary rules pertaining to offsetting receipts and offsetting collections, agencies can have negative net outlays, negative net transfers, or negative net mandatory spending. This happens when money agencies receive from certain sources exceeds the amount they spend, resulting in a surplus. For more information on this issue, see here: https://www.whitehouse.gov/wp-content/uploads/2023/03/ap_18_offsetting_fy2024.pdf.

What are the main parts of the US defense budget?

Defense spending (excluding spending on veterans) increased 3% to $994.6 billion in 2023, but was 14% lower than its 2010 peak. The largest portion (32%) compensated military and civilian personnel. There were about 1.3 million active-duty military in 2023, 41% fewer than in 1987 — the recent peak. The military also employed nearly 779,000 civilians. The military's size has been consistent since 1998, growing or shrinking by 3% or less in any year.

DEFENSE EXPENDITURES

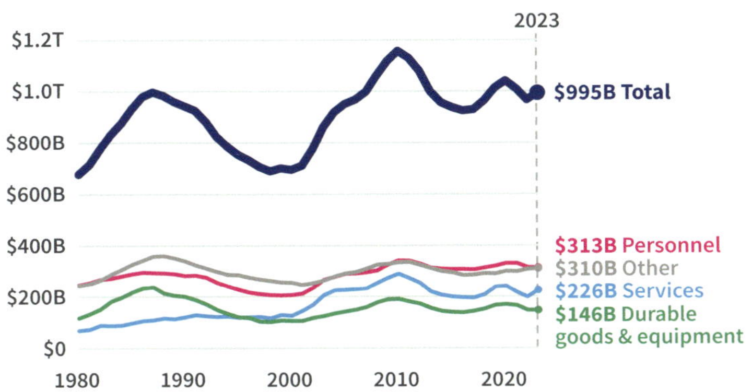

Source: Bureau of Economic Analysis
Adjusted for inflation (2023 dollars)

MILITARY PERSONNEL

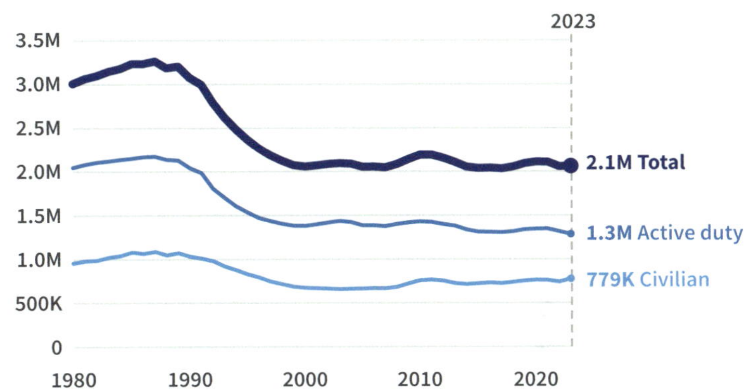

Source: Defense Manpower Data Center
Note: Data does not include reserve members, Coast Guard, or National Guard. All annual data points shown here are reflective of the source values as of Sept. 30 of the stated year.

How much does the US spend on foreign aid?

According to preliminary data, the US committed $73.9 billion to foreign aid in FY 2022; 86% of that was economic assistance. Ukraine was the largest aid recipient, with the US promising more than $13 billion. After adjusting for inflation, this was $1.1 billion more than the total aid the US had ever provided Ukraine. Partial FY 2023 data shows the US promised at least another $16.7 billion to Ukraine.

FOREIGN AID OBLIGATIONS

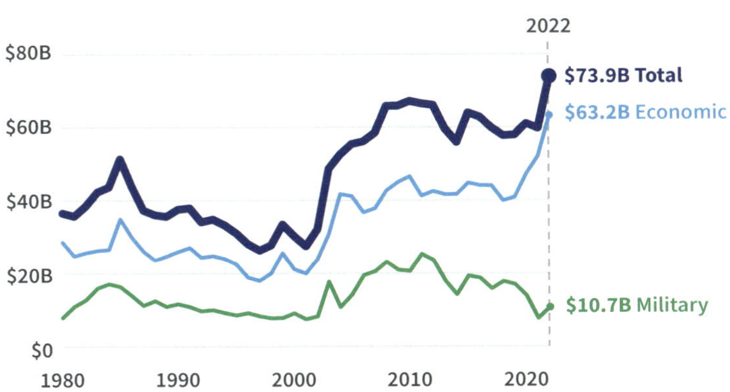

Source: US Agency for International Development and the US Department of State
Adjusted for inflation (FY 2023 dollars)
Note: Data is updated frequently and is correct as of April 3, 2024.
Data for 2022 is partially reported.

FOREIGN AID OBLIGATIONS (2012 VS. 2022)

BY TOP 8 RECEIVING COUNTRIES IN 2022

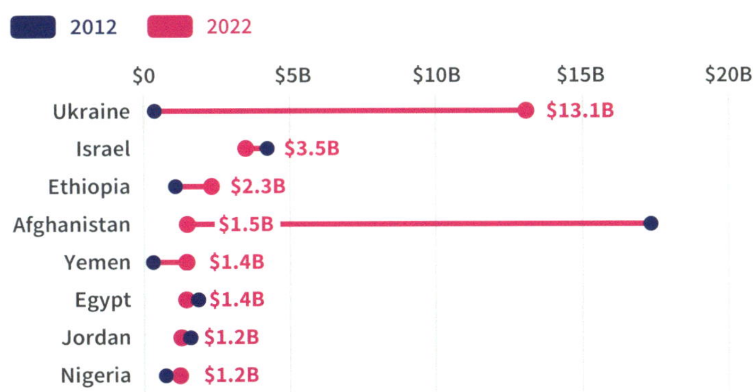

Source: US Agency for International Development and the US Department of State
Adjusted for inflation (FY 2023 dollars)
Note: Data is updated frequently and is correct as of April 3, 2024.
Data for 2022 is partially reported.

Crime

GOVERNMENT SPENDING 1980–2023
CRIME

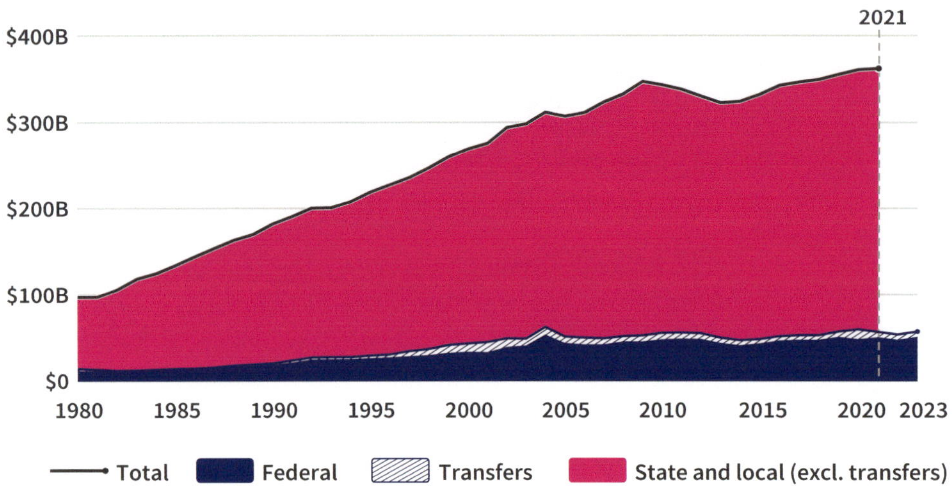

2023 FEDERAL SPENDING*

$58 billion

PERCENT OF FEDERAL SPENDING

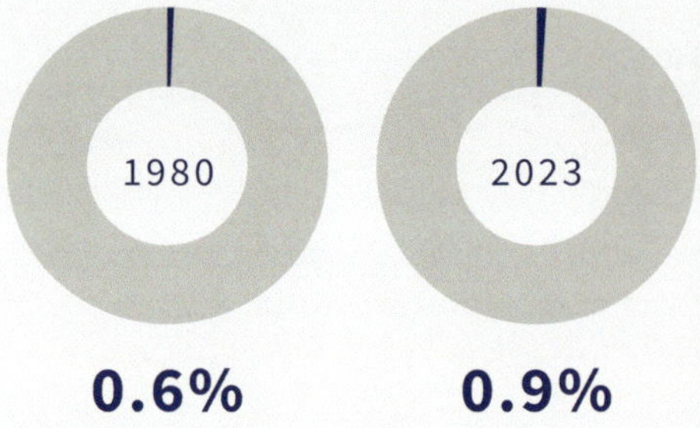

Source: USAFacts aggregation of data from the Office of Management and Budget (OMB), the Census Bureau, and the Bureau of Economic Analysis (BEA)
Adjusted for inflation (FY 2023 dollars)
Note: *Includes direct spending and transfers.

Federal agencies spending: Crime

Federal agency	Net spending in FY 2023	Share of spending transferred to state and local governments	Share of spending that was mandatory
Department of Justice	$37.8 billion	14%	23%
Judicial Branch	$8.8 billion	0%	6%
Department of Homeland Security	$7.0 billion	0%	4%
Department of the Treasury	$2.0 billion	23%	54%
Other agencies	$2.0 billion	20%	*

Source: USAFacts calculations based on the Public Budget Database from the Office of Management and Budget
*Combined, other agencies received $40 million more than they spent on mandatory crime programs. Because of budgetary rules pertaining to offsetting receipts and offsetting collections, agencies can have negative net outlays, negative net transfers, or negative net mandatory spending. This happens when money agencies receive from certain sources exceeds the amount they spend, resulting in a surplus. For more information on this issue, see here: https://www.whitehouse.gov/wp-content/uploads/2023/03/ap_18_offsetting_fy2024.pdf.

Is crime in the US rising?

Crime rates have been going down since the early 1990s. Violent crime rates dropped by 50% from 1991 to 2022, and property crime rates fell 62%. In 2022, there were 381 violent crimes per 100,000 people, the second year of decline after an increase in 2020. Meanwhile, property crime rates increased for the first time since 2001, with 1,954 property crimes per 100,000 people. This was due to a rise in larceny-theft and motor vehicle theft rates.

CRIME RATES
PER 100,000 PEOPLE

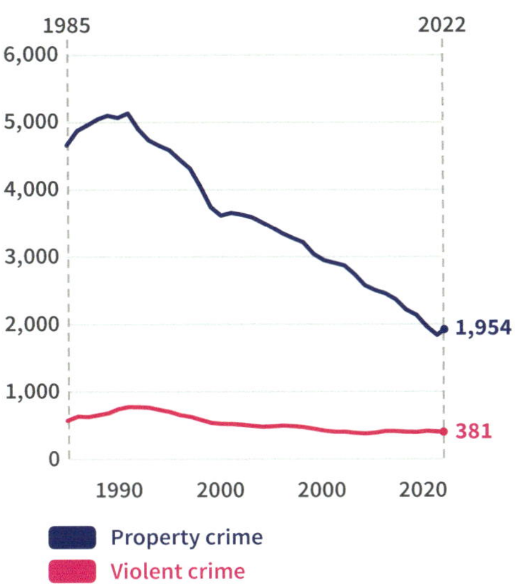

PROPERTY CRIME RATES
PER 100,000 PEOPLE

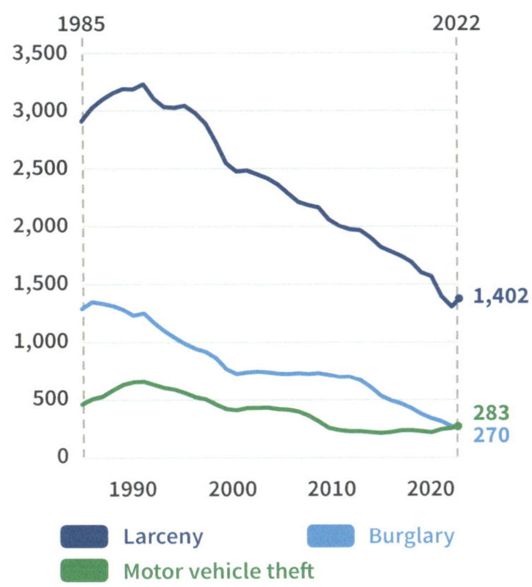

VIOLENT CRIME RATES
PER 100,000 PEOPLE

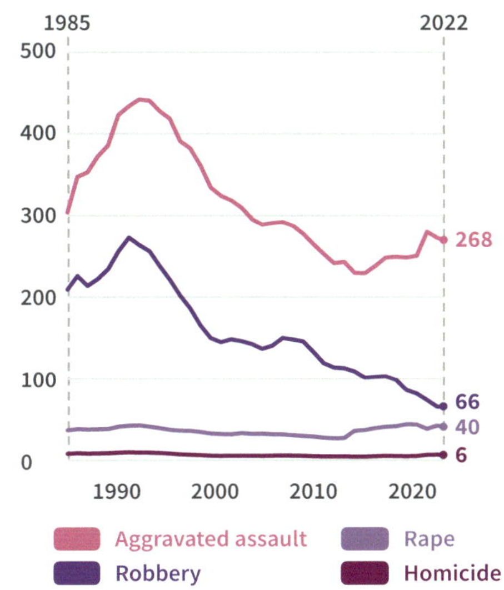

Source: Federal Bureau of Investigation

How many people are in the correctional system?

Nearly 5.7 million people were in prison, jail, or on probation when last counted in 2021. An estimated 6.9 million were admitted to jails throughout the year.[xiv] The prison population was 369 per 100,000 people in 2022 compared to a year prior, up 2%. The jailed population reached 199 per 100,000, up 4%. Both populations remain smaller than 2019 levels. Probation and parole data was not yet available for 2022 at the time of publishing.

CORRECTIONAL POPULATION
PER 100,000 PEOPLE

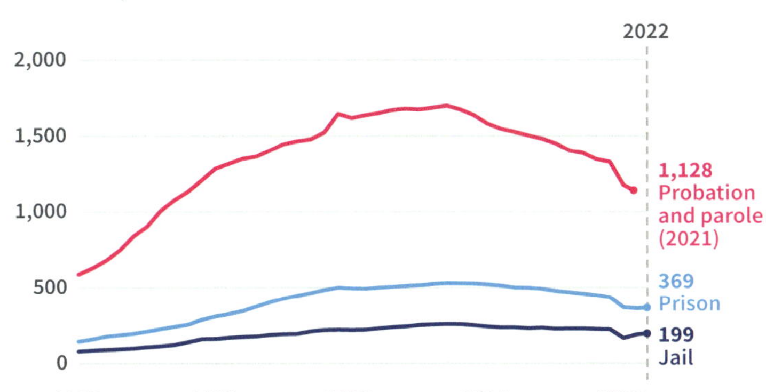

Source: Bureau of Justice Statistics

Disasters

GOVERNMENT SPENDING 1980–2023
DISASTERS

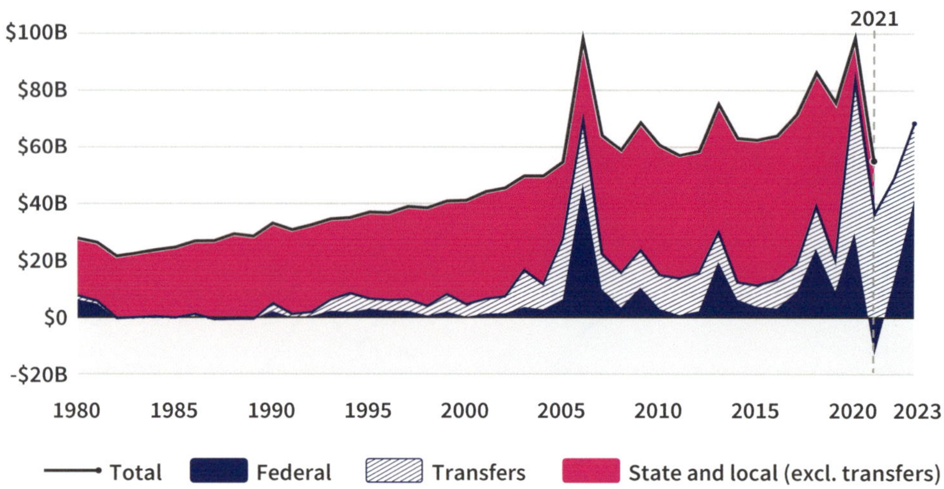

2023 FEDERAL SPENDING*

$69 billion

PERCENT OF FEDERAL SPENDING

0.3% **1%**

Source: USAFacts aggregation of data from the Office of Management and Budget (OMB), the Census Bureau, and the Bureau of Economic Analysis (BEA)
Adjusted for inflation (FY 2023 dollars)
Note: *Includes direct spending and transfers. Federal spending, transfers, and state and local spending data capture net expenditures. In some cases, this results in negative net spending.

Federal agencies spending: Disasters

Federal agency	Net spending in FY 2023	Share of spending transferred to state and local governments	Share of spending that was mandatory
Department of Homeland Security	$39.0 billion	70%	36%
Small Business Administration	$29.4 billion	0%	95%
Department of Agriculture	$123 million	0%	0%

Source: USAFacts calculations based on the Public Budget Database from the Office of Management and Budget

How many natural disasters occur in the United States and how much do they cost?

The National Oceanic and Atmospheric Administration (NOAA) tracks the lives lost due to, and the financial costs of, billion-dollar disasters. More than 80% of the financial toll of declared natural disasters is due to disasters that cost at least $1 billion.[xv] Since 1980, these disasters have resulted in the deaths of more than 16,000 people, with 470 dying in 2023, and, after adjusting for inflation, have cost a combined total of $2.7 trillion. There were 27 of these billion-dollar disasters in 2023 for a total cost of more than $89 billion. While 2023 had more billion-dollar disasters than any other year since NOAA began capturing this data, it ranked 11th in terms of cost.

COST OF BILLION-DOLLAR DISASTERS (1980–2023)

BY CATEGORY

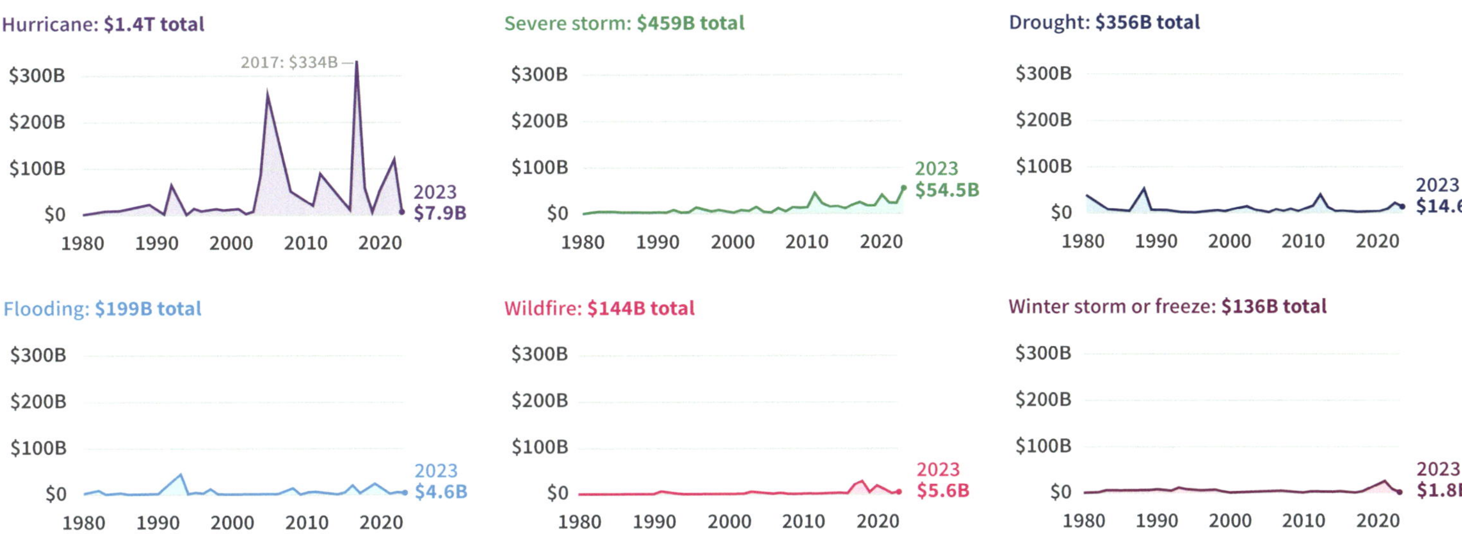

Source: National Oceanic and Atmospheric Administration

Note: Inflation adjusted by source. Source data updates monthly.

FREQUENCY OF BILLION-DOLLAR DISASTERS

BY CATEGORY

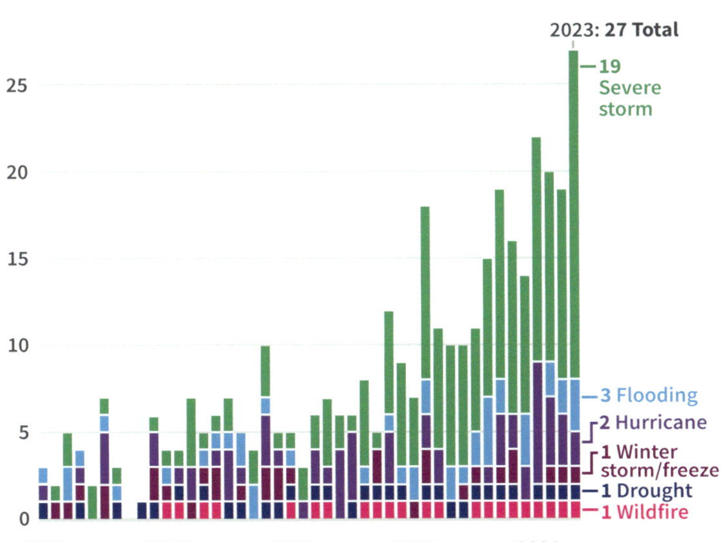

Source: National Oceanic and Atmospheric Administration

Note: Source data updates monthly.

BILLION-DOLLAR DISASTER DEATHS (1980–2023)

CUMULATIVE TOTAL, BY CATEGORY

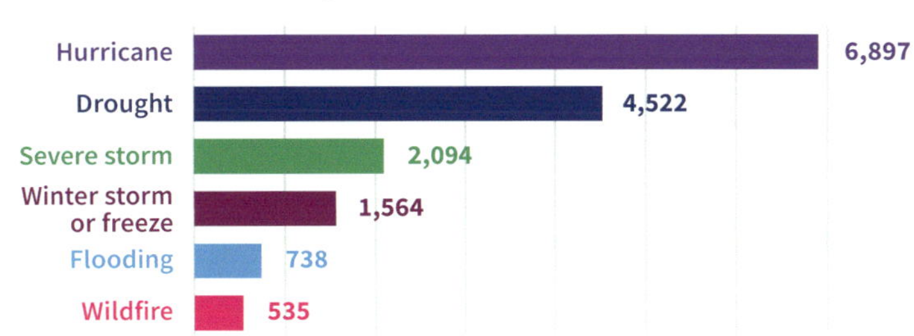

TOTAL DEATHS

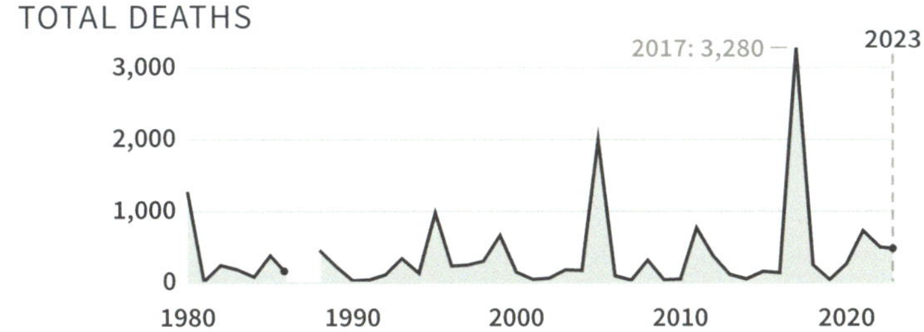

Source: National Oceanic and Atmospheric Administration

Note: Deaths from billion-dollar droughts were due to heat waves. Source data updates monthly.

Energy

GOVERNMENT SPENDING 1980–2023

ENERGY

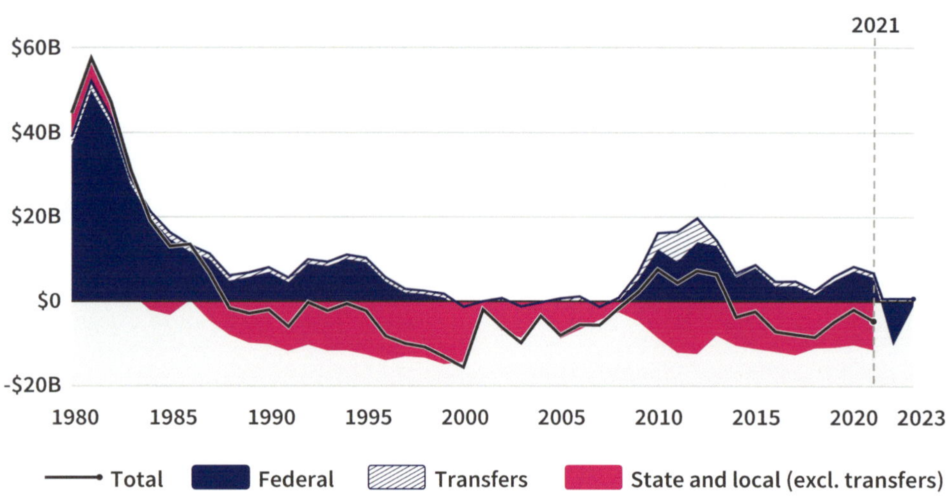

2023 FEDERAL SPENDING*

-$0.4 billion

PERCENT OF FEDERAL SPENDING

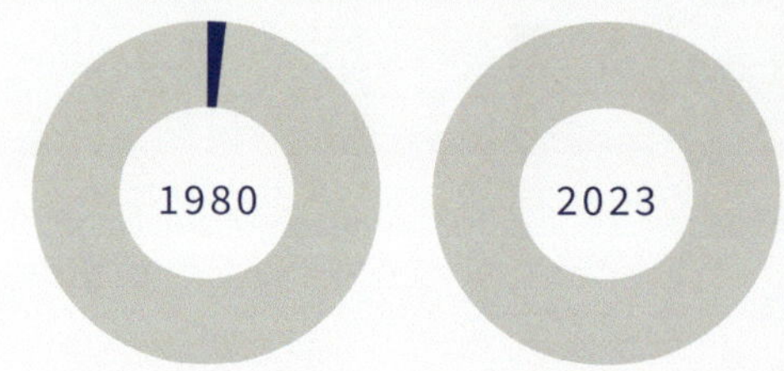

2% **0.0%**

Source: USAFacts aggregation of data from the Office of Management and Budget (OMB), the Census Bureau, and the Bureau of Economic Analysis (BEA)
Adjusted for inflation (FY 2023 dollars)
Note: *Includes direct spending and transfers. Federal spending, transfers, and state and local spending data capture net expenditures. In some cases, this results in negative net spending.

Federal agencies spending: Energy

Federal agency	Net spending in FY 2023*	Share of spending transferred to state and local governments	Share of spending that was mandatory
Department of Agriculture	$866 million	0%	**
Tennessee Valley Authority	$184 million	***	100%
Nuclear Regulatory Commission	$125 million	0%	0%
Department of Energy	-$1.8 billion	0%	****
Other agencies	$169 million	0%	98%

Source: USAFacts calculations based on the Public Budget Database from the Office of Management and Budget
*Because of budgetary rules pertaining to offsetting receipts and offsetting collections, agencies can have negative net outlays, negative net transfers, or negative net mandatory spending. This happens when money agencies receive from certain sources exceeds the amount they spend, resulting in a surplus. For more information on this issue, see here: https://www.whitehouse.gov/wp-content/uploads/2023/03/ap_18_offsetting_fy2024.pdf.
**The Department of Agriculture spent $1.1 billion on mandatory energy programs, but this was more than offset by receipts from discretionary programs.
***The Tennessee Valley Authority distributed $593 million in energy-related grants to state and local governments, but this was more than offset by receipts from other programs.
****The Department of Energy received $7.9 billion more than it spent on mandatory energy programs.

How much energy does the US use?

US energy consumption generally increased from 1949, when data collection began, through the 1990s. Total energy consumption has since trended downward. It was lower in 2023 than 2000, but more than three times higher than in 1949. After adjusting for population growth, consumption peaked in 1979 and has since dropped by 20%.

ENERGY CONSUMPTION
QUADRILLION BTUs

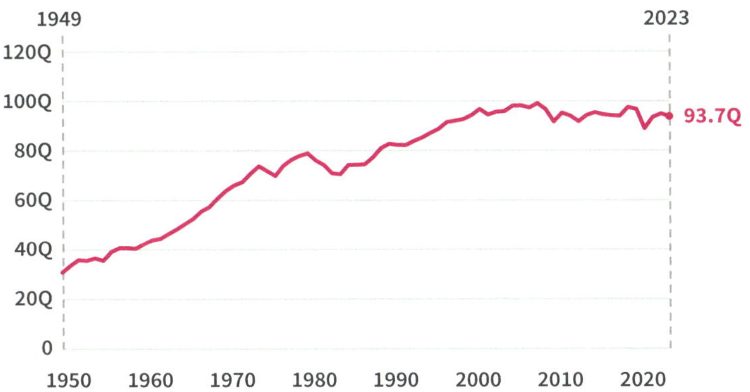

Source: Energy Information Administration
Note: Data updates frequently.

ENERGY CONSUMPTION PER CAPITA
MILLION BTUs

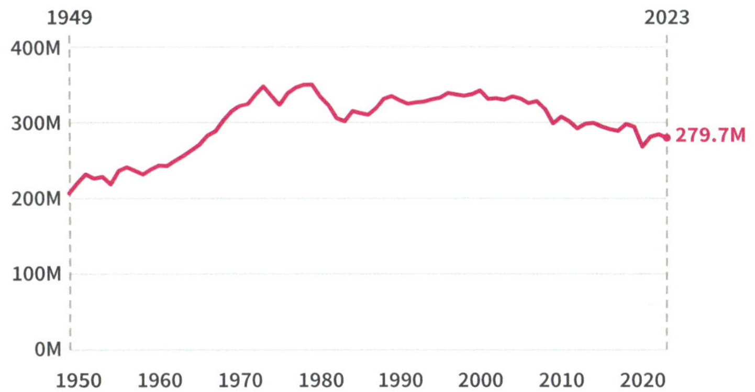

Source: Energy Information Administration
Note: Data updates frequently.

How has US energy production changed over time?

Energy production in the US rose between 2013 and 2023, mostly due to growing natural gas and crude oil production. Biomass, wind, and solar energy production also grew, but these sources were about 7% of total production in 2023. Coal production declined 41% over this period.

FOSSIL FUEL ENERGY PRODUCTION
QUADRILLION BTUs

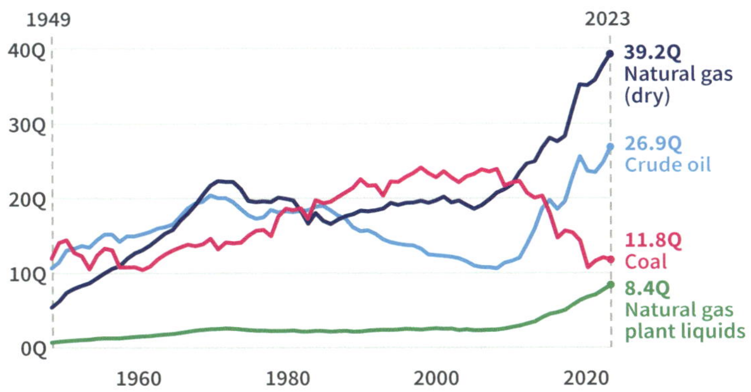

Source: Energy Information Administration
Note: Data updates frequently.

RENEWABLE AND NUCLEAR ENERGY PRODUCTION
QUADRILLION BTUs

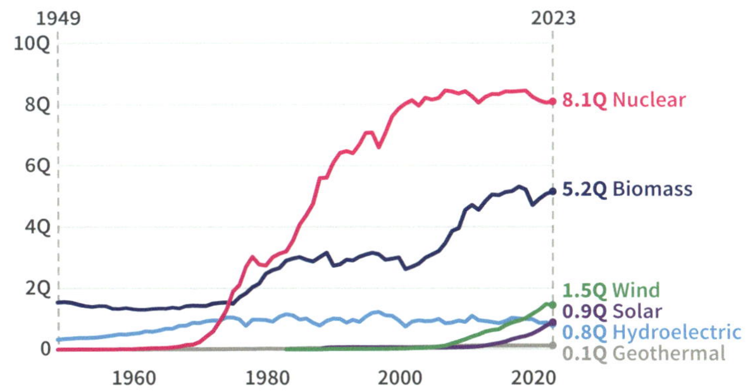

Source: Energy Information Administration
Note: Data updates frequently.

Environment & natural resources

GOVERNMENT SPENDING 1980–2023
ENVIRONMENT & NATURAL RESOURCES

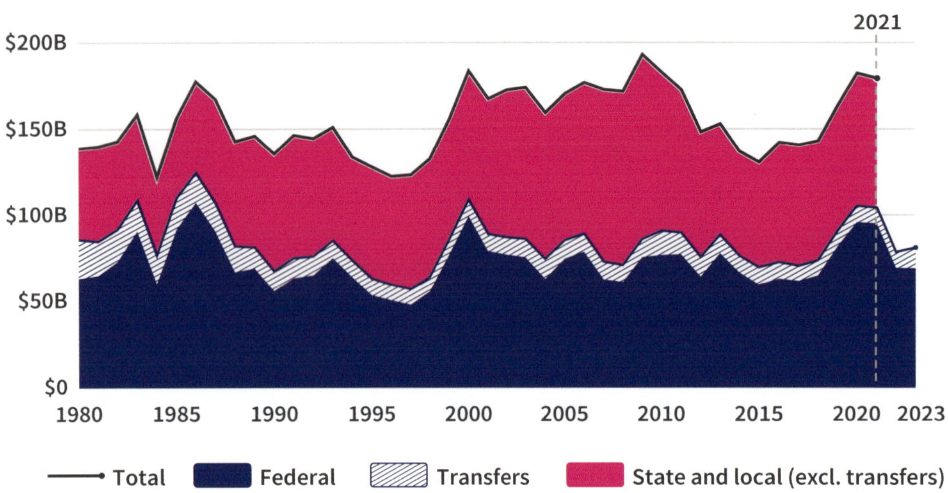

2023 FEDERAL SPENDING*

$81 billion

PERCENT OF FEDERAL SPENDING

4% **1%**

Source: USAFacts aggregation of data from the Office of Management and Budget (OMB), the Census Bureau, and the Bureau of Economic Analysis (BEA)
Adjusted for inflation (FY 2023 dollars)
Note: *Includes direct spending and transfers.

Federal agencies spending: Environment & natural resources

Federal agency	Net spending in FY 2023*	Share of spending transferred to state and local governments	Share of spending that was mandatory
Department of Agriculture	$48.7 billion	3%	65%
Environmental Protection Agency	$12.6 billion	59%	12%
Corps of Engineers–Civil Works	$7.8 billion	0%	**
Department of Commerce	$6.7 billion	7%	3%
Other agencies	$5.3 billion	50%	***

Source: USAFacts calculations based on the Public Budget Database from the Office of Management and Budget
*Because of budgetary rules pertaining to offsetting receipts and offsetting collections, agencies can have negative net outlays, negative net transfers, or negative net mandatory spending. This happens when money agencies receive from certain sources exceeds the amount they spend, resulting in a surplus. For more information on this issue, see here: https://www.whitehouse.gov/wp-content/uploads/2023/03/ap_18_offsetting_fy2024.pdf.
**The Corps of Engineers–Civil Works received $567 million more than it spent on mandatory environment programs.
***Combined, other agencies received $6.9 billion more than they spent on mandatory environment programs.

Are US air pollution levels improving?

There were fewer unhealthy air quality days in 2022 than in 2000. Thirty-five major US cities had a combined total of 597 unhealthy air quality days in 2022. The average over the last five years of data (2018–2022) was 67% lower than the average for first five years (2000–2004). Annual greenhouse gas emissions increased throughout the 1990s. They peaked in 2007 but decreased 16% by 2022.

TOTAL NUMBER OF DAYS REACHING UNHEALTHY FOR SENSITIVE GROUPS OR ABOVE ON THE AIR QUALITY INDEX

AMONG 35 MAJOR US CITIES
(FOR OZONE AND PM2.5 COMBINED)

Source: Environmental Protection Agency
Note: Sensitive groups for ozone and PM2.5 include people with heart or lung disease, older adults, children and teenagers, and people who are active outdoors.

GREENHOUSE GAS EMISSIONS

MILLIONS OF METRIC TONS,
CARBON DIOXIDE EQUIVALENT

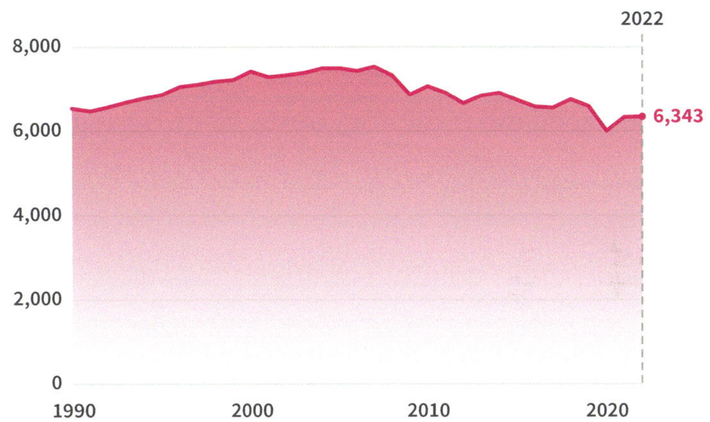

Source: Environmental Protection Agency

How has the total area of farmland in the US changed?

How much revenue did crops and animal products generate?

The US had 880.1 million acres of farmland in 2022. This was 2% less than in 2017, and nearly 8% less than in 1997. 2022's crop cash receipts totaled $278.2 billion. More than half (53%) of this came from corn and soybeans for a combined $148.5 billion. Cash receipts for animals and animal products reached $258.5 billion with cattle and calf receipts making up the largest portion of this total — $86.1 billion, or 33%.

FARMLAND IN ACRES

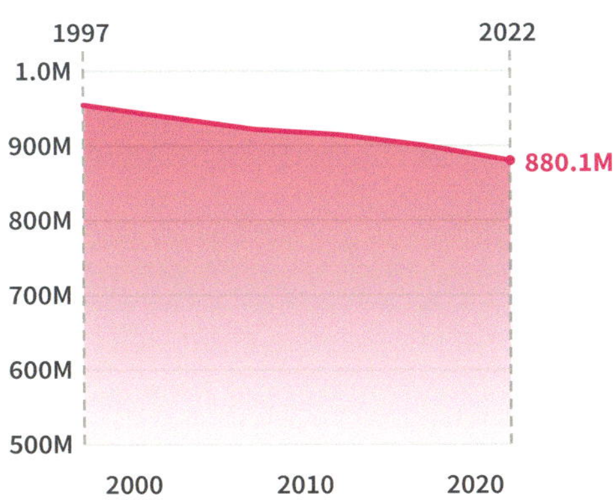

Source: Department of Agriculture

AGRICULTURE CASH RECEIPTS (2022)

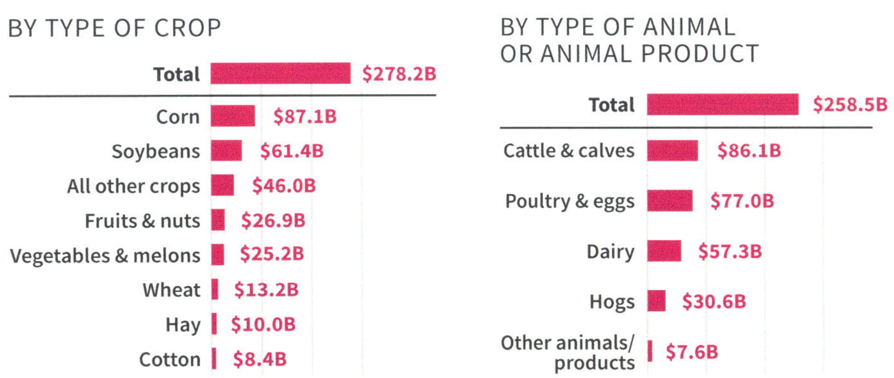

Source: Department of Agriculture
Note: Categories may not sum to total due to rounding.

Education

GOVERNMENT SPENDING 1980–2023
EDUCATION

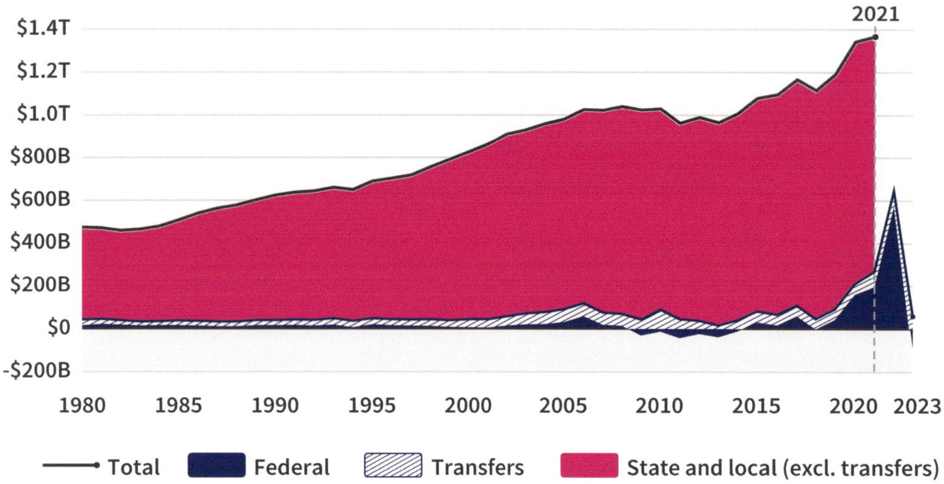

2023 FEDERAL SPENDING*

-$67 billion

PERCENT OF FEDERAL SPENDING

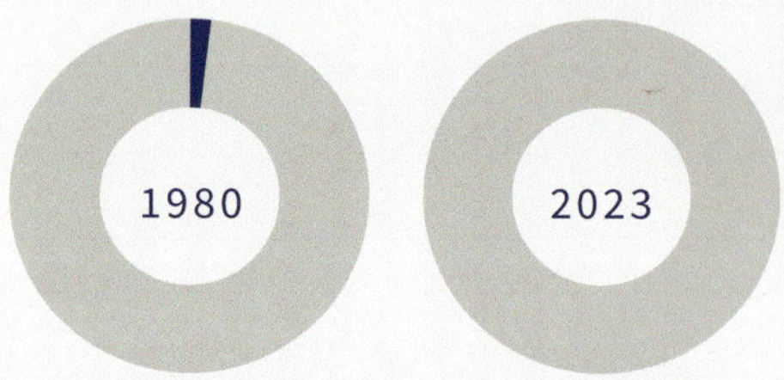

2% **-1%**

Source: USAFacts aggregation of data from the Office of Management and Budget (OMB), the Census Bureau, and the Bureau of Economic Analysis (BEA)
Adjusted for inflation (FY 2023 dollars)
Note: *Includes direct spending and transfers. Federal spending, transfers, and state and local spending data capture net expenditures. In some cases, this results in negative net spending.

Federal agencies spending: Education

Federal agency	Net spending in FY 2023*	Share of spending transferred to state and local governments	Share of spending that was mandatory
Department of the Treasury	$3.3 billion	0%	100%
Smithsonian Institution	$1.4 billion	0%	0%
Department of the Interior	$1.4 billion	9%	8%
Department of Education	-$75.2 billion**	**	***
Other agencies	$2.2 billion	51%	7%

Source: USAFacts calculations based on the Public Budget Database from the Office of Management and Budget
* Because of budgetary rules pertaining to offsetting receipts and offsetting collections, agencies can have negative net outlays, negative net transfers, or negative net mandatory spending. This happens when money agencies receive from certain sources exceeds the amount they spend, resulting in a surplus. For more information on this issue, see here: https://www.whitehouse.gov/wp-content/uploads/2023/03/ap_18_offsetting_fy2024.pdf.
** The Department of Education budget was impacted in FY 2022 and FY 2023 by President Biden's original student loan forgiveness executive order. The cost of forgiveness appeared as spending in the FY 2022 budget, but that anticipated spending was reversed in the FY 2023 budget after the Supreme Court's ruling that it was unconstitutional in Biden vs. Nebraska. As a result, total federal education spending, and Department of Education mandatory spending in particular, in the FY 2023 budget was negative.
***The Department of Education granted $64.0 billion to state and local governments for educational purposes.

How well are elementary schoolers doing in math and reading?

Between 2019 and 2022, reading and math proficiency fell among fourth and eighth graders. In 2022, 36% percent of fourth graders scored at or above proficient in math and 33% were at or above proficient in reading, compared to 41% and 35% in 2019. Among eighth graders, math proficiency fell 7 percentage points to 26% and reading proficiency fell 3 percentage points to 31%.

SHARE OF STUDENTS SCORING AT OR ABOVE PROFICIENT IN READING AND MATH

GRADE 4

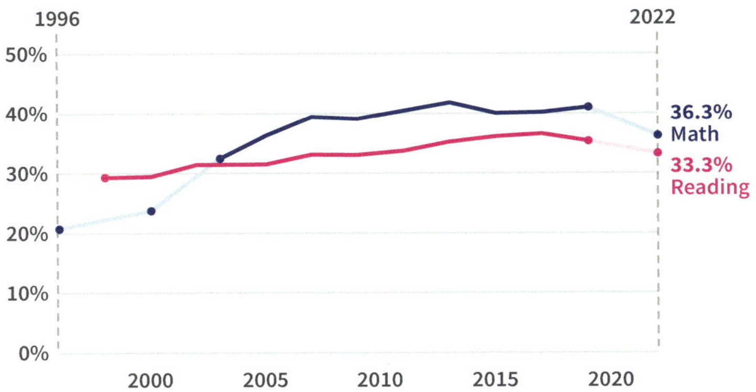

GRADE 8

Source: National Center for Education Statistics
Note: Survey not conducted in each year.

How many people attend and graduate college and how much do they borrow in loans?

Of the students who started high school in 2012, 25% completed a four-year college degree by 2022 and 6% had completed a two-year degree by 2020. Another 14% had enrolled in a four-year college the year they graduated high school but had not completed their degree and 13% had enrolled in two-year college without graduating. The mean cumulative amount of student debt borrowed for undergraduate education was almost $30,000 among students who completed their undergraduate program in 2020 and took out student loans (about 55% of the 2020 graduating class).

EDUCATIONAL ATTAINMENT

PERCENTAGE OF HIGH SCHOOL CLASS OF 2016

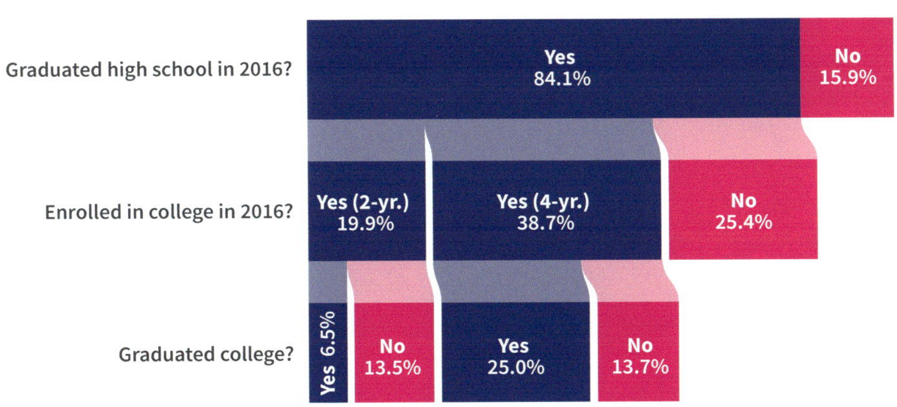

Source: National Center for Education Statistics and Census Bureau
Note: 4-year college graduation rates measure whether someone graduated within six years of enrollment. 2-year college graduation rates measure whether someone graduated within three years of enrollment.

AVERAGE CUMULATIVE UNDERGRAD STUDENT LOANS BORROWED

AMONG BORROWERS GRADUATING THAT YEAR

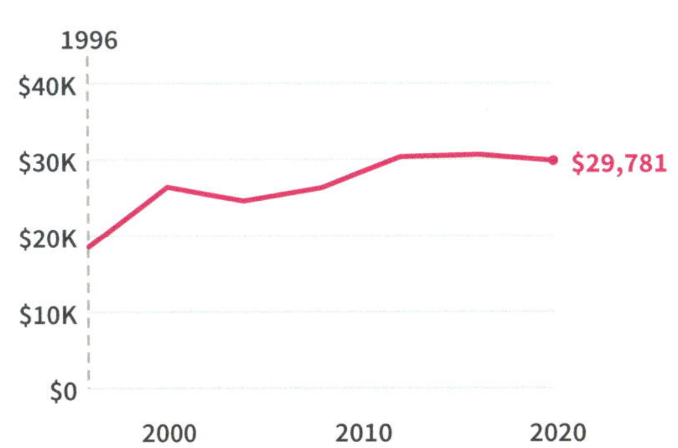

Source: National Center for Education Statistics
Note: Adjusted for inflation (2022–23 school year dollars). Study conducted once every four years.

Recommendations

Recommendations

As Congress debates issues facing the country during an election year, reliable taxpayer-funded data from government agencies should be easily available as the foundation for serious policy discussion. Good data can improve all phases of the legislative process by giving policymakers a common understanding of the current state of an issue from which to start, providing key metrics that legislation aims to affect, and creating opportunities for measuring the outcomes of policy once enacted.

Government data is one of the best sources of information for Congress and the American public, but it also has several deficiencies. USAFacts met with over 100 congressional staff from both parties and chambers during the 118th Congress to better understand their challenges in using government data. USAFacts has also encountered several challenges in accessing usable federal, state, and local data over our nine-year history, including while creating this report.

Key government data deficiencies may include:

- **Government data is outdated or delayed.** To make informed decisions, policymakers need data published on a reasonable timeline. High-priority datasets may need more frequent publication, and agencies should experiment with faster data collection and publication methods.
- **Government data is not in usable formats.** Important data is frequently locked in static, quickly outdated PDFs rather than available with historical trends in spreadsheets or tools such as data visualizations or dashboards.
- **Data on key issues is not collected or made available to decision-makers.** In some cases, the data needed to inform legislation is not collected or is collected but unpublished. Data is often not sufficiently disaggregated by geography, income, race, and other demographics, making it difficult to understand congressional districts or key population segments.
- **Governments are slow to collect new data necessary for understanding emerging issues.** Americans are confronting new technologies and issues but governments are often slow to collect and publish relevant data. Artificial intelligence, cryptocurrency, and the gig economy are new issues that are difficult to assess due to limited data.
- **It is challenging to track funding from appropriating legislation to recipients.** Congress can track very little funding holistically from authorizing legislation to distribution. Improvements to USAspending and partnerships with state and local governments that redistribute billions of federal dollars are necessary for providing clarity.
- **Data management is decentralized among federal, state, and local governments.** There are over 90,000 governments in the United States, resulting in a decentralized data infrastructure that does not support real-time, accurate decision-making. Federal, state, and local governments must work together to improve data collection and aggregation.

Congress can and should solve many of these deficiencies to help in its decision-making — and to ensure good data is available to the taxpayers who pay for it. The following recommendations outline ways Congress can improve government data and be empowered to use more data in decision-making.

Recommendations for improving data

Congress should use its legislative and oversight powers to improve government data. Over the past decade, Congress has taken several steps to improve government data and its availability to citizens. This includes the 2014 Digital Accountability and Transparency Act (DATA Act), which created USAspending. It also includes the 2018 Foundations for Evidence-Based Policymaking Act, which led to the creation of the Federal Data Strategy.

However, implementation and agency guidance is sometimes lagging or incomplete. Good data systems require balancing the information needs of the public and policymakers against important considerations like privacy and cost to taxpayers. Congress can do the following to improve government data.

Legislation

- Support the Congressional Evidence-Based Policymaking Resolution (H.Con.Res.116) and the creation of a second Commission on Evidence-Based Policymaking.
- Support the Information Quality Assurance Act (H.R.7219) to ensure that agencies rely on data and evidence to develop, issue, and inform the public on new rules and guidance.
- Support the Fiscal State of the Nation Act (H.R.6952) to ensure Congress receives annual, nonpartisan updates on the country's financial condition.
- Support the Governmentwide Executive Councils Act (H.R.7523) and specifically the reauthorization of the Federal Chief Data Officers' (CDO) Council before its scheduled sunset.
- Modernize agencies that support Congress —including the Congressional Research Service (CRS), Congressional Budget Office (CBO), and Government Accountability Office (GAO) — so they can provide real-time data, analytics dashboards, and other digital products to help the policymaking process.
- Ensure future legislation includes provisions for data collection and evaluation where possible and enables federal, state, and local governments to work together to collect, use, and share that data.

Oversight and implementation of data policy

- Instruct the GAO to audit federal data collections to identify and recommend improvements.
- Monitor the implementation of agencies' data programs to ensure efficiency, transparency, accountability, and, ultimately, good data for the American public.
- Ensure proper implementation of the Foundations for Evidence-Based Policymaking Act and the resulting Federal Data Strategy, including that:
    - Agency data publications meet standards defined by the Federal Data Strategy, including timeliness, relevance to policy conversations, and availability.
    - Agencies hire data officers, evaluation officers, and statistical officers to implement the law fully.
    - Agencies and chief data officers develop data standards and schemas for federal data collections to streamline aggregation and reduce costs.
- Encourage agencies to better work with and support how state and local governments collect, share, and report data.

Opportunities for Congress to use data

Congress should proactively leverage data to support informed and outcomes-based lawmaking. Data can improve the efficiency and efficacy of legislation and support continuous monitoring and evaluation of implementation. Lawmakers should strive to rely on nonpartisan government numbers in crafting legislation, and each major piece of legislation should involve an open discussion about relevant data and possible metrics-driven outcomes. Congress should encourage agencies to make improvements when data is unavailable, insufficient, or deficient.

- **Data should be part of legislative debate:** As part of the study process for each bill, originating committees should develop nonpartisan, government data fact sheets that provide the most relevant and up-to-date government data available to understand the problem the proposed legislation aims to address.
- **Data should be used to evaluate policy:** The legislative process should include a future-looking discussion of data that should be collected and distributed in a timely manner and effective format to evaluate the impact of each bill.
- **Data should drive oversight:** Committee oversight of federal agencies should ensure that policy implementation is creating outcomes that align with legislative intent.

Congressional support agencies should modernize their products to emphasize data provision that supports policymaking. Congress is supported by agencies such as the CRS, the CBO, and the GAO, which often produce long-form reports and analysis to guide congressional decision-making.

These reports, data, and services could be improved through the following:

- Congress should work with CRS, CBO, and GAO leadership to explore ways to better serve congressional stakeholders. For example, by providing frequently updated data dashboards, data visualizations, longitudinal studies, and short-form content.
- Congressional support agencies should expand technical assistance offered to congressional offices to help access government data, find useful insights, and create compelling visualizations.

Congressional staff should have avenues to learn data skills to support a modern Congress. Congress relies on staff who know how to access data from varying levels of government, analyze data for insights, and create data visualizations for use in the legislative process. Staff should have access to personal development funds and training opportunities.

Recommended actions include:

- Congressional offices should invest in data skills for staff to support data use by the legislative body, as now allowed by the congressional handbook.
- The Congressional Staff Academy and other congressional support entities should host professional development trainings on using data in the policy-making process.

Sources & notes

Endnotes

i. Immigrant entries by "nationality" includes new arrival green cards given to people born in the specified country. Green card data from DHS does not include breakouts by nationality. In many countries, birth in the country does not automatically provide nationality, and many people can become nationals of a country without having been born there.

ii. Department of State (2014). *The United States and China Extend Visas for Short-term Business Travelers, Tourists, and Students.* https://travel.state.gov/content/travel/en/us-visas/visa-information-resources/visas-news-archive/20141110_us-and-china-to-extend-visas-for-short-term-business-travelers-tourists-and-students.html.

iii. US Citizenship and Immigration Services (n.d.). *Obtaining Asylum in the United States.* https://www.uscis.gov/humanitarian/refugees-and-asylum/asylum/obtaining-asylum-in-the-united-states.

iv. Congressional Research Service (2023). *Asylum Process in Immigration Courts and Selected Trends.* https://crsreports.congress.gov/product/pdf/R/R47504.

v. Department of Homeland Security (2023, November 20). *Refugees and Asylees Annual Flow Report.* https://www.dhs.gov/ohss/topics/immigration/refugees-asylees-AFR. According to DHS, "A refugee is a person outside his or her country of nationality who is unable or unwilling to return to his or her country of nationality because of persecution or a well-founded fear of persecution on account of race, religion, nationality, membership in a particular social group, or political opinion. An asylee is a person who meets the definition of refugee and is already present in the United States or is seeking admission at a port of entry. Refugees are required to apply for Lawful Permanent Resident ("green card") status one year after being admitted, and asylees may apply for green card status one year after their grant of asylum."

vi. US Bureau of Labor Statistics (2024). *Industries at a Glance: Other Services.* https://www.bls.gov/iag/tgs/iag81.htm#:~:text=Establishments%20in%20this%20sector%20are,pet%20care%20services%2C%20photofinishing%20services%2C.

vii. US Bureau of Labor Statistics (2023). *Employment Projections: 2022–2023 Summary.* https://www.bls.gov/news.release/ecopro.nr0.htm.

viii. Bureau of Economic Analysis. *Prototype Measures of Economic Well-Being and Growth.* https://apps.bea.gov/well-being/.

ix. Office of Policy Development and Research (2024). *Assisted Housing: National and Local.* https://www.huduser.gov/portal/datasets/assthsg.html#.

x. Department of Agriculture (2023). *Changes to SNAP Benefit Amounts – 2023.* https://www.fns.usda.gov/snap/changes-2023-benefit-amounts#:~:text=The%20Consolidated%20Appropriations%20Act%2C%202023,amounts%2C%20without%20the%20added%20supplement.

xi. Arias, Elizabeth and others (2023). *Vital Statistics Rapid Release (Report No. 31): Provisional Life Expectancy Estimates for 2022.* https://www.cdc.gov/nchs/data/vsrr/vsrr031.pdf.

xii. National Center for Health Statistics (2023, June 26). *Health, United States, 2020–2021* (Heart Disease Deaths, Cancer Deaths). https://www.cdc.gov/nchs/hus/topics.htm?Topics=Deaths.

xiii. Substance Abuse and Mental Health Services Administration (2022). *2021–2022 National Survey on Drug Use and Health: Guide to State Tables and Summary of Small Area Estimation Methodology.* https://www.samhsa.gov/data/sites/default/files/reports/rpt44483/2022-nsduh-sae-guide-state-meth/2022-nsduh-sae-guide-state-meth.pdf.

xiv. Zeng, Zhen (2022). *Jail Inmates in 2021 – Statistical Tables.* US Department of Justice. https://bjs.ojp.gov/sites/g/files/xyckuh236/files/media/document/ji21st.pdf.

xv. Smith, AB (2023). *2022 US Billion-dollar Weather and Climate disasters in Historical Context.* NOAA. http://www.climate.gov/news-features/blogs/2022-us-billion-dollar-weather-and-climate-disasters-historical-context.

Chart sources and notes

For each chapter, all chart names are listed and additional information is provided for each.

1. Chart sources and notes are structured as follows:
   Chart title: Source(s)
   Note(s):
2. For all population-adjusted data where adjustments are not provided by the source data, we use intercensal/postcensal estimates from the US Census Bureau, unless otherwise noted. Source details can be found in the citations for the "Population" chart below.
3. USAFacts compiles data for government revenue, spending, and debt, as well as on family and individual income and taxes from various government sources, which primarily include the Office of Management and Budget (OMB), the Census Bureau, the Bureau of Economic Analysis (BEA), and the Federal Reserve. The full citations for this data are not included below; to see detailed descriptions and notes about our methodology for compiling this data, please visit: https://usafacts.org/methodology/.

Government finances

Combined government revenue: USAFacts aggregation of data from Office of Management and Budget (OMB), US Census Bureau, and Bureau of Economic Analysis (BEA).

Combined government spending: Ibid.

Federal government finances (FY 2023): Ibid.

Federal government revenue (FY 1980 vs. FY 2023): Ibid.

Federal government revenue: Ibid.

Federal government spending (FY 1980 vs. FY 2023): Ibid.

Federal government spending: Ibid.

Federal government spending (FY 2019–FY 2023): Ibid.

Federal government finances: Ibid.

Federal government debt: US Department of the Treasury (Multiple issues). *Treasury Bulletin* (Ownership of Federal Securities; TABLE OFS-1—Distribution of Federal Securities by Class of Investors and Type of Issues, TABLE OFS-2—Estimated Ownership of U.S. Treasury Securities). https://fiscal.treasury.gov/reports-statements/treasury-bulletin/current.html.
Note(s): Debt owed to the public is debt sold in credit markets in forms including bills, notes, and treasury bonds. Private US citizens, citizens of other nations, and foreign governments can all hold this debt.

Federal government debt held by the public as a percent of GDP: Ibid.

Federal government debt held by the public per capita: Ibid.

Government employment (2022): (1) For historical data before 1992: US Census Bureau (2021). *Annual Survey of Public Employment & Payroll (ASPEP) Data: Historical Data* (Public_Emp). https://www.census.gov/programs-surveys/apes/data/historical_data.html; (2) For data from 1992 on: US Census Bureau (Multiple Years). *ASPEP Datasets and Tables* ("State and Local Government Employment Data", "Federal Government Civilian Employment and Payroll Data"). https://www.census.gov/programs-surveys/apes/data/datasetstables.2022.List_1058616524.html#list-tab-List_1058616524; (3) For active duty military: Defense Manpower Data Center (DMDC) (Multiple Years). *Military and Civilian Personnel by Service/*

Agency by State/Country (Updated Quarterly) (Reports from September of each year). Office of the Secretary of Defense. https://dwp.dmdc.osd.mil/dwp/app/dod-data-reports/workforce-reports.
Note(s): (1) Federal employment data reported is from 2014; this data stopped being collected by ASPEP after that year. In 2014, federal employees made up about 17% of total government employment. (2) Civilian employment is all employees (full and part time) as of March of each year. (3) Active duty military are as of September of each year, reserves are not included (4) Civilian military employees are included in "national defense and international relations" (5) Beginning in 2017, the Census Bureau stopped reporting employment in "Water transport and terminals" for state and local governments and began reporting instead employment for a new "Sea and Inland Port Facilities" category. The employment number reported as "Water and transport terminals" takes the sum of federal employment in this category and state and local employment in the new "Sea and Inland Port Facilities" category. (6) Percent change for "Social insurance administration (Federal)" and "Judicial and legal" employment is calculated from 1982 due to lack of data availability in 1980.

Population

Population: (1) Population 1980–1989: US Census Bureau (2016, August 25). *Population Estimates 1980–1990* (rqi files beginning with "e[YY]", Month: "7[YY]", Geography: "999"). https://www2.census.gov/programs-surveys/popest/tables/1980-1990/national/asrh/; (2) Population 1990–1999: US Census Bureau (2016, December 1). *us-est90int-07-[Year]* (Intercensal Estimates of the United States Resident Population by Age and Sex: Multiple Years, July 1 Total). https://www2.census.gov/programs-surveys/popest/tables/1990-2000/intercensal/national/; (3) Population 2000–2009: US Census Bureau (2016, August 24). *us-est00int-01* (Table 1. Intercensal Estimates of the Resident Population by Sex and Age for the United States: April 1, 2000 to July 1, 2010). https://www2.census.gov/programs-surveys/popest/tables/2000-2010/intercensal/national/; (4) Population 2010–2019: US Census Bureau (2021, July 27). *NST-EST2020* (Annual Estimates of the Resident Population for the United States, Regions, States, the District of Columbia, and Puerto Rico: April 1, 2010 to July 1, 2019; April 1, 2020; and July 1, 2020). https://www2.census.gov/programs-surveys/popest/tables/2010-2020/national/totals/; (5) Population 2020–2023: US Census Bureau (2023, December 18). *NST-EST2023-POP* (Annual Estimates of the Resident Population for the United States, Regions, States, the District of Columbia, and Puerto Rico: April 1, 2020 to July 1, 2023). https://www2.census.gov/programs-surveys/popest/tables/2020-2023/state/totals/.
Note(s): (1) Population statistics are from intercensal estimates and postcensal estimates produced on July 1 of each year. These may differ from the official decennial counts which are measured as of April 1 in years ending in 0. (2) This population figure excludes territories, such as Puerto Rico.

Population growth by component: (1) 1981–1990: US Census Bureau (2016, August 24). *1981 to 1989 Intercensal Estimates of the Resident Population of States, and Year-to-Year Components of Change* (1980-1990>state>8090com.txt.txt). https://www2.census.gov/programs-surveys/popest/tables/; (2) 1991–2000: US Census Bureau (2005, November 5). *Population Estimates Tables* (1990-2000>estimates-and-change-1990-2000>2000c8_00.txt2010). https://www2.census.gov/programs-surveys/popest/tables/; (3) 2001–2010: US Census Bureau (2017, December 19). *Population Estimates* (2010>2010-eval-estimates>co-est2010-alldata.csv). https://www2.census.gov/programs-surveys/popest/datasets/; (4) 2011–2020: US Census Bureau (2021, December 17). *NST-EST2020-ALLDATA.csv* (National Population Totals). https://www.census.gov/programs-surveys/popest/technical-documentation/research/evaluation-estimates/2020-evaluation-estimates/2010s-totals-national.html; (5) 2021–2023: US Census Bureau (2023, December 18). *NST-EST2023-ALLDATA.csv.* https://www.census.gov/data/tables/time-series/demo/popest/2020s-national-total.html
Note(s): Population change shows the estimate of change in population as measured on July 1 of each year compared to July 1 of the previous year.

Death rate: (1) For 1900–1998: National Center for Health Statistics (NCHS) (2015). *Mortality Data: HIST290A* (Unpublished Tables: HIST290A_0039; _4049; _5059; _6067; _6878; _7998). Centers for Disease Control and Prevention (CDC). https://www.cdc.gov/nchs/nvss/mortality/hist290a.htm; (2) For 1999-2020: CDC (2022). *CDC WONDER Underlying Cause of Death, 1999–2020 Request* (Group Results by: "Year"). https://wonder.cdc.gov/ucd-icd10.html (3) For 2021–2023: CDC (2024). *CDC WONDER Provisional Mortality Statistics, 2018 through Last Month Request* (Group Results by: "Year"). https://wonder.cdc.gov/controller/datarequest/D176.
Note(s): (1) Detailed mortality data between 1900–1932 was only available in certain areas, referred to as "Death Registration Areas". For these years, we report the age-adjusted death rates reported by NCHS, which are calculated using only the death and population counts of the Death Registration Areas in a given year. (2) The 2023 death count is calculated from provisional CDC data that is updated frequently. The death rate calculated here uses provisional numbers current as of 3/27/2024.

Birth rate: (1) For 1980–2006: NCHS (2019). *Health, United States - 2019* (Table 1. Crude birth rates, fertility rates, and birth rates, by age, race, and Hispanic origin of mother: United States, selected years 1950–2018). CDC. https://www.cdc.gov/nchs/data/hus/2019/001-508.pdf; (2) For 2007–2022: CDC (2024). *CDC WONDER Natality, 2007-2022 Request* (Group By: "Year", Measures selected: "Birth rate"). https://wonder.cdc.gov/controller/datarequest/D66; (3) For 2023: CDC(2024). *CDC WONDER Provisional Natality, 2023 Through Last Month* (Group By: "Year", Measures selected: "Births"). https://wonder.cdc.gov/controller/datarequest/D192.
Note(s): (1) Birth rate is calculated as total number of live births per 100,000 people in the population. (2) Birth rate for 2021–2023 calculated by USAFacts using CDC births data and Census population data. Birth rate for all other years reported as calculated by CDC.

Components of population change (2022 vs. 2023), by state: US Census Bureau (2023, December 18). *NST-EST2023-ALLDATA.csv*. https://www.census.gov/data/tables/time-series/demo/popest/2020s-national-total.html

Share of population, by age group: (1) 1980–1989: US Census Bureau (2021, October 9). *State Intercensal Tables: 1980–1990* (State Population Estimates and Demographic Components of Change: 1980 to 1990, by Single Year of Age and Sex). https://www.census.gov/data/tables/time-series/demo/popest/1980s-state.html; (2) 1990–1999: CDC (2020). CDC WONDER: Bridged-Race Population Estimates 1990–2020 Request (Group by: "Age", "Yearly July 1st Estimates"). https://wonder.cdc.gov/Bridged-Race-v2020.HTML; (3) 2000–2009: US Census Bureau (2021, December 17). Population and Housing Unit Estimates Tables - 2009 (National Intercensal Tables: 2000–2010, Sex and Age, Table 1. Intercensal Estimates of the Resident Population by Sex and Age for the United States: April 1, 2000 to July 1, 2010). https://www.census.gov/programs-surveys/popest/data/tables.2009.List_58029271.html; (4) 2010–2019: US Census Bureau (2021, October 8). State Population by Characteristics: 2010–2020 (Age, Sex, Race, and Hispanic Origin - 6 race groups (5 race alone groups and one multiple race group), Annual State Resident Population Estimates for 6 Race Groups (5 Race Alone Groups and Two or More Races) by Age, Sex, and Hispanic Origin: April 1, 2010 to July 1, 2019; April 1, 2020; and July 1, 2020 (SC-EST2020-ALLDATA6)). https://www.census.gov/programs-surveys/popest/technical-documentation/research/evaluation-estimates/2020-evaluation-estimates/2010s-state-detail.html; (5) 2020–2023: US Census Bureau (2024, April 11). nc-est2023-agesex-res.csv (Annual Estimates of the Resident Population by Single Year of Age and Sex for the United States: April 1, 2020 to July 1, 2023). https://www.census.gov/data/tables/time-series/demo/popest/2020s-national-detail.html.
Note(s): This population figure excludes territories, such as Puerto Rico.

Share of households, by household type: (1) US Census Bureau (2023, November). *Historical Households Tables* (Tables; Table HH-1. Households by Type: 1940 to Present, Table HH-4. Households by Size: 1960 to Present). https://www.census.gov/data/tables/time-series/demo/families/households.html; (2) US Census Bureau (2023, November). *Historical Families Tables* (Tables, Table FM-1. Families by Presence of Own Children Under 18: 1950 to Present). https://www.census.gov/data/tables/time-series/demo/families/families.html.
Note(s): Other includes both other family households (such as two single relatives living together), as well as other nonfamily households (such as nonmarried partners living together, or roommates).

Share of population, by race/ethnicity: US Census Bureau (2023, June 20). *National Population by Characteristics: {Multiple Years}* (Annual Estimates of the Resident Population by Sex, Race, and Hispanic Origin for the United States: April 1, 2020 to July 1, 2022 (NC-EST{Year}-SR11H)). https://www.census.gov/data/tables/time-series/demo/popest/2020s-national-detail.html.
Note(s): (1) The Census first allowed respondents to select more than one race in the 2000 Census. Comparisons between pre-2000 and post-2000 data should be made with caution. (2) The Census Bureau added the racial category of 'Two or more races' beginning in 2000.

Population (2000 vs. 2022), by race/ethnicity: US Census Bureau (2023, June 20). *National Population by Characteristics: {Multiple Years}* (Annual Estimates of the Resident Population by Sex, Race, and Hispanic Origin for the United States: April 1, 2020 to July 1, 2022 (NC-EST{Year}-SR11H)). https://www.census.gov/data/tables/time-series/demo/popest/2020s-national-detail.html.

Immigration and border security

Government spending 1980–2023, immigration & border security: USAFacts aggregation of data from OMB, Census Bureau, and BEA.

New immigrant arrivals: (1) Green cards: DHS (Multiple Years). *Yearbook of Immigration Statistics* (Lawful Permanent Residents [Year] Data Tables, Table 6. Persons Obtaining Lawful Permanent Resident Status by Type and Major Class of Admission). https://www.dhs.gov/immigration-statistics/yearbook; (2) Visas: DOS (2022). *Nonimmigrant Visa Statistics* (Nonimmigrant Visa Issuances by Visa Class and by Nationality, FY1997-2022 NIV Detail Table). https://travel.state.gov/content/travel/en/legal/visa-law0/visa-statistics/nonimmigrant-visa-statistics.html; (3) Refugees: Refugee Processing Center (2024, January 31). *Admissions and Arrivals* (Refugee Admissions Report). DOS. https://www.wrapsnet.org/admissions-and-arrivals/; (4) Asylees: DHS (2024, February 26). *Yearbook of Immigration Statistics* (Refugees and Asylees 2022 Data Tables, Table 16. INDIVIDUALS GRANTED ASYLUM AFFIRMATIVELY OR DEFENSIVELY: FISCAL YEARS 1990 TO 2022). https://www.dhs.gov/immigration-statistics/yearbook.
Note(s): (1) The data shown in this chart is reported on a federal fiscal year basis. The federal fiscal year runs from October 1 of the previous calendar year to September 30 of the current calendar year. (2) New arrival green card data only includes green cards granted to new immigrants to the US. It excludes green cards granted through an adjustment of status to immigrants who are already in the US on a visa. (3) Non-tourist visa data excludes temporary visitors for business or pleasure (including with Border Crossing Cards), transit aliens, and transit crew (airline, cruise ship, etc.).

New immigrant arrivals (2022): (1) Green cards: US Department of Homeland Security (DHS) (2023, November 20). *Yearbook of Immigration Statistics* LPR Yearbook Tables 8 to 11 Expanded, Table 10. (PERSONS OBTAINING LAWFUL PERMANENT RESIDENT STATUS BY TYPE AND BROAD CLASS OF ADMISSION AND REGION AND COUNTRY OF BIRTH). https://www.dhs.gov/immigration-statistics/readingroom/lpr/table_8_to_11_expanded; (2) Visas: US Department of State (DOS) (2022). *Nonimmigrant Visa Statistics* (Nonimmigrant Visa Issuances by Visa Class and by Nationality, FY1997-2022 NIV Detail Table). https://travel.state.gov/content/travel/en/legal/visa-law0/visa-statistics/nonimmigrant-visa-statistics.html; (3) Refugees: DHS (2024, February 26). *Yearbook of Immigration Statistics* (Refugees and Asylees [Multiple years] Data Tables, Table 14. REFUGEE ARRIVALS BY REGION AND COUNTRY OF NATIONALITY). https://www.dhs.gov/immigration-statistics/yearbook/; (4) Asylees: DHS (2024, February 26). *Yearbook of Immigration Statistics* (Refugees and Asylees [Multiple years] Data Tables; Table 17. INDIVIDUALS GRANTED ASYLUM AFFIRMATIVELY BY REGION AND COUNTRY OF NATIONALITY: FISCAL YEARS [multiple years], Table 19. INDIVIDUALS GRANTED ASYLUM DEFENSIVELY BY REGION AND COUNTRY OF NATIONALITY: FISCAL YEARS [multiple years]). https://www.dhs.gov/immigration-statistics/yearbook.
Note(s): (1) The data shown in this chart is reported on a federal fiscal year basis. The federal fiscal year runs from October 1 of the previous calendar year to September 30 of the current calendar year. (2) For consistency among detailed categories, this chart uses DHS estimates for all components except for visa issuances, which comes from State Department data. Other charts in this report that use refugee data use State Department refugee data for recency. Therefore, the total number of new arrivals shown in this chart may not exactly match the number of new arrivals shown in other charts.

New immigrant arrivals, by country of birth/nationality: Ibid.
Note(s): The data shown in this chart is reported on a federal fiscal year basis. The federal fiscal year runs from October 1 of the previous calendar year to September 30 of the current calendar year.

Annual border enforcement actions: US Customs and Border Protection (CBP) (2024, February 13). *Nationwide Encounters.* https://www.cbp.gov/newsroom/stats/nationwide-encounters.
Note(s): (1) Encounters by the Office of Field Operations (OFO) include ineligible people turned away at ports of entry. USBP encounters include people apprehended while illegally entering the US between legal ports of entry. Due to the COVID-19 pandemic, between 2020 and 2023, both OFO and USBP expelled certain people at the border without opportunity to seek asylum. Regular expulsion flights were held to Haiti, Mexico, Ecuador, Guatemala, Honduras, and El Salvador. (2) The data shown in this chart is reported on a federal fiscal year basis. The federal fiscal year runs from October 1 of the previous calendar year to September 30 of the current calendar year.

Monthly border enforcement actions: Ibid.
Note(s): Encounters by the Office of Field Operations (OFO) include ineligible people turned away at ports of entry. USBP encounters include people apprehended while illegally entering the US between legal ports of entry. Due to the COVID-19 pandemic, between 2020 and 2023, both OFO and USBP expelled certain people at the border without opportunity to seek asylum. Regular expulsion flights were held to Haiti, Mexico, Ecuador, Guatemala, Honduras, and El Salvador.

Asylum application cases received: DHS (2024, February 26). *Refugees and Asylees Annual Flow Report* (Refugees and Asylees: [Multiple years]). https://www.dhs.gov/ohss/topics/immigration/refugees-asylees-AFR.
Note(s): The data shown in this chart is reported on a federal fiscal year basis. The federal fiscal year runs from October 1 of the previous calendar year to September 30 of the current calendar year.

Decisions for asylum cases: Executive Office for Immigration Review (EOIR) (2023, October 12). *Adjudication Statistics* (Asylum Decision Rates). https://www.justice.gov/d9/pages/attachments/2020/02/12/11_asylum_decision_rates.pdf.
Note(s): The data shown in this chart is reported on a federal fiscal year basis. The federal fiscal year runs from October 1 of the previous calendar year to September 30 of the current calendar year.

Individuals granted affirmative or defensive asylum: DHS (Multiple Years). *Yearbook of Immigration Statistics* (Refugees and Asylees [Year] Data Tables; Table 17. INDIVIDUALS GRANTED ASYLUM AFFIRMATIVELY BY REGION AND COUNTRY OF NATIONALITY, Table 19. INDIVIDUALS GRANTED ASYLUM DEFENSIVELY BY REGION AND COUNTRY OF NATIONALITY). https://www.dhs.gov/immigration-statistics/yearbook.
Note(s): (1) DHS continues to revise estimates for past years with each new Yearbook of Immigration Statistics. Because of the nature of the reporting, total, affirmative, and defensive asylum claims granted statistics are historically revised through 1990. Meanwhile, asylum claims by region are only revised for the ten years previous to each year's report. Because of this, regional breakdowns may not sum to the total number of asylum claims granted for years more than 10 years in the past. (2) Data for defensive asylum claims granted for people from Oceania and unknown regions are withheld for 2014, 2015, 2017, and 2018. Therefore, the asylum claims granted reported in those years for each region only reflect

affirmative asylum claims, and regional breakdowns for those years will also not sum to the total number of asylum claims granted. Similarly, data has been withheld for affirmative asylum claims granted for people from Oceania and unknown regions in 2021. According to DHS, data was withheld from these regions in these years to protect the privacy of individuals represented in categories with small numbers of asylees. (3) The data shown in this chart is reported on a federal fiscal year basis. The federal fiscal year runs from October 1 of the previous calendar year to September 30 of the current calendar year.

Refugee ceilings and admissions: Refugee Processing Center (2024, January 31). *Admissions and Arrivals* (Refugee Admissions Report). DOS. https://www.wrapsnet.org/admissions-and-arrivals/.
Note(s): The data shown in this chart is reported on a federal fiscal year basis. The federal fiscal year runs from October 1 of the previous calendar year to September 30 of the current calendar year.

Refugees admitted, by region: DHS (2024, February 26). *Yearbook of Immigration Statistics* (Refugees and Asylees [Multiple years] Data Tables, Table 14. REFUGEE ARRIVALS BY REGION AND COUNTRY OF NATIONALITY). https://www.dhs.gov/immigration-statistics/yearbook/.
Note(s): The data shown in this chart is reported on a federal fiscal year basis. The federal fiscal year runs from October 1 of the previous calendar year to September 30 of the current calendar year.

Noncitizen removals: DHS (2024, February 26). *Yearbook of Immigration Statistics 2022* (Immigration Enforcement Actions Data Tables, Table 39. NONCITIZEN REMOVALS, RETURNS, AND EXPULSIONS: FISCAL YEARS 1892 TO 2022). https://www.dhs.gov/ohss/topics/immigration/yearbook/.
Note(s): (1) The data shown in this chart is reported on a federal fiscal year basis. The federal fiscal year runs from October 1 of the previous calendar year to September 30 of the current calendar year. (2) Data for 1976 includes the 15 months from July 1, 1975 to September 30, 1976 because the end date of fiscal years was changed from June 30 to September 30.

Noncitizen returns: Ibid.
Note(s): (1) The data shown in this chart is reported on a federal fiscal year basis. The federal fiscal year runs from October 1 of the previous calendar year to September 30 of the current calendar year. (2) Data for 1976 includes the 15 months from July 1, 1975 to September 30, 1976 because the end date of fiscal years was changed from June 30 to September 30.

Immigration courts caseload: EOIR (2023, October 12). *Adjudication Statistics* (Pending Cases, New Cases, and Total Completions). https://www.justice.gov/d9/pages/attachments/2020/01/31/1_pending_new_receipts_and_total_completions.pdf.
Note(s): (1) The data shown in this chart is reported on a federal fiscal year basis. The federal fiscal year runs from October 1 of the previous calendar year to September 30 of the current calendar year. (2) Includes data about removal, deportation, exclusion, asylum-only, and withholding only cases.

Foreign-born population: (1) For 1970–2000: Gibson, C. and Jung, K. (2006, February). *Working Paper No. 81, HISTORICAL CENSUS STATISTICS ON THE FOREIGN-BORN POPULATION OF THE UNITED STATES: 1850 TO 2000* (Table 12. Citizenship Status of the Foreign-Born Population: 1890 to 1950 and 1970 to 2000). US Census Bureau, Population Division. https://www.census.gov/content/dam/Census/library/working-papers/2006/demo/POP-twps0081.pdf; (2) For 2005–2010: Data retrieved from ACS table listed above through ACS API at https://www.census.gov/data/developers/data-sets/acs-1year.2005.html; (3) For 2010–2022: US Census Bureau (Multiple Years). *American Community Survey (ACS) 1-Year Estimates Subject Tables* (S0501 SELECTED CHARACTERISTICS OF THE NATIVE AND FOREIGN-BORN POPULATIONS). https://data.census.gov/table?q=foreign%20born&d=ACS%201-Year%20Estimates%20Selected%20Population%20Profiles.
Note(s): This excludes 2020 data that relies on the American Community Survey because of the pandemic's impact on data collection and quality. For more information, see: https://usafacts.org/articles/what-low-response-rates-mean-for-2020-acs-data/.

Estimated unauthorized immigrant population: DHS (Multiple Years). *Estimates of the Unauthorized Immigrant Population Residing in the United States* (Estimates of the Unauthorized Immigrant Population Residing in the United States). https://www.dhs.gov/immigration-statistics/population-estimates/unauthorized-resident.
Note(s): Estimation methodology changed in 2015, though estimates from 2015–2018 continued to rely on the 2010 Census.

Foreign-born residents, as a share of the population: (1) For 1970–2000: Gibson, C. and Jung, K. (2006, February). *Working Paper No. 81, HISTORICAL CENSUS STATISTICS ON THE FOREIGN-BORN POPULATION OF THE UNITED STATES: 1850 TO 2000* (Table 12. Citizenship Status of the Foreign-Born Population: 1890 to 1950 and 1970 to 2000). US Census Bureau, Population Division. https://www.census.gov/content/dam/Census/library/working-papers/2006/demo/POP-twps0081.pdf; (2) For 2005–2010: Data retrieved from ACS table listed above through ACS API at https://www.census.gov/data/developers/data-sets/acs-1year.2005.html; (3) For 2010–2022: US Census Bureau (Multiple Years). *American Community*

Survey (ACS) 1-Year Estimates Subject Tables (S0501 SELECTED CHARACTERISTICS OF THE NATIVE AND FOREIGN-BORN POPULATIONS). https://data.census.gov/table?q=foreign%20born&d=ACS%201-Year%20Estimates%20Selected%20Population%20Profiles.
Note(s): This excludes 2020 data that relies on the American Community Survey because of the pandemic's impact on data collection and quality. For more information, see: https://usafacts.org/articles/what-low-response-rates-mean-for-2020-acs-data/.

Selected characteristics of foreign- and native-born populations (2022): US Census Bureau (2023). *American Community Survey (ACS) 1-Year Estimates Subject Tables* (S0501 SELECTED CHARACTERISTICS OF THE NATIVE AND FOREIGN-BORN POPULATIONS). https://data.census.gov/table?q=foreign%20born&d=ACS%201-Year%20Estimates%20Selected%20Population%20Profiles.

Labor force participation rate, by nativity: (1) Foreign-born: BLS (2024, February 2). *FRED* (Labor Force Participation Rate - Foreign Born [LNU01373395]). Federal Reserve Bank of St. Louis. https://fred.stlouisfed.org/series/LNU01373395; (2) Native-born: BLS (2024, February 2). *FRED* (Labor Force Participation Rate - Native Born [LNU01373413]). Federal Reserve Bank of St. Louis. https://fred.stlouisfed.org/series/LNU01373413.

Unemployment rate, by nativity: (1) Foreign-born: BLS (2024, February 2). *FRED* (Unemployment Rate - Foreign Born [LNU04073395]). Federal Reserve Bank of St. Louis. https://fred.stlouisfed.org/series/LNU04073395; (2) Native-born: BLS (2024, February 2). *FRED* (Unemployment Rate - Native Born [LNU04073413]). Federal Reserve Bank of St. Louis. https://fred.stlouisfed.org/series/LNU04073413.

Civilian labor force level, total and foreign-born: (1) Foreign-born: BLS (2024, February 2). *FRED* (Civilian Labor Force Level - Foreign Born [LNU01073395]). Federal Reserve Bank of St. Louis. https://fred.stlouisfed.org/series/LNU01073395; (2) Native-born: BLS (2024, February 2). *FRED* (Civilian Labor Force Level - Native Born [LNU01073413]). Federal Reserve Bank of St. Louis. https://fred.stlouisfed.org/series/LNU01073413.

Percent of the civilian labor force that is foreign born (2022), by state: Census Bureau (2023). *American Community Survey 1-Year Estimates PUMS* (MDAT, Custom query). https://data.census.gov/mdat/#/search?ds=ACSPUMS1Y2022&cv=NATIVITY&rv=ucgid,ESR_RC1&nv=NAICSP,ES-R%281,2,3%29,POWSP&wt=PWGTP&g=0400000US01,02,04,05,06,08,09,10,11,12,13,15,16,17,18,19,20,21,22,23,24,25,26,27,28,29,30,31,32,33,34,35,36,37,38,39,40,41,42,44,45,46,47,48,49,50,51,53,54,55,56&ESR_RC1=%7B%22S%22%3A%22Employment%20status%20recode%20re-code%22,%22R%22%3A%22ESR%22,%22W%22%3A%22PWGTP%22,%22V%22%3A%5B%5B%221,2,3,4,5%22,%22Labor%20force%22%5D%5D%7D.

Foreign-born employment level (2022), by industry: Census Bureau (2022, October 31). *Characteristics of the Foreign-Born Population by Nativity and U.S. Citizenship Status* (Table 1.8 Industry of Employed Civilian Workers 16 Years and Over by Sex, Nativity, and U.S. Citizenship Status: 2022). https://www.census.gov/data/tables/2022/demo/foreign-born/cps-2022.html.

Share of workers that are foreign-born (2022), by industry: Ibid.

Work visas granted: DOS (2023). *Nonimmigrant Visa Statistics* (Nonimmigrant Visa Issuances by Visa Class and by Nationality, FY1997-2022 NIV Detail Table). https://travel.state.gov/content/travel/en/legal/visa-law0/visa-statistics/nonimmigrant-visa-statistics.html.
Note(s): (1) The data shown in this chart is reported on a federal fiscal year basis. The federal fiscal year runs from October 1 of the previous calendar year to September 30 of the current calendar year. (2) "Temporary agricultural workers" is for H-2A visas; "Specialty occupations workers" is for H-1B; "Temporary non-agricultural workers" is for H-2B; "Foreign diplomats, officials, and staff" is for A-1, A-2, or A-3 (A-2 visas were the 4th-largest individual visa category by number of visas granted in 2022); "Intracompany transferees" is for L-1.

Economy

Government spending 1980–2023, economy: USAFacts aggregation of data from OMB, Census Bureau, and BEA.

Consumer price index: BLS (2024). *CPI for All Urban Consumers* (CPI-U) (All items in U.S. city average, all urban consumers, seasonally adjusted [CUSR0000SA0]; More formatting options: "12-Month Percentage Change" view). https://data.bls.gov/timeseries/CUSR0000SA0.

Percent change in Consumer Price Index from January 2021: (1) BLS (2024). *CPI for All Urban Consumers (CPI-U)* (Energy in U.S. city average, all urban consumers, seasonally adjusted [CUSR0000SA0E]). https://data.bls.gov/timeseries/CUSR0000SA0E; (2) BLS (2024). *CPI for All Urban Consumers (CPI-U)* (Food in U.S. city average, all urban consumers, seasonally adjusted [CUSR0000SAF1]). https://data.bls.gov/timeseries/CUSR0000SAF1; (3) BLS (2024). *CPI for All Urban Consumers (CPI-U)* (Shelter in U.S. city average, all urban consumers, seasonally adjusted [CUSR0000SAH1]). https://data.bls.gov/timeseries/CUSR0000SAH1.

Personal Consumption Expenditures Price Index: BEA (2024, February). *FRED* (Personal Consumption Expenditures: Chain-type Price Index [PCEPI]). Federal Reserve Bank of St. Louis. https://fred.stlouisfed.org/series/PCEPI.

Federal funds rate: Board of Governors of the Federal Reserve System (2024, April 1). *FRED* (Federal Funds Effective Rate [FEDFUNDS]). Federal Reserve Bank of St. Louis. https://fred.stlouisfed.org/series/FEDFUNDS.

Annual percent change in real gross domestic product (GDP): BEA (2024, February 28). *National Income and Product Accounts* (Table 1.1.1. Percent Change From Preceding Period in Real Gross Domestic Product, Series: "Annual"). https://apps.bea.gov/iTable/?reqid=19&step=2&isuri=1&categories=survey#eyJhcHBpZCI6MtksInN0ZXBzIjpbMSwyLDNdLCJkYXRhIjpbWyJjYXRlZ29yaWVzIiwiU3VydmV5Il0sWyJOSVBBX1RhYmxlX0xpc3QiLCIxIl1dfQ==.

Percent change in real GDP (2022 vs. 2023), by state: BEA (2024, March 29). *State annual gross domestic product (GDP) summary* ([SAGDP1] Real gross domestic product (million of chained 2017 dollars)). https://apps.bea.gov/itable/?ReqID=70&step=1&_gl=1*1asldyu*_ga*NTIwMjY0NDY5LjE2MzAwOTQwNjM.*_ga_J4698JNNFT*MtcxMjAxMDk1MC45MS4xLjE3MTIwMTA5NjQuNDYuMC4w#eyJhcHBpZCI6NzAsInN0ZXBzIjpbMSwyOSwyNSwzMSwyNiwyNywzMF0sImRhdGEiOltbIlRhYmxlSWQiLCI1MzEiXSxbIk1ham9yX0FyZWEiLCIwIl0sWyJTdGF0ZSIsWyIwIl1dLFsiQXJlYSIsWyJYWCJdXSxbIlN0YXRpc3RpYyIsWyIxIl1dLFsiVW5pdF9vZl9tZWFzdXJlIiwiTGV2ZWxzIl0sWyJZZWFyIixbIjIwMjMiXV0sWyJZZWFyQmVnaW4iLCItMSJdLFsiWWVhcl9FbmQiLCItMSJdXX0=.

Net change in employment (jobs): BLS (2024). *Employment, Hours, and Earnings from the Current Employment Statistics survey (National)* (All employees, thousands, total nonfarm, seasonally adjusted (CES0000000001); Data type: "All employees, thousands", Super sector: "Total nonfarm", More formatting options: "12-Month Net Change" view). https://data.bls.gov/PDQWeb/ce.
Note(s): (1) Data reflect December over December employment change for the stated year. (2) Data up-to-date as of April 8, 2022.

Percent change in annual average employment (2022 vs. 2023), by state: BLS (2024). *State and Metro Area Employment, Hours, & Earnings* (Table 1. Employees on nonfarm payrolls in States and selected areas by major industry). https://www.bls.gov/sae/tables/annual-average/home.htm.

Unemployment rate: Bureau of Labor Statistics (BLS) (2024). *Labor Force Statistics from the Current Population Survey* ((Seas) Unemployment Rate (LNS14000000); Labor force status: "Unemployment rate", Periodicity: "Monthly"). https://data.bls.gov/PDQWeb/ln.

Unemployment rate (2023 average), by state: BLS (2024, March 1). *Unemployment Rates for States, 2023 Annual Averages.* https://www.bls.gov/lau/lastrk23.htm.

Job openings rate: BLS (2024, March). *Job Openings and Labor Turnover Survey* (Table A. Job openings, hires, and total separations by industry, seasonally adjusted). Retrieved from BLS One-Screen Data Search, Job Openings and Labor Turnover Survey. https://data.bls.gov/PDQWeb/jt.

Job openings rate (2023 average), by state: BLS (2024). *Job Openings and Labor Turnover Survey* (Industry: "Total nonfarm"; Data Elements: "Job openings"; Rate and/or level: "Rate"; Seasonal Adjustment: "Not seasonally adjusted"). https://data.bls.gov/PDQWeb/jt.

Labor force participation rate: BLS (2024). *Labor Force Statistics from the Current Population Survey* ((Seas) Labor Force Participation Rate (LNS11300000); Labor force status: "Civilian labor force participation rate", Periodicity: "Monthly"). https://data.bls.gov/PDQWeb/ln.

Labor force participation rate, by age group: BLS (2024). *Labor Force Statistics from the Current Population Survey* (Age: "16 to 19", "20 to 24", "25 to 54" "55 and older", "Labor force status: "Civilian labor force participation rate", Periodicity: "Monthly"). https://data.bls.gov/PDQWeb/ln.

Labor force participation rate (2023 average), by state: BLS (2024, March 1). *Table 1. Employment status of the civilian noninstitutional population 16 years of age and over by region, division, and state, 2022-23 annual averages.* https://www.bls.gov/news.release/srgune.t01.htm.

Percentage point change in the labor force participation rate (2019 vs. 2023), by state: (1) For 2019: BLS (2020, August 12) *Geographic Profile of Employment and Unemployment, 2019* (Table 14. Employment status of the civilian noninstitutional population, by gender, age, race, Hispanic or Latino ethnicity, and marital status, 2019 annual averages). https://www.bls.gov/opub/geographic-profile/2019/home.htm; (2) For 2023: BLS (2024, March 1). *Table 1. Employment status of the civilian noninstitutional population 16 years of age and over by region, division, and state, 2022-23 annual averages.* https://www.bls.gov/news.release/srgune.t01.htm.
Net trade balance: BEA (2024, February 7). *International Trade in Goods and Services* (Current Release, U.S. Trade in Goods and Services,

1960-present, Table 1. U.S. International Trade in Goods and Services). https://www.bea.gov/data/intl-trade-investment/international-trade-goods-and-services.

Net trade balance with top trading partners: BEA (2024, March 7). *International Trade in Goods and Services* (Current Release, U.S. Trade in Goods and Services by Selected Countries and Areas, 1999–present, Table 3. U.S. International Trade by Selected Countries and Areas). https://www.bea.gov/data/intl-trade-investment/international-trade-goods-and-services.

Standard of living

Government spending 1980–2023, standard of living: USAFacts aggregation of data from OMB, Census Bureau, and BEA.

Real gross domestic product, per capita: Bureau of Economic Analysis (2024). FRED (Real gross domestic product per capita (A939RX0Q048SBEA)). Federal Reserve Bank of St. Louis. https://fred.stlouisfed.org/series/A939RX0Q048SBEA#0.

Real GDP per capita (2023), by state: Bureau of Economic Analysis (2024, March 29). Real gross domestic product (GDP) by state: Millions of chained 2017 dollars (SAGDP1). https://apps.bea.gov/itable/?ReqID=70&step=1&_gl=1*1asldyu*_ga*NTIwMjY0NDY5LjE2MzAwOTQwNjM.*_ga_J4698JNNFT*MTcxMjAxMDk1MC45MS4xLjE3MTIwMTA5NjQuNDYuMC4w#eyJhcHBpZCI6NzAsInN0ZXBzIjpbMSwyOSwyNSwzMSwyNiwyNywzMCw-zMF0sImRhdGEiOltbIlRhYmxlSWQiLCI1MzEiXSxbIk1ham9yX0FyZWEiLCIwIl0sWyJTdGF0ZSIsWyIwIl1dLFsiQXJlYSIsWyJYWCJdXSxbIlN0YXRpc3RpY-yIsIjEiXSxbIlVuaXRfb2ZfbWVhc3VyZSIsIkxldmVscyJdLFsiWWVhciIsWyIyMDIzIiwiMjAyMiJdXSxbIllllYXJCZWdpbiIsIi0xIl0sWyJZZWFyX0VuZCIsIi0xIl1d-fQ==.

Percent change in real GDP per capita (2022 vs. 2023), by state: Ibid.

Average total market income (2000 vs 2022): USAFacts calculations using data from the Internal Revenue Service and the US Census Bureau.

Average taxes paid, Average transfers received (2000 and 2022): Ibid.

Average savings from selected deductions and tax credits (2022): Ibid.

Median annual wages: BLS (2024, April 3). *Occupational Employment and Wage Statistics* (Multiple Years, National, XLS Version). https://www.bls.gov/oes/tables.htm.
Note(s): BLS calculates annual wages by multiplying the hourly mean wage by the equivalent of year-round, full-time hours (2,080 hours).

Median annual wages (2023), by state: BLS (2024, April 3). *Occupational Employment and Wage Statistics* (2022, State, XLS Version). https://www.bls.gov/oes/tables.htm.
Note(s): BLS calculates annual wages by multiplying the hourly mean wage by the equivalent of year-round, full-time hours (2,080 hours).

Poverty rate: US Census Bureau (2023). *Historical Poverty Tables: People and Families - 1959 to 2022* (Table 2. Poverty Status of People by Family Relationship, Race, and Hispanic Origin: 1959 to 2022; Table 3. Poverty Status of People by Age, Race, and Hispanic Origin: 1959 to 2022). https://www.census.gov/data/tables/time-series/demo/income-poverty/historical-poverty-people.html.

Poverty rate (2022), by state: US Census Bureau (2023). *Historical Poverty Tables: People and Families - 1959 to 2022* (Table 20. Percent of People in Poverty by State: 2020, 2021, and 2022). https://www.census.gov/data/tables/time-series/demo/income-poverty/historical-poverty-people.html.

Share of households that are housing burdened: (1) For renters: US Census Bureau (2023). *American Community Survey: (Multiple Years) 1-year estimates* (B25070 Gross Rent as a Percentage of Household Income in the Past 12 Months). https://data.census.gov/table/ACSDT1Y2022.B25070?q=B25070:%20GROSS%20RENT%20AS%20A%20PERCENTAGE%20OF%20HOUSEHOLD%20INCOME%20IN%20THE%20PAST%2012%20MONTHS&g=010XX00US,$0400000&tid=ACSDT1Y2019.B25070; (2) For homeowners: US Census Bureau (2023). *American Community Survey: (Multiple years) 1-year estimates* (B25091 Mortgage Status by Selected Monthly Owner Costs as a Percentage of Household Income in the Past 12 Months). https://data.census.gov/table/ACSDT1Y2022.B25091?q=B25091:%20MORTGAGE%20STATUS%20BY%20SELECTED%20MONTHLY%20OWNER%20COSTS%20AS%20A%20PERCENTAGE%20OF%20HOUSEHOLD%20INCOME%20IN%20THE%20PAST%2012%20MONTHS&g=010XX00US,$0400000&tid=ACSDT1Y2021.B25091.

Note(s): Denominator excludes households for which a percentage of household income spent on housing was not computed.

Share of households that are housing burdened (2022), by state: Ibid.
Note(s): Denominator excludes households for which a percentage of household income spent on housing was not computed.

Subsidized housing units available: (1) For 2004–2008: Department of Housing and Urban Development (2023). *Picture of Subsidized Households for 2004–2008* (Select Year, "U.S. total", "Total for all HUD programs", "total_units") https://www.huduser.gov/portal/picture/query.html; (2) For 2009–2023: HUD (2024). *Picture of Subsidized Households* (Select Year, "U.S. total", "Summary of all HUD programs", "Subsidized units available") https://www.huduser.gov/portal/datasets/assthsg.html#2009-2017_query; (3) For 2023 data by state: HUD (2023). *Picture of Subsidized Households* (Select "2023 based on 2020 census", "State", "Summary of all HUD programs", "Subsidized units available") https://www.huduser.gov/portal/datasets/assthsg.html#2009-2017_query.

Average months on subsidized housing waitlist: (1) For 2004–2008: Department of Housing and Urban Development (2023). *Picture of Subsidized Households for 2004–2008* (Select Year, "U.S. total", "Total for all HUD programs", "months_waiting") https://www.huduser.gov/portal/picture/query.html; (2) For 2009–2023: HUD (2024). *Picture of Subsidized Households* (Select Year, "U.S. total", "Summary of all HUD programs", "Average months on waiting list") https://www.huduser.gov/portal/datasets/assthsg.html#2009-2017_query; (3) For 2023 data by state: HUD (2024). *Picture of Subsidized Households* (Select "2023 Based on 2020 Census", "State", "Summary of all HUD programs", "Average months on waiting list") https://www.huduser.gov/portal/datasets/assthsg.html#2009-2017_query.

Share of households that are food insecure: US Department of Agriculture (USDA) Economic Research Service (2023, October 25). *Food Security in the US* (Food Security Data file, "Food security, all households"). https://www.ers.usda.gov/topics/food-nutrition-assistance/food-security-in-the-u-s/interactive-charts-and-highlights/#trends.

Share of households that are food insecure (2020–2022 average), by state: US Department of Agriculture (USDA) Economic Research Service (2023, October 25). *Food Security in the US* (Food Security Data file, "Food security by State"). https://www.ers.usda.gov/topics/food-nutrition-assistance/food-security-in-the-u-s/interactive-charts-and-highlights/#trends.

Nutrition assistance (SNAP) average monthly recipients: USDA Food and Nutrition Service (2024, January 12). *SNAP Data Tables* (National Level Annual Summary: Participation and Costs, 1969–2023). https://www.fns.usda.gov/pd/supplemental-nutrition-assistance-program-snap.

Nutrition assistance (SNAP) average monthly benefit per person: Ibid.

Wealth and savings

Government spending 1980–2023, wealth & savings: USAFacts aggregation of data from OMB, Census Bureau, and BEA.

Wealth, by income percentile: Board of Governors of the Federal Reserve System (2024, March 22). *Distribution of Household Wealth in the U.S. since 1989* (Units: "Levels ($)", Distribute by: "Income percentile"). https://www.federalreserve.gov/releases/z1/dataviz/dfa/distribute/chart/.

Share of wealth, by income percentile: Board of Governors of the Federal Reserve System (2024, March 22). *Distribution of Household Wealth in the U.S. since 1989* (Units: "Shares (%)", Distribute by: "Income percentile"). https://www.federalreserve.gov/releases/z1/dataviz/dfa/distribute/chart/.

Personal savings rate: BEA (2024). *FRED* (Personal Savings Rate [PSAVERT], Units: "Percent", Frequency: "Monthly"). Federal Reserve Bank of St. Louis. https://fred.stlouisfed.org/series/PSAVERT#0.
Note(s): The savings rate reflects personal savings as a percentage of disposable personal income, which is personal income minus taxes and consumer spending.

Share of families with retirement accounts: Board of Governors of the Federal Reserve System (2023, March 24). *Survey of Consumer Finances, 1989–2022.* https://www.federalreserve.gov/econres/scf/dataviz/scf/chart/#series:Retirement_Accounts;demographic:all;population:1;units:have;range:1989,2022.

Median value of retirement accounts: Ibid.

Homeownership rates: 1) National: Census Bureau (2023 March 15). *Housing Vacancies and Homeownership (CPS/HVS)* (Table 14. Homeownership Rates by Area: 1960 to 2022). https://www.census.gov/housing/hvs/data/prevann.html; 2) Census Bureau (2023 March 15). *Housing Vacancies and Homeownership (CPS/HVS)* (Table 17. Homeownership Rates by Age of Householder and Family Status for the United States). https://www.census.gov/housing/hvs/data/prevann.html.

Median net housing value: Board of Governors of the Federal Reserve System (2022, October). *Changes in US Family Finances from 2019 to 2022* (Figure A. Net Housing Values, 1998–2022). https://www.federalreserve.gov/publications/october-2023-changes-in-us-family-finances-from-2019-to-2022-accessible-version.htm#xbox3figurea-nethousingvalues1998202-74ca179a.

Housing affordability: Board of Governors of the Federal Reserve System (2022, October). *Changes in US Family Finances from 2019 to 2022* (Figure C. Housing Affordability, 1998–2022 surveys). https://www.federalreserve.gov/publications/october-2023-changes-in-us-family-finances-from-2019-to-2022-accessible-version.htm#xbox3figurea-nethousingvalues1998202-74ca179a.

Social Security retirement and Disability Insurance recipients: (1) For social security: Social Security Administration (SSA) (2024). *Benefits Paid by Type of Beneficiary* (Time series report; Select beneficiary type(s): All under "Retired workers & dependents" and "Survivors"; Frequency: "Monthly" (September of each year)). https://www.ssa.gov/oact/ProgData/icp.html; (2) For disability insurance: SSA (2024). *Benefits Paid by Type of Beneficiary* (Time series report; Select beneficiary type(s): All under "Disabled workers & dependents"; Frequency: "Monthly" (September of each year)). https://www.ssa.gov/oact/ProgData/icp.html.

Average monthly benefit, Social Security and Disability Insurance: Ibid.

Medicare enrollment: CMS (2023). *Medicare Trustees Report* (Table V.B3.--Medicare Enrollment). https://www.cms.gov/oact/tr/2023.

Average Medicare cost per beneficiary: CMS (2023). *Medicare Trustees Report* (Table V.D1.--HI and SMI Average Incurred per Beneficiary Costs. https://www.cms.gov/oact/tr/2023.

Health

Government spending 1980–2023, health: USAFacts aggregation of data from OMB, Census Bureau, and BEA.

Health risk factors: (1) National Center for Chronic Disease Prevention and Health Promotion (NCCDPHP). *Behavioral Risk Factor Surveillance System, Behavioral Risk Factor Surveillance System (BRFSS) Prevalence Data (2011 to present)* (Topics: 'BMI Categories', 'Current Smoker Status', 'Binge Drinking'; Location: 'US'). CDC. https://chronicdata.cdc.gov/Behavioral-Risk-Factors/Behavioral-Risk-Factor-Surveillance-System-BRFSS-P/dttw-5yxu/data; (2) NCCDPHPH. *Behavioral Risk Factor Surveillance System, Behavioral Risk Factor Surveillance System (BRFSS) Prevalence Data (2010 and prior)* (Topics: 'BMI Categories', 'Current Smoker Status', 'Binge Drinking'; Location: 'US'). CDC. https://chronicdata.cdc.gov/Behavioral-Risk-Factors/Behavioral-Risk-Factor-Surveillance-System-BRFSS-P/y4ft-s73h/data.
Note(s): (1) The Behavioral Risk Factor Surveillance System (BRFSS) survey from which this data is sourced underwent methodological changes in 2011. Users should take caution when comparing data from 2011 and onward to data from 2010 and earlier. See https://www.cdc.gov/brfss/factsheets/pdf/DBS_BRFSS_survey.pdf. (2) Data shows the median of all states, DC and Territories (3) Rates are crude prevalence rates of people of age 18 or over.

Life expectancy at birth: (1) For 1960–2019: NCHS (2021). *Life expectancy at birth, age 65, and age 75, by sex, race, and Hispanic origin: United States, selected years 1900-2019.* CDC. https://www.cdc.gov/nchs/data/hus/2020-2021/LExpMort.pdf; (2) For 2020: NCHS (2022). *Mortality in the United States, 2021.* CDC. https://www.cdc.gov/nchs/data/databriefs/db456.pdf; (3) For 2021–2022: NCHS (2022). *Provisional Life Expectancy Estimates for 2022.* CDC. https://www.cdc.gov/nchs/data/vsrr/vsrr031.pdf.

Top five causes of death: (1) For 1999–2020: CDC (2021). *CDC WONDER Underlying Cause of Death, 1999–2020* (Group Results By: "UCD - 15 Leading Causes of Death"; Year/Month: [Multiple Years]). https://wonder.cdc.gov/ucd-icd10.html; (2) For 2020–2022: CDC (2024). *CDC WONDER Provisional Mortality Statistics, 2018 through Last Month Request* (Group Results By: "UCD - 15 Leading Causes of Death"; Year/Month: "2022 (provisional)", "2021", "2020"). https://wonder.cdc.gov/mcd-icd10-provisional.html.
Note(s): 2022 numbers are provisional as of June 15, 2023.

Accidental deaths, by type of accident: (1) For 1999–2020: CDC (2021). *CDC WONDER Underlying Cause of Death, 1999–2020* (Group Results By: "ICD-10 113 Cause List"; Year/Month: [Multiple Years]; Cause of death: #Accidents (unintentional injuries) and subcategories). https://wonder.cdc.gov/ucd-icd10.html; (2) For 2020–2022: CDC (2024). *CDC WONDER Provisional Mortality Statistics, 2018 through Last Month Request* (Group Results By: "ICD-10 113 Cause List"; Year/Month: "2022 (provisional)", "2021", "2020"; Cause of death: #Accidents (unintentional injuries) and subcategories). https://wonder.cdc.gov/mcd-icd10-provisional.html.

Drug-involved overdose deaths: (1) For 1999–2021: CDC (June 2023). *CDC WONDER National Drug Overdose (OD) Deaths, 1999–2021* (Table: Rate Drug OD Deaths). https://view.officeapps.live.com/op/view.aspx?src=https%3A%2F%2Fnida.nih.gov%2Fsites%2Fdefault%2Ffiles%2FOverdose_data_1999-2021%25201.19.23.xlsx&wdOrigin=BROWSELINK; (2) For 2022: CDC (2024). *CDC WONDER Provisional Mortality Statistics, 2018 through Last Month Request* (Group Results By: "State"; Year/Month: "2022 (provisional); Underlying cause of death: Drug/Alcohol Induced Causes, Drug poisoning (overdose) categories; Multiple cause of death: MCD – ICD-10 Codes, [Multiple selections]). https://wonder.cdc.gov/mcd-icd10-provisional.html.

Cumulative drug overdose deaths (2013–2022), by state: (1) For 2013–2020: CDC (2021). *CDC WONDER Underlying Cause of Death, 1999–2020* (Group Results By: "State", "Year"; Cause of death: Drug/Alcohol Induced Causes, Drug poisoning (overdose) categories). https://wonder.cdc.gov/ucd-icd10.html; (2) For 2021–2022: CDC (2024). *CDC WONDER Provisional Mortality Statistics, 2018 through Last Month Request* (Group Results By: "State", "Year"; Cause of death: Drug/Alcohol Induced Causes, Drug poisoning (overdose) categories). https://wonder.cdc.gov/mcd-icd10-provisional.html.

Cumulative drug overdose deaths (2013–2022), by race/ethnicity, age, and gender: (1) For race and ethnicity 2013–2020: CDC (2021). *CDC WONDER Underlying Cause of Death, 1999–2020* (Group Results By: "Race", "Hispanic Origin", "Year"; Cause of death: Drug/Alcohol Induced Causes, Drug poisoning (overdose) categories). https://wonder.cdc.gov/ucd-icd10.html; (2) For race and ethnicity 2021–2022: CDC (2024). *CDC WONDER Provisional Mortality Statistics, 2018 through Last Month Request* (Group Results By: "Race", "Hispanic Origin", "Year"; Cause of death: Drug/Alcohol Induced Causes, Drug poisoning (overdose) categories). https://wonder.cdc.gov/mcd-icd10-provisional.html; (3) For age groups 2013–2020: CDC (2021). *CDC WONDER Underlying Cause of Death, 1999–2020* (Group Results By: "Year"; Demographics: [Select ages in group]; Cause of death: Drug/Alcohol Induced Causes, Drug poisoning (overdose) categories). https://wonder.cdc.gov/ucd-icd10.html; (4) For age groups 2021–2022: CDC (2024). *CDC WONDER Provisional Mortality Statistics, 2018 through Last Month Request* (Group Results By: "Year"; Demographics: [Select ages in group]; Cause of death: Drug/Alcohol Induced Causes, Drug poisoning (overdose) categories). https://wonder.cdc.gov/mcd-icd10-provisional.html; (5) For gender 2013–2020: CDC (2021). *CDC WONDER Underlying Cause of Death, 1999–2020* (Group Results By: "Gender", "Year; Cause of death: Drug/Alcohol Induced Causes, Drug poisoning (overdose) categories). https://wonder.cdc.gov/ucd-icd10.html; (6) For gender 2021–2022: CDC (2024). *CDC WONDER Provisional Mortality Statistics, 2018 through Last Month Request* (Group Results By: "Gender", "Year; Cause of death: Drug/Alcohol Induced Causes, Drug poisoning (overdose) categories). https://wonder.cdc.gov/mcd-icd10-provisional.html.

Share of people that had any mental illness in the past year: Substance Abuse and Mental Health Services Administration (SAMHSA). *Interactive NSDUH State Estimates* (Outcome: "Any Mental Illness in the Past Year (through 2019)"; Age Group: "18 to 25" and "26 or older"). https://datatools.samhsa.gov/saes/state.

Share of people that had any mental illness in the past year (2021–2022), by state: SAMHSA (14 February 2024). *2021–2022 National Survey on Drug Use and Health: Model-Based Prevalence Estimates* (Table 31. Any Mental Illness in the Past Year: Among People Aged 18 or Older; by Age Group and State, Annual Average Percentages, 2021 and 2022). https://view.officeapps.live.com/op/view.aspx?src=https%3A%2F%2Fwww.samhsa.gov%2Fdata%2Fsites%2Fdefault%2Ffiles%2Freports%2Frpt44484%2F2022-nsduh-sae-tables-percent-CSVs%2F2022-nsduh-sae-tables-percent.xlsx&wdOrigin=BROWSELINK.

Share of people that had a major depressive episode in the past year: Substance Abuse and Mental Health Services Administration (SAMHSA). *Interactive NSDUH State Estimates* (Outcome: "Major Depressive Episode in the Past Year (through 2019)"; Age Group: "12 to 17", "18 to 25", and "26 or older"). https://datatools.samhsa.gov/saes/state.

Share of people that had a major depressive episode in the past year (2021–2022), by state: SAMHSA (14 February 2024). *2021–2022 National Survey on Drug Use and Health: Model-Based Prevalence Estimates* (Table 34. Major Depressive Episode in the Past Year: Among People Aged 12 or Older; by Age Group and State, Annual Average Percentages, 2021 and 2022). https://view.officeapps.live.com/op/view.aspx?src=https%3A%2F%2Fwww.samhsa.gov%2Fdata%2Fsites%2Fdefault%2Ffiles%2Freports%2Frpt44484%2F2022-nsduh-sae-tables-percent-CSVs%2F2022-nsduh-sae-tables-percent.xlsx&wdOrigin=BROWSELINK.

Health insurance coverage, share of people: (1) For 1987–1998: US Census Bureau (Multiple Years). *1997 Health Insurance Data Tables: Health Insurance Historical Tables - Original Series* (Table HI-1. Health Insurance Coverage Status and Type of Coverage by Sex, Race and Hispanic Origin: 1987–2005; Table A-1. Health Insurance Coverage Status and Type of Coverage by Sex, Race and Hispanic Origin: 1987–2005--Continued). https://www.census.gov/topics/health/health-insurance/data/tables.1987.List_198970099.html; (2) For 1999–2012: US Census Bureau (2021). *Health Insurance Historical Tables - HIB Series* (Table HIB-1. Health Insurance Coverage Status and Type of Coverage by Sex, Race and Hispanic Origin: 1999–2012). https://www.census.gov/data/tables/time-series/demo/health-insurance/historical-series/hib.html; (3) For 2013–2016: US Census Bureau (2018). *Health Insurance Time Series Tables* (Table HIC-1. Health Insurance Coverage Status and Type of Coverage by Sex, Race and Hispanic Origin: 2013–2017). https://www2.census.gov/programs-surveys/demo/tables/health-insurance/time-series/hic/; (4) For 2017–2022: US Census Bureau. (Health Insurance Historical Tables - HHI CPS), Table HHI-01. Health Insurance Coverage Status and Type of Coverage--All Persons by Sex, Race, and Hispanic Origin: 2017–2022). https://www2.census.gov/programs-surveys/demo/tables/health-insurance/time-series/hic/.
Note(s): Starting in 2017, people covered under TRICARE are counted as receiving private insurance rather than government insurance. According to the Census Bureau, "The CPS ASEC time series goes back to 1987. Making comparisons over time requires caution, since annual estimates reflect survey improvements, including (a) the addition of a verification question in 1999, (b) redesign of the questionnaire in 2014, and (c) improvements to the CPS ASEC processing system in 2018."

Health insurance coverage, number of people: Ibid.

Health insurance spending per enrollee: Centers for Medicare and Medicaid Services (CMS) (2023). *Historical National Health Expenditure Data* (NHE Tables, Table 21. Expenditures, Enrollment, and Per Enrollee Estimates of Health Insurance). https://www.cms.gov/Research-Statistics-Data-and-Systems/Statistics-Trends-and-Reports/NationalHealthExpendData/NationalHealthAccountsHistorical.

Infrastructure

Government spending 1980–2023, infrastructure: USAFacts aggregation of data from OMB, Census Bureau, and BEA.

Federal transportation and infrastructure spending: Ibid.

Federal Emergency Management Agency (FEMA) infrastructure spending after natural disasters: Federal Emergency Management Agency (FEMA) (2024). *OpenFEMA Dataset: Public Assistance Funded Projects Details - v1.* https://www.fema.gov/openfema-data-page/public-assistance-funded-projects-details-v1.

Share of roads in unsatisfactory condition: Bureau of Transportation Statistics (BTS) (2022). *State Transportation Statistics: Road Condition.* US Department of Transportation (USDOT). https://www.bts.gov/content/condition-us-roadways-functional-system.
Note(s): Original data is reported as the International Roughness Index (IRI) in inches per mile. Lower IRI represents smoother riding roadways. "Unsatisfactory condition" corresponds to an IRI of >170. Percentages capture share of miles that are in unsatisfactory condition. U.S. includes the 50 states, the District of Columbia, and Puerto Rico.

Share of highway bridges, by condition: BTS (2023). *State Transportation Statistics: Bridge Condition.* USDOT. https://www.bts.gov/content/condition-us-highway-bridges.
Note(s): Percentages capture share of square meters that are in poor condition. U.S. totals include the 50 states, the District of Columbia, Guam, Puerto Rico, and U.S. Virgin Islands.

Traffic injuries: National Highway Traffic Safety Administration (2023). *Traffic Safety Facts Annual Report Tables: National Statistics; Table 2. People Killed and Injured and Fatality and Injury Rates; Table 4. People Killed and Injured, by Person Type and Vehicle Type.* US Department of Transportation. https://cdan.dot.gov/tsftables/tsfar.htm.
Note(s): (1) The numbers of people injured are estimates, not actual counts, based on a nationally representative sample of crashes. (2) The data for 2019–2021 is subject to change with future releases of the Traffic Safety Facts Annual Report from the source.

Traffic fatalities: Ibid.
Note(s): The data for 2019–2021 is subject to change with future releases of the Traffic Safety Facts Annual Report from the source.

Flights on-time performance: BTS (2024). *On-Time Performance - Reporting Operating Carrier Flight Delays at a Glance.* https://www.transtats.bts.gov/HomeDrillChart.asp.

Note(s): The BTS releases seasonally adjusted air traffic data based on monthly reports from commercial U.S. air carriers. This data is often retroactively updated and is current as of May 26, 2023.

Number of air carrier accidents (2013–2022): National Transportation Safety Board (2023). *2003–2022 Accident Statistics* (Table 29. Accident Aircraft 20003 through 2022 US Civil Aviation). https://www.ntsb.gov/safety/Pages/research.aspx.
Note(s): Data included is for scheduled flights operated by US regional and major airlines. Federal regulation defines serious injury when an injury meets any of these four criteria: 1) requires more than 48 hours hospitalization, 2) fracture of any bone, 3) severe hemorrhage, nerve, muscle or tendon damage, 4) injury to an internal organ, 5) second or third-degree burns, or any burn over more than 5% of the body.

Rail transit assets in a state of good repair: Department of Transportation (2023). *2021 TAM Data Summary: A Snapshot of Asset-Related Data Reported to the National Transit Database.* https://www.transit.dot.gov/sites/fta.dot.gov/files/2023-03/2021-TAM-Data-Snapshot.pdf.

Rail transit accidents (2018 vs. 2021): BTS (2024). *Transit Safety Data by Mode for All Reported Accidents.* USDOT. https://www.bts.gov/content/transit-safety-data-modea-all-reported-accidentsb.
Note(s): Accidents include transit vehicle collisions with motor vehicles, objects, and people (excluding suicides), as well as derailments / vehicles going off the road. Accident figures do not include fires, security events, or not otherwise classified safety events. The definition of light rail changed, so we only show light rail data for 2015 and onwards.

Share of people without a fixed broadband subscription (2022), by state: USAFacts analysis of Census Bureau data (February 2024). *ACS 1-Year Estimates Public Use Microdata Sample, Custom Table* (Vintage: 2022, Weighting: PUMS person weight). https://data.census.gov/mdat/#/.

Share of people without a fixed broadband subscription (2022), by race/ethnicity, household income, and homeownership: Ibid.

Other key topics

DEFENSE, VETERANS, AND FOREIGN AID

Government spending 1980–2023, defense, veterans support, and foreign aid: USAFacts aggregation of data from OMB, Census Bureau, and BEA.

Defense expenditures: BEA (2024, January 25). *National Income and Product Accounts* (Table 3.11.5. National Defense Consumption Expenditures and Gross Investment by Type, Series: "Annual"). https://apps.bea.gov/iTable/?reqid=19&step=2&isuri=1&categories=survey#eyJhcHBpZCI6MTk-sInN0ZXBzIjpbMSwyLDNdLCJkYXRhIjpbWyJjYXRlZ29yaWVzIiwiU3VydmV5Il0sWyJOSVBBX1RhYmxlX0xpc3QiLCIxMDgiXV19.

Military personnel: (1) Active duty 1980–1993: DMDC (2023). *Historical Reports - FY 1954 - 1993 (Not DMDC Data).* Washington Headquarters Services (WHS), Statistical Information Analysis Division (SIAD). https://dwp.dmdc.osd.mil/dwp/app/dod-data-reports/workforce-reports; (2) Active duty 1994–2012: DMDC (2023). *Historical Reports - FY 1994 - 2012.* https://dwp.dmdc.osd.mil/dwp/app/dod-data-reports/workforce-reports; (3) Active duty 2013–2023: DMDC (2023). *Active Duty Military Personnel by Service by Rank/Grade (Updated Monthly)* (For each year, either "FY [year]" Excel file or "September [year]" PDF file). https://dwp.dmdc.osd.mil/dwp/app/dod-data-reports/workforce-reports; (4) Civilian 1980–2001: DMDC (2023). *Civilian Personnel* (DoD Civilian Strength (FY 1950 - FY 2001)). https://dwp.dmdc.osd.mil/dwp/app/dod-data-reports/workforce-reports; (5) Civilian 2002–2007: DMDC (2023). *Civilian Personnel* (DoD Employment by Organization and Function, Historical Reports - FY 1996–2011). https://dwp.dmdc.osd.mil/dwp/app/dod-data-reports/workforce-reports; (6) Civilian 2008–2023: DMDC (2023). *Military Personnel, Military and Civilian Personnel by Service/Agency by State/Country (Updated Quarterly)* (For each year, either "FY [year]" or "September [year]" file). https://dwp.dmdc.osd.mil/dwp/app/dod-data-reports/workforce-reports.

Foreign aid obligations: United States Agency for International Development (2024). *Complete dataset.* https://www.foreignassistance.gov/data.
Note(s): Obligations are binding agreements that will result in payment either in the same year or in the future. Negative values reflect revisions of previous agreements.

Foreign aid obligations (2012 vs. 2022), by top 8 receiving countries in 2022: Ibid.
Note(s): Obligations are binding agreements that will result in payment either in the same year or in the future. Negative values reflect revisions of previous agreements.

CRIME

Government spending 1980–2023, crime: USAFacts aggregation of data from OMB, Census Bureau, and BEA.

Crime rates: FBI (2023, May 1). *Crime Data Explorer, Crime* (Trend of Property/Violent Crime from 1985 to 2022). https://cde.ucr.cjis.gov/LATEST/webapp/#/pages/explorer/crime/crime-trend.
Note(s): The FBI switched its crime data collection from the SRS system to the NIBRS system in 2021. As a result of differences in data collection, data is not completely comparable between the two. Trends over time should only be calculated using data from one data collection system. The FBI has indicated that it will continue updating the historical crime rate time series that was previously estimated using SRS data once the NIBRS system reaches higher participation rates from law enforcement agencies.

Correctional population: (1) Bureau of Justice Statistics (BJS) (2021, May 11). *Key Statistics* (Total Correctional Population). US Department of Justice (DOJ). https://bjs.ojp.gov/data/key-statistics; (2) For 2021–2022 prison population: Carson Ph.D., E. A. (2022, December). *Prisoners in 2021 - Statistical Tables* (NCJ 305125). DOJ, BJS. https://bjs.ojp.gov/library/publications/prisoners-2021-statistical-tables; (3) For 2021–2022 jail population: Zeng Ph.D., Z. (2022, December). *Jail Inmates in 2021 - Statistical Tables* (NCJ 304888). DOJ, BJS. https://bjs.ojp.gov/library/publications/jail-inmates-2021-statistical-tables; (4) For 2021 community supervision population: Kaeble, D. (2023, February). *Probation and Parole in the United States, 2021* (NCJ 305589). DOJ, BJS. https://bjs.ojp.gov/library/publications/probation-and-parole-united-states-2021.
Note(s): All probation, parole, and prison counts are for December 31, while jail counts are for the last weekday in June.

DISASTERS

Government spending 1980–2023, disasters: USAFacts aggregation of data from OMB, Census Bureau, and BEA.

Cost of, frequency of, and deaths from billion dollar disasters: National Centers for Environmental Information (2024). *U.S. Billion-Dollar Weather and Climate Disasters.* NOAA. https://www.ncdc.noaa.gov/billions/time-series.
Note(s): (1) Billion-dollar disasters were determined by inflation-adjusting the cost of the disaster at the time to present dollars. Costs include physical damage, business interruption, public infrastructure, and more, but do not capture health care related losses or losses associated with loss of life. (2) “Other” includes costs related to flooding, freezes, and winter storms.

ENERGY

Government spending 1980–2023, energy: USAFacts aggregation of data from OMB, Census Bureau, and BEA.

Energy consumption: Energy Information Administration (EIA) (2024, March 26). *Monthly Energy Review* (Table 1.3 Primary Energy Consumption by Source). https://www.eia.gov/totalenergy/data/browser/?tbl=T01.03#/?f=A.

Energy consumption per capita: Ibid.

Fossil fuel energy production: EIA (2024, March 26). *Monthly Energy Review* (Table 1.2 Primary Energy Production by Source). https://www.eia.gov/totalenergy/data/browser/?tbl=T01.02#/?f=A.

Renewable and nuclear energy production: Ibid.

ENVIRONMENT AND NATURAL RESOURCES

Government spending 1980–2023, environment and natural resources: USAFacts aggregation of data from OMB, Census Bureau, and BEA.

Total number of days reaching unhealthy for sensitive groups or above on the air quality index: EPA (2023). *Our Nation's Air: Trends Through 2022.* https://gispub.epa.gov/air/trendsreport/2023/#home.

Greenhouse gas emissions: US Environmental Protection Agency (EPA) (2023, May 16). *Greenhouse Gas Inventory Data Explorer* (Sector: “Economic sectors”, “All sectors”; Break out by: “Economic sector”). https://cfpub.epa.gov/ghgdata/inventoryexplorer/#allsectors/allsectors/allgas/econsect/all.
Note(s): Carbon dioxide equivalent is used to standardize emissions from different greenhouse gases, based on their ability to trap heat in the atmosphere over time.

Farmland in acres: Department of Agriculture (February 2024). *Census of Agriculture* (Table 1. Historical Highlights: 2022 and Earlier Census Years). https://www.nass.usda.gov/Publications/AgCensus/2022/Full_Report/Volume_1,_Chapter_1_US/.

US agriculture cash receipts (2022): Department of Agriculture (February 2024). Farming and Farm Income. https://www.ers.usda.gov/data-products/ag-and-food-statistics-charting-the-essentials/farming-and-farm-income/.

EDUCATION

Government spending 1980–2023, education: USAFacts aggregation of data from OMB, Census Bureau, and BEA.

Share of students scoring at or above proficient in reading and math: NCES (2023). NAEP Data Explorer (Subject: "Mathematics" and "Reading"; Grade: "Grade 4" and "Grade 8"; Year: "All Years"; Scale: "Composite Scale"; Statistic: "at or above Proficient"). https://www.nationsreportcard.gov/ndecore/xplore/NDE.
Note(s): (1) Represents students scoring at proficient or above. Proficiency represents solid academic performance on the National Assessment of Educational Progress (NAEP) exam. (2) Excludes test years for which accommodations were not permitted. (3) Data included from public and private schools.

Educational attainment: (1) High school graduation: NCES (2022, December). Digest of Education Statistics (Chapter 2. Elementary and Secondary Education, 219. High School Completers and Dropouts, Table 219.46. Public High School 4-year Adjusted Cohort Graduation Rate (ACGR), by Selected Student Characteristics and State). https://nces.ed.gov/programs/digest/d22/tables/dt22_219.46.asp; (2) College enrollment: CPS School Enrollment Supplement ("PESTYPE", "PEHSPNON", "PEYRDIP", "PTDTRACE"). Retrieved from US Census Bureau. https://data.census.gov/mdat/#/; (3) College graduation: NCES (2024/2023, January). Digest of Education Statistics (Chapter 3. Postsecondary Education; 326. Completion and Retention Rates; Table 326.10. Graduation rate from First Institution Attended for First-time, Full-time Bachelor's Degree-Seeking Students at 4-year Postsecondary Institutions, by Race/Ethnicity, Time to Completion, Sex, Control of Institution, and Percentage of Applications Accepted: Selected Cohort Entry Years, 1996 through 2016; Table 326.20. Graduation Rate from First Institution Attended within 150 Percent of Normal Time for First-time, Full-time Degree/Certificate-seeking Students at 2-year Postsecondary Institutions, by Race/Ethnicity, Sex, and Control of Institution: Selected Cohort Entry Years, 2000 through 2018). https://nces.ed.gov/programs/digest/current_tables.asp.
Note(s): (1) High school graduation rates are for public high school students only and measure whether someone graduated within 4 years of beginning 9th grade, after adjusting for transfers into/out of a school and deaths of students. This is known as the adjusted cohort graduation rate (ACGR). (2) College enrollment rates measure the proportion of people who graduated high school in 2019 who were enrolled in college in October of 2019.

Average cumulative undergrad student loans borrowed: NCES (Multiple years). *DATALAB* (National Postsecondary Student Aid Study; Analysis Type: Averages, Medians, & Percents; Columns: BORAMT1 ["Average" De-select "Include zeroes"]; Filters: UGDEG ["Certificate", "Associate's degree", "Bachelor's degree"], PROGSTAT ["Yes"]). https://nces.ed.gov/datalab.
Note(s): Excludes Parent PLUS loans given to parents of dependent students.

Photo credits

Cover: Photos by: Brett Jordan on Unsplash, Corbin Mathias on Unsplash, hartcreations on iStock

Inside cover: Photo by Deane Bayas on Pexels

Page 01: Photo by Adam Gerhold on Unsplash

Page 04: Photo by Luke Michael on Unsplash

Page 07: Photo by Molly Hutson on Unsplash

Page 19: Photo by Pauline Bernfeld on Unsplash

Page 24: Photo by ConvertKit on Unsplash

Page 36: Photo by Kelly on Pexels

Page 44: Photo by Braxton Apana on Unsplash

Page 54: Photo by Alexander Grey on Unsplash

Page 61: Photo by cottonbro studio on Pexels

Page 70: Photo by Daniel Lee on Unsplash

Page 77: Photo by Patrick Tomasso on Unsplash

Page 90: Photo by Cole Miller on Unsplash

Page 94: Photo by Mika Baumeister on Unsplash

USAFACTS

To request additional printed copies, please contact:

congress@usafacts.org